D0782889

Political Consciousness
and American Democracy

Political Consciousness

and American Democracy

by
James F. Lea

Foreword by
Cecil L. Eubanks

UNIVERSITY PRESS OF MISSISSIPPI
JACKSON

This Volume is Authorized and Sponsored by the
University of Southern Mississippi

COPYRIGHT © 1982 BY THE UNIVERSITY PRESS OF MISSISSIPPI
MANUFACTURED IN THE UNITED STATES OF AMERICA
ALL RIGHTS RESERVED

Library of Congress Cataloging in Publication Data

Lea, James F.
  Political consciousness and American democracy.
  Includes index.
  1. Political participation—United States.
  2. Political socialization—United States.
  I. Title.
  JK1764.L4   323'.042'0973   81-13133
  ISBN 0-87805-150-3   AACR2
  ISBN 0-87805-150-1 (pbk.)

All material from M.Q. Sibley's *Nature and Civilization: Some Implications for Politics* (1977) has been reproduced by permission of the publisher, F.E. Peacock Publishers, Inc., Itasca, Illinois.

3.042
62p

To the children

David, Stephen, Kelly, Michael,
Wendy, Cindy, Chris, Susan, Amy,
Amy, Susan, Jo Ann, Josh, Nicole, Ben
and those to come

198101

"Only that day dawns to which we are awake."

Thoreau, *Walden*

Contents

Foreword

"I think only those people who want to be free are human." With those words that indefatigable creation of Nikos Kanzantzakis, Zorba the Greek, utters the truth and the hope of this book. The American political culture is permeated with the symbols and language of freedom. They are the foundation of our democratic consciousness, that consciousness of freedom which is the central focus of this study. The family, the school, political leaders, the media and the workplace are all the subject of scrutiny in terms of how they contribute to the consciousness of the free, inquiring democratic citizen. Yet, they are examined in a critical light, for there is much in the American political culture that is disturbing and not particularly conducive to the development of that freedom loving human being. It should be noted that Zorba says those who *want* to be free are human, not those who *are* free. Freedom is not something to be found; it is to be sought. It is a struggle.

The struggle is witness to the terrible burdens of freedom and to the many false masks we create to alleviate those burdens. If it is human to want to be free, it is just as human to want to escape that freedom. Illusory and comforting dogmas are preferable. Such were the masks of the nineteenth and twentieth century ideologies of communism and fascism. As this book points out, we moderns have found still another mask, both more subtle and cynical than any ideology. It is the mask of resignation. Democracy, we are told, is not for the many; and those who speak of the need for participation by the many, in other words, of freedom, are destined to be the victims of authoritarian politics. We have exchanged illusory hope for skeptical nihilism.

The temptation to accept this logic is great, especially in an age where the family's influence on our communal life has diminished, where work has lost its dignity and schools have abandoned their mission, where political institutions feed on image and the most powerful instrument of social control has become mass advertising, that paragon of falsehood and corrupter of language. The temptation is great, but the logic is that of the debtor's prison. We cannot be free, because we know not how; and we do not know how, because we are not free.

Yet, somewhere between the false hopes and the despairing

resignation lies the truth of Zorba's assertion about freedom. A twentieth century theologian, Paul Tillich, provided a clue toward understanding that truth. He characterized the human as that being possessed of "finite freedom." Freedom is the ability of the self to act as a whole person, and it is the fact of our having possibility. In the first instance freedom is that capacity to be a self, to discover the conflict that divides our self (such as love and hate, or guilt and pride) and to *free* ourselves from this inner division and become whole, in other words, to become free. In the second instance, freedom is the infinite possibility of human beings to transcend the given world, to project themselves into the future, or, as Nietzsche put it, to make promises. The problem, of course, is that we are constantly divided against ourselves and our ability to transcend the given world is limited. That is finitude!

Finite freedom, the kind of freedom a democratic consciousness requires, insists that we face the anxiety of our given world with the courage of our hopes. Striking a balance between this anxiety and courage is both the dilemma and the challenge of democratic politics. Tillich often refers to that balance as walking on the boundary. What lies on that boundary is a high sense of tragic expectation. It is true that freedom is not to be found on this earth. It is true that unmasking is a difficult endeavor accompanied by anguish. Certitude is more pleasant. In spite of that knowledge, we struggle. As another of Kazantzakis' creations, Father Yanaros of *The Fratricides*, puts it: "We struggle to obtain the unattainable— that is what separates man from beasts."

Cecil L. Eubanks
Louisiana State University

Preface

The noted British author Doris Lessing writes:

> We are what we learn.
> It often takes a long and painful time.[1]

We learn most of our political beliefs and inclinations through political socialization. This transmits, by way of major social agencies like schools, media, the family, and others, the political culture of a society and in so doing influences political consciousness. The nature of this learning process in the United States and its implications for American democracy is the concern of this study.

Does the dominant thrust of American political culture and socialization encourage a democratic political consciousness, where citizens possess a sense of efficacy, community, tolerance, and independence? It is precisely this democratic consciousness that we need to develop in order to rationally address the major problems faced by our technological society. The presence or absence of this will determine in large part whether we will have a technocracy, an "advanced" society run by elites, or a technological democracy, a sophisticated society imbued with effective popular control of major institutions. For it is at the level of the citizenry, and not elites, that the *ultimate* potentiality for democratic self-government does or does not exist, as the case may be. This has not always been given sufficient emphasis. One might profitably recall Tolstoy's caution against the neglect of mass behavior.

> To study the laws of history we must completely change the subject of our observation, must leave aside kings, ministers, and generals, and study the common, infinitesimally small elements by which the masses are moved. No one can say in how far it is possible for man to advance in this way toward an understanding of the laws of history; but it is evident that only along that path does the possibility of discovering the laws of history lie, and that as yet not a millionth part as much mental effort has been applied in this direction by historians as has been devoted to describing the actions of various kings, commanders, and ministers and propounding the historians' own reflections concerning these actions.[2]

[1]Doris Lessing, *The Summer Before the Dark* (New York: Alfred A. Knopf, 1973), p.7.
[2]Leo Tolstoy, *War and Peace*, trans. by Louise and Aylmer Maucle (New York: Simon and Schuster, Inc., 1942), pp. 919–20.

xi

A politicized, democratic mass consciousness and set of activist behavioral predispositions are particularly important in the United States due to the nature of the Madisonian system. The many checks and balances, the separation of institutions, indirect selection processes for some top decision-makers, and extraordinary majorities required on constitutional change, plus the vertical fragmentation of the government over a federal system, all enormously complicate political life for the American citizen. This may discourage clear political understanding and the inclination to participate.

With this belief in the need for a democratic political consciousness in mind, the goal of this study is to describe, analyze and assess, to paraphrase Tolstoy, the "common, infinitesimally small elements" by which the American citizenry are inclined to particular ways of thinking and feeling about political things. The three major subdivisions of the study explore American "political culture," "socialization" and "consciousness." In these sections I hope to clarify the foundations of politically relevant values, and patterns of behavior in America, to set forth the manner in which they are passed on through various agencies, and to assess their possible impact on our potential for democratic citizenship.

Unfortunately, while widespread democratic political beliefs are necessary for effective popular control, which is the essence of democracy, they are insufficient in themselves. This is due in large part to interrelated social and economic factors. The social structure of roles and statuses, plus wealth and income distribution, offers certain unique contextual constraints and possibilities for each citizen. It also mediates the political learning of cultural values, or political socialization. Thus, in examining political consciousness and American democracy I will keep in focus the interplay of socioeconomic status with the internalization of political culture values and the consequent implications for political consciousness and orientations.

In concluding this exploration of the sociocultural base of American political life I will abandon the descriptive and analytical approach and try to carefully evaluate the implications of political socialization for American democracy. Also, I hope to sketch how the process might be improved so as to enhance democratic possibilities.

This book began in the mid-seventies as an outgrowth of several things. First, in trying to understand the sociocultural substratum shaping electoral politics, I taught a seminar on American political socialization. Second, in seeking to understand the factors influencing governmental institutions I wrote a paper in 1975 on the presidency and political culture while participating in a National Endowment for the Humanities "Summer Seminar for College Teachers" at the University of Virginia under the superb direction of Henry J. Abraham. Henry provided invaluable stimulation and guidance. Third, and most important, with my mentor and good friend Cecil L. Eubanks of Louisiana State University I laid the initial plans for this study.

Cecil later took on administrative responsibilities—first graduate director and then department chairman—which necessitated his withdrawal from the project, but not before he had contributed much of chapter 1, virtually all of chapter 2, and the concluding section of chapter 7, plus many good suggestions and ideas. He also edited the nearly completed manuscript in an early draft and, of course, graciously consented to prepare the foreword. For all these things and because he first taught me the importance of ideas, I am eternally grateful and to him I obviously owe the greatest intellectual debt.

I want to express a special thanks to my friend and colleague Ed Wheat. Ed is simply the best reader I have encountered in our profession and—although always on a busy schedule of teaching, writing, and reviewing—he was unfailingly willing to be an intellectual sounding board and to critique a chapter. Three reviewers who took the time and trouble to do more than merely peruse the manuscript, who contributed lengthy assessments with many suggestions as to how the study might be improved, are also owed thanks. They are Ruth Bamberger of Drury College, Donald Lutz of the University of Houston, and Herb Reid of the University of Kentucky.

The concluding chapter grew from a paper which I presented to an Ethical Issues Seminar jointly sponsored by the National Endowment for the Humanities and the American Political Science Association in the summer of 1980. The stimulating discussions at the two weekend sessions in Washington, D.C., a critique of the paper by the distinguished seminar director, Roland Pennock, and subsequent interchanges with one member of the group in particular, Bette Novit-Evans, contributed to both the substance and form of the chapter. Suffice to say, many of the above-mentioned names do not agree with various conclusions contained in this book and none are in any way responsible for errors or incorrect interpretations.

At a truly critical point in this endeavor, my delightful editor Seetha Srinivasan provided absolutely indispensable encouragement. Her combination of sensitivity and efficiency is rare. Marcia Brubeck provided thorough, detailed copy editing, which sharpened as much as was possible often belabored, wooden prose and eliminated an incalculable number of errors. To both these individuals I am grateful, as I am to the many students who contributed in ways they will never know and to the people at the University of Southern Mississippi like Bill Hatcher who helped me to get the time and research funds necessary to undertake this project. Thanks also go to Diane Van Zandt who, in doing much of the typing, patiently and expertly corrected more mistakes of spelling, punctuation, and grammar than I like to remember.

Any author with a family who spends several years of researching, writing and pondering over a manuscript knows who is owed the debt that mere acknowledgement does not even begin to repay. In my case it is Cindy, and our boys, Chris, Josh, and Ben.

Part One

Political Culture and American Democracy

The Origins of Political Consciousness
and the Social Psychology of Political Life

*The moral man is not he who merely wills and does that
which is right—not the merely innocent Man—but he who
has the consciousness of what he is doing.*
Hegel (about Socrates), *The Philosophy of History*

*It is not the consciousness of men that determines their
being but, on the contrary, their social being that
determines their consciousness.*
Marx, *A Contribution to the Critique of Political Economy*

*. . . if the brain is a machine of ten billion nerve cells
and the mind can somehow be explained as the summed
activity of a finite number of chemical and electrical
reactions, boundaries limit the human prospect—we are
biological and our souls cannot fly free.*
E. O. Wilson, *On Human Nature*

There is little if any evidence to suggest that the human race ever
lived in an asocial state. Thus there is some legitimacy to the notion
that we humans are naturally social, perhaps naturally political,
creatures. Yet early political existence was instinctual in character
and tribal in organization and the force of custom ruled the community. A vital missing ingredient in these primitive societies was
political consciousness: the deliberate attempt to order the affairs
of the community on consciously held principles of law, politics,
and government.

Why and how did political consciousness first emerge, and what
precisely is its nature? What is the relevance of political consciousness to the particular shape of American democracy? What are the
major social and cultural sources of political consciousness? I will
begin by addressing these questions. Let us look first at the way
political consciousness might have originated. This preliminary
discussion will provide an appropriate background for a consideration of its precise nature and significance.

THE ORIGINS OF POLITICAL CONSCIOUSNESS

What specifically occasioned in early societies the beginnings of political consciousness and thus political civilization is unclear, although we know that Israel and Greece provided settings.[1] In Israel by the time of Moses (1200 B.C.) law and order had begun to emerge in a tribal civilization. The transition to political society was nearly completed by the time of the great Greek city-states, such as Athens, several hundred years after Moses.

Our understanding of the perplexing and brutal nature of this passage from barbarism to civilization, from the tribe to the polis, is enhanced considerably by the Greek tragedian Aeschylus in the final years of the sixth century B.C. In the *Oresteia* (*Agamemnon*, *The Libation Bearers*, and *The Eumenides*)[2] Aeschylus relates a familiar story to his Greek audiences, the tale of the house of Atreus. It is a horrifying account of tribal passions, murder, and intrigue. Clytaemnestra, wife of the commander of the forces sent to avenge the seduction of Helen of Troy and sister of Helen, murders her husband and his mistress Cassandra. In so doing, she avenges the death of her sacrificed daughter and the insult of Cassandra. Clytaemnestra and her lover Aegisthus become rulers of Argos. Orestes, son of Agamemnon and Clytaemnestra, is commanded by the god Apollo to avenge these crimes, and he, in turn, kills Aegisthus and his mother. The sin of matricide is too much for Orestes, and he is pursued by his guilt, in the person of the Furies, to Apollo's shrine. Apollo cannot release Orestes from the Furies, although the god purifies Orestes of blood guilt and sends him to Athena for a final resolution. Athena must bring some meaningful order out of a world that has gone awry. Hers is the political task.

Athena succeeds in an extraordinary fashion. First, she appoints a group of citizens to try Orestes on the charge of manslaughter, thereby establishing a court of law, the Areopagus. Human beings must be involved in this resolution. The court, however, is hopelessly and evenly divided, and Athena herself must cast the deciding

[1]For an excellent account of the rise of political consciousness in ancient Hebrew and Greek civilizations, see part 1 of Mulford Q. Sibley, *Political Ideas and Ideologies: A History of Political Thought* (New York: Harper and Row, 1970). An equally useful study is John G. Gunnell, *Political Philosophy and Time* (Middletown, Conn.: Wesleyan University Press, 1968).

[2]Aeschylus, *Oresteia: Agamemnon, The Libation Bearers, The Eumenides,* in *The Complete Tragedies* ed. and trans. Richmond Lattimore, 5 vols. (Chicago: University of Chicago Press, 1960), vol. 1.

vote. She acquits Orestes while at the same time persuading the Furies to become more benevolent patrons of Athens. The chorus, in the final lines of *The Eumenides*, rejoices over this resolution and the beginnings of a new order. Tribal barbarism has given way to political civilization.

The vote by Athena and her establishment of the Areopagus are significant evidence that the concerns of the city of Athens will be favored over those of the house of Atreus or any other tribal unit. Indeed, Athena explains her actions in terms of political wisdom:

> . . . you may deserve and have salvation for your citadel,
> your land's defence,
> such as is nowhere else found among men. . . .
> I establish this tribunal. It shall be untouched
> by money-making, grave but quick to wrath, watchful
> to protect those who sleep, a sentry on the land.[3]

As one commentator noted, the secret of Athena's achievement "lies in the use of reason which both restores the individual to sanity and founds a community like Athens."[4]

Aeschylus teaches us, then, that the movement from tribalism to political civilization involves questions of rational and moral self-consciousness. Conscience and consciousness in this respect seem to be synonymous, or at least intertwined. We cannot speak of possessing a conscience without having some degree of self-awareness, of consciousness.[5] Aeschylus also instructs us in the tragic quality of the balance that is struck between our animal natures and our rational natures. (Nineteenth- and twentieth-century nationalisms provide ample evidence that it is easy for civilizations to slip back into tribalisms.) What interests us is the phenomenon of political consciousness as it has been introduced by the Greek tragedian.

Political consciousness, we have seen, is a general awareness of the need to order the affairs of the community rationally. Aeschylus insists that this rational ordering involves a concern not solely for order but also for moral order, for justice. To achieve this state of

[3]Ibid., *The Eumenides*, p. 160.

[4]Richard Kuhns, *The House, the City, and the Judge: The Growth of Moral Awareness in the Oresteia* (New York: Bobbs-Merrill, 1962), p. 79.

[5]For an interesting discussion of the unity of consciousness and conscience as well as a historical and literary survey of the role each has played in the human drama, see Edward Engelberg, *The Unknown Distance: From Consciousness to Conscience, Goethe to Camus* (Cambridge, Mass.: Harvard University Press, 1972).

consciousness, it is necessary to be aware of one's self as a self and to be aware of other selves. These two coexistent forms of consciousness—an awareness of one's individual subjective personality and an awareness of the group of selves represented by the tribe, the state, or the community—are the roots of political consciousness. They precede any concern for equality, political participation, law making, elections, or other institutional forms of politics. They precede all of the secondary, albeit sophisticated, forms that political consciousness can take with which we moderns are familiar. Aeschylus describes for us how these roots take hold in a tribal setting, how Orestes' personal, self-conscious guilt over the slaying of his mother and her lover is transformed into a moral and rational concern for political order in Athens. He tells us of the beginnings of political consciousness. It falls to another Greek, Socrates (especially as analyzed by the nineteenth-century political philosopher Georg W. Hegel), to illustrate fully the fundamental nature of consciousness and why it leads to the concern for rational and moral order.

In his *Philosophy of History* and *Phenomenology of the Mind*[6] Hegel desribes the journey of human consciousness. We need not be Hegelians to appreciate the value of his analysis. The journey Hegel describes is, in one sense, deceptively simple. Humankind becomes aware of itself at some juncture in history. This self-consciousness is troubling, subjective, highly individualistic. It sets one's self apart from the tribe. We would call this awareness estrangement. In a very fundamental sense such estrangement is the beginning and foundation of politics. Why is this so? Because the human who is so estranged by this new self-consciousness seeks to find himself/herself again, to return to the group self. A complete return may not be possible but the attempt, Hegel argues, is ever present in our history and is none other than this same search for political order that we saw in Aeschylus. What is the pivotal moment in history wherein this self-consciousness emerges? The answer is difficult for obvious anthropological reasons. Still, in the recorded history of Western civilization we do have a "first representation" of such a consciousness in the figure of Socrates.

Socrates was, of course, arrested and condemned to death for not

[6]G. W. Hegel, *The Philosophy of History*, trans. J. Sibree (New York: Dover, 1956); *The Phenomenology of Mind*, trans. J. B. Baillie, 2nd ed. (New York: Macmillan, 1931).

believing in the gods of the state and for corrupting the young.[7] The charges against Socrates were not entirely unfounded from the point of view of the Athenian leaders. It was true that through his own life of disdain for material wealth and power, and through the climate of doubt he created with his constant questioning, Socrates was challenging the "authority" of the Athenian regime. Yet Socrates loved Athens and refused escape from it after his sentence. He did not, after all, challenge the rule of law. It is also true that Socrates was critical of the practice of religion that was based upon excessive reliance on empty ritual. Plato's *Euthyphro* is a classic account of Socrates' attempts, much in the vein of Old Testament prophets such as Amos, to purify common notions of piety. Yet Socrates believed in the traditional religious forms of his beloved Greece.

What set Socrates apart, and what is important for the discussion of him in connection with consciousness, is his contention that he had an inner daimon to which he listened and which instructed him in matters of goodness and beauty. By virtue of this attribute, as Hegel points out, in Socrates "the principle of subjectivity . . . attained free expression."[8] Socrates taught the principle of individuality to all, for he argued that human beings could discover what was right and good for themselves. Hegel summarizes his impact in philosophical and religious terms: "Socrates—in assigning to insight, to conviction, the determination of men's actions—posited the Individual as capable of a final moral decision, in contraposition to Country and to Customary Morality, and thus made himself an Oracle, in the Greek sense."[9]

Even though Socrates remained loyal to the city of Athens until his death, his primary allegiance was to the world of rational thought. Athens recognized the danger of subjectivity represented in Socrates. Tragically and ironically, by recognizing Socrates and the possibility of subjective self-consciousness, the city made the discovery that the principle had already taken root within its walls.[10]

This principle of subjectivity, of individual self-consciousness,

[7]For an account of the trial and character of Socrates, see Plato, *Euthyphro, The Apology, Crito, and Phaedo*, trans. F. J. Church (New York: Bobbs-Merrill, 1956).
[8]Hegel, *The Philosophy of History*, p. 269.
[9]Ibid., pp. 269–70.
[10]Ibid., p. 270.

has had a tremendous impact on art and philosophy—and on politics. This self-conscious individuality sets the individual apart from the tribal community and begins the process by which a return to communal order is attempted through a rational calculation of the purposes of the community and the proper means for achieving them. That calculation, of course, is the political task.

From Socrates' notions of self-consciousness comes political consciousness, which has, then, a dialectical quality. On the one hand, it stems from an awareness of one's individuality, and on the other it is accompanied by appreciation of the rights of individuals. At the same time, there comes a sense of loss, of separation from the world of others. Thus the conscious self turns to the world of politics with its emphasis on rational order that makes it possible to be both an individual with rights and a member of the political community with responsibilities. These are, of course, the central elements of citizenship, and in this way the role of citizens becomes one of the first concerns of political consciousness. So the estrangement of the conscious self leads to the search for the political community, which will inevitably involve authority and leadership. The nature of these and the relationship to them in which citizens function is the other major concern of the newly awakened political consciousness and brings us to a significant question raised by the case of Socrates which has plagued social theorists since his time. To what extent was Socrates influenced by his culture; or in a more general sense, can the history of consciousness be explained in terms of biological evolution? Or was Socrates, as he contended, a free man?

It is apparent that the phenomenon of self-consciousness inevitably leads to questions of freedom and requires us to broaden the scope of our discussion to include the debate over the influences on human consciousness of biology and enviroment.

BIOGENETIC THEORIES OF CONSCIOUSNESS

Ironically, Socrates' pupil, Plato, articulated the classic theory of innate distinctions in human capacity, by which he justified inequalities of political and economic power and position. In the *Republic* he presented a tripartite division of the human organism into the rational element, the spirited element, and the appetitive element. Not all individuals are equally possessed of these faculties: "Some of you have the power of command and in the composition of these he [God] has mingled gold, wherefore also they have the greatest honour; others he has made of silver, to be auxiliaries; others again who are to be husbandmen and craftsmen he has composed of brass and iron."[11] It is probably true that over much of the course of Western civilization this belief in innate differences in human capability dominated, particularly since such distinctions served to legitimize monarchies, aristocracies, oligarchies, and other ruling elites.

The theory was given a scientific twist in the nineteenth century when Herbert Spencer misapplied Darwin's findings about evolutionary biology to society, producing the powerful theory known as Social Darwinism. To interfere in the process of social evolution where the fittest people survive and flourish, so the reasoning went, impeded the natural scheme of things, thereby weakening society. This pseudoscientific social philosophy rationalized the elite consolidation of power in industrializing post-Civil War America. Social Darwinism received its most enthusiastic response in the United States.

The politically most important proposition of those who hold to a biologically based theory of human behavior is that personality predispositions, whether cooperative and sociable or aggressive and antisocial, are endemic in the human organism. Aristotle, a biologist by training, asserted in *The Politics* that "a social instinct is implanted in all men by nature."[12] Both the defects and abilities of human beings impel them to form political socieites.

The defects of man which are said to make him dependent on a political community are that he is incapable of feeding, clothing, and protecting himself and of sustaining physical existence alone. The abilities which distinguish him from animals and make him a political being are his unique capacity for abstract thought and complex speech, which can only be developed in interaction with others. Absent this development he never becomes "human."

Some anthropology and archaeology reinforces Aristotle's view of the innate sociability of man. For example, the Tasadays, a tribe found in the depths of a Philippine rain forest in 1971, were a marvelously warm community, with no words to denote hate, war, or homocide. Also, the recent incredible find in Kenya of the remains of a community of *Homo habilis* some 2.5 million years old

---

[11]Plato, *The Republic*, trans. Benjamin Jowett (New York: Vintage Books, 1955), p. 125.
[12]Aristotle, *The Politics*, trans. T. A. Sinclair (Baltimore, Md.: Penguin Books, 1962), pp. 28–30.

indicates, according to paleoanthropologist Richard Leakey, that man is inherently sociable. Leakey wrote, "The evidence coming out is that man owes his existence today to the fact he is innately co-operative."[13] Originally the human "social contract," in Leakey's interpretation, called for an economy based on reciprocity and sharing which is unique among primates and which fostered language, and conceptual and technological skills. With Rousseau Leakey views warlike activities as a result of the rise in economic disparity between rich and poor and not as a result of human nature.

The most famous theory of the innateness of antisocial, individualistic and competitive personality and behavioral inclinations is found in the thought of Thomas Hobbes. Born into a prepolitical state of nature, man has the liberty to "use his own power, as he will himself, for the preservation of his own nature—that is to say, of his own life—and consequently of doing anything which, in his own judgement and reason, he shall conceive to be the aptest means thereunto." Because men are of comparable ability by nature "there arises equality of hope in the attaining of our ends." Consequently, "if any two men desire the same thing, which nevertheless they cannot both enjoy, they become enemies; and on the way to their end, which is principally their own conservation, and sometimes their desire only, endeavor to destroy or subdue one another." Because of this propensity "the life of man is solitary, poor, nasty, brutish, and short."[14] The solution that Hobbes advances amounts to a contract for a powerful Leviathan, or state, to impose restrictions on human selfishness.

Konrad Lorenz, Nikolas Tinbergen, and Robert Ardrey have concluded that man is a "naked, killer ape," motivated by aggression and a territorial imperative. Some impute the motivations for war, and for surrogate wars like the space race and international athletic events, to innate aggressiveness.[15] It is, however, with the dramatic explanations of the genetic base of human behavior offered by the rapidly expanding and controversial school of sociobiology that we confront the gravest social implications of the current thrust of genetic determinism.

From its inception at Harvard, sociobiology has stimulated de-

[13]Quoted in Patrick Young, "He Survived by Co-operating," *National Observer*, March 20, 1976. See also Richard Leakey and Roger Lewin, *People of the Lake* (New York: Anchor Books, 1978).

[14]Thomas Hobbes, *Leviathan* (New York: Bobbs-Merrill, 1958), bk. 13, pp. 104–9.

[15]Cited in Theodore Couloumbis and James Wolfe, *Introduction to International Relations* (Englewood Cliffs, N.J.: Prentice-Hall, 1978), pp. 159–60.

bate in academic departments and political and professional meetings over its thesis that life is a function of the conflict of genes for survival.[16] Darwin's emphasis on the individual as the unit for survival fails, in the view of sociobiologists, to explain altruistic behavior, and they also fault Ardrey's and Lorenz's identification of the aggressive group as the primary unit of selection as too simplistic. Aggression is only one tactic used in survival strategies. Sociobiologists assert that all living things predicate existence on a genetic calculus of kinship. Genes, not individuals or groups, are the primary unit of selection. While selfishness, conflict, and competition motivate the atomized genetic struggle, other factors, such as altruism, may enter into the evolutionary equation. Mothers sacrifice themselves so that their children can survive in emergencies, and brothers may do likewise. Soldier termites explode themselves when the colony is attacked, spraying poison on the invaders. Daughter ants, wasps, and bees become voluntarily sterile workers who devote three-fourths of their time to raising and caring for sisters because they share three-fourths of their genetic material with their sisters and the queen. While the genetic push is less powerful for humans, since facultative genes dominate and those can be influenced by the environment, sociobiologists nevertheless attribute such emotions as love, hate, and fear, as well as behavioral inclinations to heroism, conformism, brotherhood, and homosexuality, at least partially to a genetic base. They also attribute such sentiments as national loyalty, willingness to defend one's country, and support for religious and other community institutions, when these might not appear in the best interests of individuals, to the belief that such actions and support will enhance the overall prospect for genetic survival. Robert Trivers describes this as a "back-scratching" theory of reciprocal altruism.[17]

[16]The sociopolitical implications of this relatively new school of scientific research are being assessed by social scientists, although there has not been any significant public discussion on the matter. Two good analyses by political scientists are Elliott White, "Sociobiology and Politics," *Political Science Reviewer* 8 (1978), pp. 263–86; and Fred H. Wilhoite, Jr., "Primates and Political Authority: A Biobehavioral Perspective," *American Political Science Review* 70 (1976), pp. 1110–26. Two authoritative scientific works on the topic are Edward O. Wilson, *Sociobiology: The New Synthesis* (Cambridge, Mass.: Harvard University Press, 1975); and his *On Human Nature* (Cambridge, Mass.: Harvard University Press, 1978). A useful place to begin reading is Michael S. Gregory et al., eds., *Sociobiology and Human Nature* (San Francisco: Jossey-Bass, 1978).

[17]Robert Trivers, "Sociobiology and Its Implications" (Paper delivered in the Honors Lecture Series, University of Southern Mississippi, Hattiesburg, Miss., January 9, 1978).

Sociobiology has been called everything from "so-so biology" to "souped-up Hobbes" by its critics. Some object to its obvious devaluation of free will. Others fear the precept that superior genes, which prosper by developing over time the most effective survival strategies, may become identified with dominant races or classes or with the dominant sex. Sociobiologist Edward Wilson disclaims support for the proposition that groups can legitimately justify dominance by claiming genetic superiority. He says that genetic evolution has been too brief for such a result, and furthermore, the genetic component is only one of many, accounting for perhaps as little as 10 percent of the shaping forces of human behavior. Nevertheless he does concede that the theory suggests "loose coordination of some of the genetically determined traits with success."[18] This is, to some, a form of "genetic capitalism," uncomfortably close to Social Darwinism and to the slave apologist, Nazi, and sexist biological arguments of black, Jewish, and female inferiority.

Perhaps more importantly, to adopt a theory of the inherent aggressiveness of man as a function of genetic individual or group struggle rationalizes the process by which a political Leviathan is superimposed over the citizen. Not only can the theory become the father to reality in this manner but it may become self-fulfilling. It is at least arguable that repression is likely to provoke the very aggressiveness that justifies its existence. Scottish psychologist R. D. Laing warned, "If our experience is destroyed, our behavior will be destructive."[19] Above all else, political Leviathans destroy experience.

The biogenetic theory of consciousness and human behavior has much more explaining to do, however, as a science and a philosophy of determinacy. Despite evidence suggesting some biogenetic sources of human behavior, sociobiology is far from an explanation of the interrelationship between gene and environment, neurophysical structures and consciousness. There are some, like Marshall Sahlins, who believe the sociobiologists have by and large simply encoded our own cultural propensities, meaning a libertarian capitalist system, into the animal kingdom, nay, into the genetic world.[20] What is perhaps most startling about sociobiologists like Edmund O. Wilson, as well as about his equally insistent but environmentally determinist counterpart, B. F. Skinner, is their apparent lack of

[18]Quoted in *Time*, August 1, 1977, p. 58.
[19]R. D. Laing, *The Politics of Experience* (New York: Random House, 1967), p. 12.
[20]Marshall Sahlins, *The Use and Abuse of Biology: An Anthropological Critique of Sociobiology* (Ann Arbor: University of Michigan Press, 1976).

doubts about their promethean claims for world betterment. Wilson refers to a "democratically contrived eugenics" and opines (at the end of *On Human Nature*) that as genetic technology develops, "the human species can change its own nature. What will it choose?"[21] Wilson and Skinner forget that in their worlds where consciousness is the offspring of genetic conflict and/or environmental conditioning, there is no choice.

SOCIOCULTURAL THEORIES OF CONSCIOUSNESS

Sociobiology is a relatively new science and has only recently become influential in the world of scholarship. Social scientists have been rather more interested in sociocultural theories of consciousness. This is true in part because no genetic theory has yet offered a satisfactory explanation of human behavior. As we have seen, even the most hard-line genetic determinist or Darwinist has to acknowledge some influence by the environment. More important, social scientists have embraced the sociocultural theory of consciousness because of the influence of behaviorism in modern psychology and its much broader cousin, behavioralism, in political science and sociology. Whereas behavioralism merely looks at the "behavior" of individuals and groups (usually quantifying it), behaviorism is a rigorous attempt to explain the "laws" of human behavior by means of a stimulus-response paradigm. Both, of course, have roots in the positivistic desire to create a science of society.

The more extreme behaviorists reject the notion of consciousness altogether. Instead, they focus on the environment as it molds human behavior, and develop the techniques like operant conditioning to manipulate that environment and thereby shape behavior. Behaviorism, then, is a theory of behavior as well as a therapy.

B. F. Skinner argues that as a science of human behavior, behaviorism is fundamentally incompatible with any notion of personal freedom. Skinner's philosophical tract on this subject, *Beyond Freedom and Dignity*,[22] maintains that we are now possessed of the manipulative technology necessary to solve many of the problems

---

[21]Wilson, *On Human Nature*, p. 208.
[22]B. F. Skinner, *Beyond Freedom and Dignity* (New York: Alfred A. Knopf, 1971). For an excellent analysis of the political implications of Skinner's work, upon which the discussion relies heavily, see Walt Anderson, *Politics and the New Humanism* (Pacific Palisades, Calif.: Goodyear Publishing, 1973), pp. 24-34.

of the world and to create a happy citizenry without further reference to our outworn notions of personal freedom. That Skinner is correct about the power of existing behaviorist technologies is attested by mass advertising and by the behavior modification therapy used in our prisons, mental institutions, and schools. Still, the value of abandoning our ideas about freedom for a world governed by the principles of operant conditioning has yet to be demonstrated. Indeed, it cannot be done: Skinnerian psychology does not logically justify the choice of any one particular form of conditioning over any other. And the kind of utopia envisaged by Skinner seems merely an extension of technological efficiency to achieve a rigidly-ordered society.

Behaviorism, then, is not so much a theory of the roots of self-consciousness as a denial of it and of anything remotely resembling subjectivity. A far more sophisticated and more influential theory of sociocultural influence has been the Marxian attempt to explain human behavior and consciousness on the basis of economics. Marxism owes a debt to the same desire to create a science of society that behaviorism does. Still, there is in Marxism no denial of the phenomenon of consciousness, just the assertion typical to much of socialist thinking that environment conditions that consciousness. Marx and Engels describe this relationship between environment and consciousness in the *Communist Manifesto*. "Man's ideas, views and conceptions, in one word, man's consciousness, changes with every change in the social conditions of his material existence, in his social relations and in his social life. . . ."[23]

What are the social conditions of material existence? Taken together they comprise what is called the "infrastructure" of a society. They include, first, the state of development of technology in a particular social setting, as well as the production, commerce, and consumption such a society engages in, in other words, its "productive forces." The infrastructure also includes the productive relations built upon these productive forces, or the interactions between those who produce and those who own the means of production, whom Marx calls the "living agents" of production. Of course, these productive relations are best understood in terms of labor as well as in terms of the existence of inequities in the distribution of income. In order to understand a society, then—in order to understand the nature of

[23]Karl Marx and Friedrich Engels, *The Communist Manifesto* (New York: International, 1948), p. 28.

consciousness—it is necessary, first, to examine the technological mode of production that exists in that society and, second, to know which classes control that mode of production, as well as which ones do not. Consciousness, therefore, is primarily class consciousness. It may be that there are other determinants of consciousness in a society, but class is dominant. Marx, of course, had great faith that the suffering of a particular class, the workers, would lead to the development of a revolutionary consciousness. That, in turn, would result in a transformation of society so that classes and exploitation disappeared and consciousness became free and spontaneous.

Marx's dream dominates a host of schemes for transforming the world which begin by asserting an environmental basis for consciousness. If we transform the environment, the argument goes, we transform the person, eliminate exploitation, and change society. One need not be a Marxist to appreciate the power that environment and culture exert over human beings. One need not be a Marxist to reconize that the economic factors in the culture may be crucial in determining the character of a social system. Social scientists have emphasized sociocultural influences for some time. This book will follow their lead.

Nevertheless, there is something as troubling in Marx as there was in B. F. Skinner or E. O. Wilson. Consciousness, in these three cases, rests upon some determining faculty, whether it is genetic makeup, operant conditioning, or economic class. Yet always—and usually on the part of the major spokesman for that determinant—there is the insistence (sometimes explicit, sometimes implicit) that some are exempted from the forces of biology or culture. Some have transcended their genetic potential; others have risen above their class position to understand the world more correctly and change it more compassionately. Each advocate has insisted, despite the determinancy of his or her position, that a small niche of freedom remains in which to make claims of value. While human consciousness is most assuredly influenced by genes and environment, some of it transcends that influence, transforms it. Each advocate has insisted, by implication, that Socrates was ultimately a free man.

Perhaps the most intriguing response to these advocates of biological and environmental determining comes from a rather amorphous and large group of existentialist thinkers who range from the Danish Christian philosopher-theologian Sören Kierkegaard, to the French atheist-Marxist author Jean-Paul Sartre. There is in existentialism a strong echo of the Socratic insistence, expressed, for example, in *The Apology*, on the duty assigned to man by god, to become nothing less than he can be.[24] We are our own "projects," to use Sartre's phrase, "condemned" to make of our lives what they may become and responsible for the outcome. The existentialists do not deny the influence of biological or cultural forces. They assert that the human being is free to react to these determinants, to absorb them, change them, overcome them. Freedom, and the estrangement that goes with it, are part of the human condition. Viewed in this light freedom is, *ultimately*, a situation whereby each moment becomes a unique, fresh possibility in which an individual chooses—of his or her own free will—from alternative experiences. Hence life constitutes a perpetual process of self-creation. The individual human "essence" or "nature" tomorrow, or next year, or ten years from now, is shaped by what a person does (or what is done to one) between now and that future. Thus what we do, our behavior, and also how we understand and reflect on this experience, our consciousness, become of critical importance in determining who and what we are.

Is such existential freedom possible? Clearly it is possible only in a limited and paradoxical sense. Necessarily, finitude surrounds us in the form of our physical and mental limitations as well as environmental contingencies including economic ones. Freedom involves our creating a self within those limitations. As Spinoza put it, freedom involves a "recognition of necessity."[25] At various times and places people have sought to escape their freedom and personal responsibility by blaming their fate on innumerable and infinitely varied "gods." They have sought understanding, explanation, and prediction of this fate by analyzing lifelines, entrails, and tea leaves, by studying the movement of animals, and by reading the heavens. The world of scholars, as we have seen, has similarly sought to reduce the complex world of human consciousness to the "simplicities" of biology and culture. Yet even in the deterministic musings of a Skinner or a Wilson or a Marx, one finds evidence of a longing for that existential freedom, evidence of an assertion of will. This is the political manifestation of that will which Hegel regarded Socrates as symbolizing. Hegel wrote, "As soon as Thought arises, it investigates the various political constitutions: as the result of its investigations it forms for itself an idea of an improved state of society, and demands

---

[24]Plato, *The Apology*, pp. 21–49.
[25]Quoted in Rollo May, *Love and Will* (New York: W. W. Norton, 1969), p. 269.

that this ideal should take the place of things as they are."[26] In other words, we have seen not only the assertion, however reluctant, of a free self-consciusness, but also the stirrings of a political consciousness.

Conclusion

Conceptions of citizenship, authority, and leadership, plus notions of the proper relationship of citizens to their officials, are perhaps the fundamental concerns of political consciousness. These arise from the estrangement inhering in the subjective awareness of self and others. While ultimately such subjective conceptions are grounded in freedom, they are not unaffected by biology or culture. There is often a tendency to attribute even greater power to these factors than is merited by the evidence. This is due partially to the surprisingly burdensome nature of freedom. "Nothing," in Dostoevsky's words, "is a greater cause of suffering."[27] How much simpler to blame factors beyond one's control, like biology or culture, for such things as one's share in the distribution of socioeconomic and political power. There is a particularly strong temptation in capitalist societies like the United States, which are by definition less egalitarian than social democracies, to impute inordinate power to the biogenetic base of life. This is because dominant groups can thereby rationalize their privileges, both to themselves and to others. It is possible also that subordinate groups allay anxieties about their own low status by blaming biology. Given the limited and often inconsistent evidence supporting this model of human consciousness, justifying one's destiny by means of biogenetic factors is an "inauthentic response," to use a major existentialist concept. Such justification also carries repressive social implications.

Of more significance to individual and collective human existence, including political life, are sociocultural factors. It is undeniable that everything we do, including the clothes we choose each morning and the time and manner we choose for rest in the evening, as well as all the events of the day and dreams of the night, is conditioned by our culture. To recognize this is not to fall into the trap of cultural determinism. At its essence human life is largely

[26]Hegel, *Philosophy of History*, p. 268.
[27]Fyodor Dostoevsky, *The Grand Inquisitor on the Nature of Man*, trans. Constance Garnett (New York: Liberal Arts Press, 1948), p. 180.

unfathomable and unpredictable. Still, as key sociocultural institutions (schooling, economics, and television, for example) become more influential, then the role of the culture in human choice assumes greater importance. The interaction of culture and consciousness greatly affects the nature of the political society. The process may result in a politically alert citizenry imbued with genuine democratic norms and behavioral inclinations—or it may not. Thus whether or not we have a functioning democracy, and the particular configuration it takes, depend in large measure on American political culture, the political socialization process by which it is transmitted, and the political consciousness which permeates it. Of particular importance is the democratic form of the interaction between culture and consciousness, not only because the American political system fancies itself democratic, but because democracy is that form of rational and moral order which conforms most closely to the authentic or free self-conscious being.

Political consciousness and American democracy are complex concepts indeed. Before the analysis proceeds let us first gain a clearer idea of what is meant by that emotionally powerful but intellectually ambiguous phrase "American democracy."

II

Models of American Democracy:
Cultural Prerequisites

Our constitution is named a democracy, because it is in the hands not of the few but of the many.
Pericles, "The Funeral Oration"

There is no democratic theory—there are only democratic theories.
Robert Dahl, *A Preface to Democratic Theory*

The tendency of democracies is, in all things, to mediocrity.
James Fenimore Cooper, *The American Democrat*

Democracy, as any citizen of ancient Athens would agree, is "rule by the people." In Greece during the fifth century B.C. the citizens themselves, through a general assembly, made policy directly. The history of democratic thought since then has recorded continual attempts to adapt that simple method for use in more complex social settings—and to answer certain questions about "rule by the people."

What do we mean by "rule"? Can rule be indirect, i.e., representative, and still be democratic? Who are the people? The opinion of what portion of them is necessary for the making of public policy? How can the intensity of their opinions be measured? Exploring the history of American political thought for concrete, meaningful answers to these questions can be an enticing, yet elusive task, for as Daniel Boorstin wrote: "No nation has ever believed more firmly that its political life was based on a perfect theory. And yet no nation has ever been less interested in politicial philosophy or produced less in the way of theory."[1]

A survey of what little theory we have generated reveals two facts: first, there is a distinct body of what we shall call liberal Jeffersonian thought that closely resembles the classical Greek theory of democracy, Second there have been strong objections to that body of thought. These objections have given rise to at least two major

---

[1] *The Genius of American Politics* (Chicago: University of Chicago Press, 1953), p. 8.

opposing views: the conservative and the pluralist theories of democracy.[2]

Each of the three competing ideas of American democracy requires certain cultural foundations for success. The vital "political culture is the set of attitudes, beliefs, and sentiments which give order and meaning to a political process and which provide the underlying assumptions and rules that govern behavior and the political system."[3] Hence as the basis of political consciousness, the political culture may well be the key to political life in this country and all others. I will now examine the three theories of democracy which have historically vied for allegiance in the United States and the cultural prerequisites of each.

LIBERAL JEFFERSONIAN DEMOCRACY

The liberal Jeffersonian theory embodies the approach to problems of democratic governance which evolved from Enlightenment thinkers and the communitarian, majoritarian belief system that developed on American shores during the colonial era and was dominant during the revolutionary era. It was advanced by Jeffersonian Republicans of the eighteenth century, such men as Thomas Jefferson, Thomas Paine, John Taylor, and Samuel Adams. The first and perhaps most basic axiom of this approach is that the majority shall prevail; government is to be organized so as to enable the majority to make public policy. But there are to be limits, for Jefferson recognized more quickly than most that "one hundred and seventy-three despots would surely be as oppressive as one." He summed up the qualifications to majority rule in his first inaugural address:

> All, too, will bear in mind this sacred principle, that though the will of the majority is in all cases to prevail, that will, to be rightful, must be reason-

[2]The notion that there are three basic alternatives in American democratic theory is conventional wisdom by now, but their development owes a great deal to three stimulating discussions of the theories: John D. Livingston and Robert G. Thompson, *The Consent of the Governed*, 2nd ed. (New York: Macmillan, 1966), a work upon which this section has relied heavily, especially pp. 99–133; R. Joseph Monsen, Jr., and Mark W. Cannon, *The Makers of Public Policy: American Power Groups and Their Ideologies* (New York: McGraw-Hill, 1965); and the classic by Robert A. Dahl, *A Preface to Democratic Theory* (Chicago: University of Chicago Press, 1956). A counterinterpretation of basic democratic alternatives is now beginning to emerge. Look for these models to be increasingly questioned.

[3]Lucien W. Pye, "Political Culture," *International Encyclopedia of Social Science*, Vol. 12, pp. 218–24.

able; that the minority possess their equal rights, which equal laws must protect, and to violate which would be oppression.[4]

Jefferson first noted that for a majority to rule with legitimacy, it must do so in a climate of reason. It must have been created in the course of a rational discussion of how justice and the common good, or the public welfare, can best be defined and implemented. Self-centeredness and self-interest must all be set aside by the majority. They must be public persons when acting as rulers, considering the needs of all people and not merely themselves.

The Jeffersonian's second qualification to majority rule is the vigorous protection of those particular freedoms which make discussion, dissent, and minority-majority interchangeabality possible, namely freedom of speech, religion, press, association, and assembly. Because majorities and minorities are impermanent in character, all must show allegiance to a process which places limits on the power of temporary majorities and guarantees certain rights for temporary minorities. Moreover, this limit on majority rule is not given by a tolerant and beneficent majority to the minority. It is a necessary prerequisite to legitimate rule by any majority.

It can be readily seen that the emphasis of liberal Jeffersonian democracy, as it has been described up to this point, is procedural in nature. The emphasis has been on how decisions are to be made, in a broad, general manner, and what protections are to be given to the citizens as they attempt to participate in that process. Like all procedural frameworks for decision making, however, liberal democracy needs a supporting culture to promote the particular political consciousness that is compatible with it.

The Cultural Prerequisites of the Liberal Jeffersonian Model

A framework of ideas, values, and/or beliefs always serves to explain and justify a particular political system, and this generally includes statements about the nature of human beings and society and the purpose of the state. For example, what justifies the liberal Jeffersonian belief that the majority can be expected to restrain its self-interest or selfishness in the name of something called the public good? What will keep the majority from exceeding its powers and depriving the minority of its rights, indeed of its very existence?

[4]Thomas Jefferson, *The Life and Selected Writings of Thomas Jefferson*, ed. Adrienne Koch and William Peden (New York: Random House, The Modern Library, 1944), p. 315.

The answers to these questions and others of similar cast are to be found in the liberal Jeffersonian view of human nature.

Each person is regarded as an independent, moral, and (most important) rational being, wholly capable of ordering his or her affairs. It is this optimistic view of rational human beings, coupled with an almost mystical belief in their equality, that justifies the liberal's faith in making every man and woman a ruler and in trusting the rights of minorities to the majority. Still, the Jeffersonians were not so naive as to suppose that humans were going to act rationally at all times. They knew, as Samuel Adams would put it, that power is intoxicating. And those who have it "often discover a disposition to make ill use of it."

The key, then, to the liberal view of human nature is the word "capable." Humans are capable of governing rationally. In expressing such optimism the liberals are not so much describing human nature as developing a view of what it ought to be. The reasoning faculty, the mind, of human beings is the source of their dignity, their "humanness." The highest purpose of society and government is to foster and cultivate that dignity. So we have a right to make our own choices, we are independent, but we also have a moral responsibility to develop our intellectual and ethical qualities and to use them for the common good.

Jefferson, like the ancient Greeks, identifies the good person with the good citizen. The fundamental remedy for the abuse of power is education, to give persons free access to ideas and to encourage the discussion of those ideas. Free universal education is a necessary condition for a liberal society. The Jeffersonians believed that men do ill merely because they do not know good.

A final ideological safeguard against majority tyranny is the liberal Jeffersonian belief in natural rights. Because we are rational and have the capacity to make moral decisions, we are endowed with natural rights which are not subject to the jurisdiction of any political institution and which, of course, no majority can violate.

The history of political thought in America and elsewhere is replete with attempts to classify the content as well as the source of this body of natural rights. Jeffersonian democrats have been fairly insistent that the freedoms of thought, speech, press, and assembly are among the more important natural rights. Thus the procedural limitations on majority rule are buttressed by a sanction of natural rights as well. If political institutions and social organizations, which according to the Jeffersonians cannot make similar claims to naturalness, become destructive of these rights, then those institutions and organizations may be altered or abolished. Natural rights provide one more means of making majority rule legitimate and of reinforcing the concept of self-government.

The populist foundation of the liberal Jeffersonian theory of democracy can be summarized as resting on an optimistic view of human nature, a fundamental faith in our capacity for rationality and educability, buttressed by a belief that our right to life, liberty, and the pursuit of happiness are natural and are not subject to the whims of temporary rulers.

Conservative Federalist Democracy

There were thinkers who could not accept what they considered to be the overly optimistic philosophy of the liberal Jeffersonians. In the eighteenth century John Adams, in particular, pointed to a long and unhappy history of human relations in order to prove that the average person is not kindly and rational but rather naturally indolent, selfish, given to incredible shortsightedness and jealousy and tending toward faction or internal group conflict. Human beings are motivated not by ideals but by needs, not by reason but by the desire for goods.[5] The pursuit of economic gain is likely to dominate politics. But Adams and his followers considered themselves democrats, albeit of a nature different from that of liberals. The theory of democracy which was developed as a result of these views has been called the conservative, Madisonian, or Federalist theory (after the group that advocated the United States Constitution of 1787 among whom were James Madison, Alexander Hamilton, and John Adams). Like many variations of the more classic form of democratic thought it is as much a reaction against liberal democracy as it is an original model in its own right.

The Federalists viewed human nature as a paradox. Humans may not be completely depraved, but they are caught up in conflicts between reason and passion, between self-interest and public interest. In such conflicts natural tendencies are likely to prevail, and those natural tendencies are essentially predatory and antisocial. Consequently, there is in the conservative Federalist model of democracy a strong implication that humans need more than a

---

[5]John Adams, *The Political Writings of John Adams*, ed. George A. Peek, Jr. (New York: Bobbs-Merrill, 1954), pp. 148–49, 206.

commitment to reasoned choice to bind them together. They require a symbolic or mythogical attachment to community and tradition with attendant spiritual and moral implications. Human beings need a sense of shared values and common purpose which reason alone cannot give. This insistence on the usefulness of community and symbolic allegiance to tradition is best stated in the works of the late Felix Frankfurter, justice of the U.S. Supreme Court and a twentieth-century judicial conservative.

> National unity is the basis of national security. . . . It is fostered by all those agencies of the mind and spirit which may serve to gather up the traditions of a people, transmit them from generation to generation, and thereby create that continuity of a treasured common life which constitutes a civilization.[6]

Still another point of disagreement between the conservative Federalists and liberal Jeffersonians concerns faith in popular majorities and natural equality. These elements of liberalism are considered to be fatal attacks on the natural distinctions between human beings. As John Adams put it, there will always be a better sort, a middling sort, and a meaner sort, and the better sort, the natural aristocrat of superior ability who is motivated by a strong sense of civic duty, must be allowed to put his or her talents to use for the good of the community. It is clear that the conservatives end by creating an elitist version of democracy, although they remain consistent to their skeptical theory of human nature by insisting that once in power, this minority ruling group of aristocrats must also be limited. (It should be noted that many Jeffersonians supported, or at least tolerated, restrictions on civil and political rights based on lack of property or on race and gender.) Finally, while the conservative Federalists do not disagree with the liberals' view that government ought to protect the rights of the people, they insist that the property of the people enjoy similar safety.

On the basis of the above assumptions (which include an emphasis on human frailty, the need for a sense of community, and the necessity for seeing to it that a government of a natural but limited elite protect both property and liberty), the conservative Federalists erect the imposing structure of government based on fragmenting and separating power through a system of checks and balances.

[6]*Minersville School District* v. *Gobitis* (1940), quoted in C. Herman Pritchett, *The American Constitution*, 2nd ed. (New York: McGraw-Hill, 1968), p. 558.

John Adams was frequently accused of being Dr. Balance, and the principle of balance remains an essential ingredient of the Federalist model, where a carefully constructed constitution of separated powers and checks and balances serves to neutralize the efforts of majority and minority groups or factions to gain power and invade the rights of others. On the positive side this same constitution will allow for the influence of a more reasoned approach to public policy, for decisions must be arrived at not by the "superior force of an interested and overbearing majority" but "according to the rules of justice."[7]

If the constitutional scheme of dividing power and balancing it, particularly in achieving social balance of classes, was the treatment for the symptoms of group dissension, the cure would be, according to James Madison, a "republican remedy" through the "successive filtration of popular power." Indirect elections one or two steps removed from the people would filter out the whims of a majority of the moment and would allow for the virtuous elite to govern.

The conservative Federalist theory of democracy begins, then, with a reaction to the liberal view of human nature, taking a decidedly more pessimistic view, and ends with the belief that the dangers of direct popular rule can be mitigated by combining the principles of fragmenting and balancing power and a limited, responsible elite. This elite would govern on the basis of adherence to the sacrosanct traditions of a unified community and a sense of duty or obligation to the public.

Liberal Jeffersonian and Conservative Federalist Democracies Compared

Despite the fact that there are very real differences between the two theories of democracy presented so far, especially in their appraisal of human nature, they share some goals and purposes. They are both struggling to create a process by which public policy is founded in a climate of reason and directed toward the pursuit of the common good. They differ primarily in how these goals are to be achieved.

In a very real sense the two theories represent the two fundamental types of democratic theory, two solutions to the conflict between liberty and equality. As Leslie Lipson eloquently noted, there are

[7]James Madison, Federalist, No. 10, in *The Federalist* ed. Edward M. Earle, (New York: Random House, The Modern Library, 1937), p. 54.

essentially two species of democracy. One is "primarily libertarian in tone and individualistic in temper. Zealous in protecting minorities, it devises political institutions to hedge in the rule of the majority. . . . The other species has a predilection for equality. . . . The majority dominates."[8] The former is the conservative approach to democratic rule, and the latter represents the Jeffersonian ideal.

The issues put forth in the two theories represent, for the most part, the framework for the debates over the U.S. Constitution of 1787 and for much of our subsequent political history. Indeed, it is tempting to view the U.S. Constitution of 1787 as a conservative Federalist victory. Subsequent political and historical growth such as the rise of political parties, the reforms of Jacksonian democracy, the successes of the Populist movement in the late nineteenth century, and the decisions of the Supreme Court under Chief Justice Earl Warren (1954-1969) are then regarded as a move toward majoritarian democracy of the Jeffersonian type. While this observation has some validity, it is deceptively simple, for in fact a new theory of democracy, called pluralist democracy, has arisen and bases itself initially upon assumptions that differ slightly from those of either the Jeffersonian or the Federalist model. Yet the new concept is directly traceable to the American past and to the debate on the nature and uses of power that took place in 1787, during the controversy over the ratification of the U.S. Constitution, and again in the middle of the nineteenth century, when slavery and the nature of the union were at issue.

PLURALIST DEMOCRACY

The pluralist theory of democracy began as a more descriptive approach to democracy and represents an attempt by group theorists, such as Arthur Bentley and David Truman, and behavioralist political scientists of the 1950s, such as Robert Dahl, to make democratic theory more consistent with the realities of political behavior. Yet as I noted above, the pluralist approach is not new. It has its historical roots in James Madison's tenth Federalist Paper, written in 1787, and John Calhoun's *Disquisition on Government*, published in 1853.

Madison discussed the inevitable presence of groups, or as he

---

[8]Leslie Lipson, *The Democratic Civilization* (New York: Oxford University Press, 1964), p. 583. See also George H. Sabine, "The Two Democratic Traditions," *Philosophical Review* 51 (1952), pp. 451–74.

called them, factions, in society in his brilliant Federalist Paper No. 10. The causes of these factions are primarily economic, although Madison makes it clear that differences of opinion on a variety of other matters such as religion and government will suffice to cause group conflict. He thus anticipates the modern theorists not only in his notion of the inevitability of groups but also in his conclusions that it is the function of government to regulate "these various and interfering interests."

The basic difference between Madison's view of factions and modern group theorists' view is that Madison and many of the conservative Federalists believed that the influence of these factions must be neutralized through a system of fragmented power. Then a rational approach to the public welfare would be reflected in policy decisions. In other words, policy was not to be simply the result of compromise between clashing groups. Some attempt was to be made to assess what the public welfare was and to enact legislation consistent with that public good. Modern pluralist democracy is content to allow public policy to reflect a balance of the many and varied private interest groups present in the political system without insisting on any abstract notion of the common good.[9] Thus while Madison anticipated the pluralist notions of a group-oriented society, he did not share their conclusions regarding the operation of those groups in the political system. Somewhat ironically, it fell to John C. Calhoun, a nineteenth-century political theorist and apologist for slavery—and former vice president—to anticipate the conclusions of the group theorists regarding pluralistic politics, but in a distinctly negative fashion.

Democractic government for Calhoun was simply government by consent of the governed, but this meant consent of associations of groups of human beings as well as individuals. Consequently, the only solution to the problem of democratic decision making was to give each group or interest an equal voice, including a veto, in policymaking and demand that there be universal agreement to a policy before its implementation. Obviously in such a situation universal agreement would never be achieved unless there was a good deal of compromise, and indeed Calhoun recognized this as an essential element of his system.

In Calhoun's time, the 1840s and 1850s, the groups or interests

[9]Livingston and Thompson, *The Consent of the Governed*, p. 119. Livingston and Thompson use the term "Broker rule," whereas I use the more commonly accepted "pluralistic democracy."

were sectional or, more specifically, state oriented and the concur-
rent majority thesis, as his theory was called, was designed to
support the status quo of the plantation slave system. This in part
accounts for the fact that his theories were not readily accepted in
the twentieth century. Modern pluralists go to great lengths to
separate their theories from Calhoun's, but as their critics point out,
pluralism is subject to the same criticism that Calhoun's theories
were, that is, it too is wedded to a system of decision making by
compromise and tends to make significant social change difficult if
not impossible.

The contempory model of pluralist democracy had these historical antecedents. The first modern statement of the theory was
developed by Arthur F. Bentley, an American political scientist, in
1908 in *The Process of Government* but not until the 1950s, when
Bentley and Calhoun were rediscovered and republished, did the
theory gain any significant foothold in American political philosophy.[10]

Like the adherents to the conservative Federalist model, the
pluralists were disenchanted with classic liberal democracy. Some
felt that while both liberal and conservative approaches to democracy supported the notion of a common good, they failed to develop
any workable and recognizable conception of it.[11] Others indicted
liberal democracy because of its lack of any systematic treatment of
the problems raised when one accepted both majority rule and
minority rights.[12] How is it possible, for example, to take into
account the intensity of a minority's feelings on a subject as opposed
to the majority's sheer numerical power?

Almost all of the pluralists came to the conclusion that both the
liberal Jeffersonians and the conservative Federalists were talking
in terms of an ideal and not in terms of the real world of political
systems with its voter irrationality and group egoism.[13] Whereas

[10]Arthur F. Bentley, *The Process of Government* (Evanston: The Principia Press of
Illinois, 1949). The two classic explications of Bentley's thesis that gave it so much
impetus during the early fifties are Earl Latham, *The Group Basis of Politics* (Ithaca,
N.Y.: Cornell University Press, 1952), and David B. Truman, *The Governmental
Process* (New York: Alfred A. Knopf, 1951).

[11]See, for example, Joseph Schumpeter, *Capitalism, Socialism, and Democracy*
(New York: Harper and Row, 1942).

[12]See, for example, Dahl, *A Preface to Democratic Theory.*

[13]The pioneering works in this direction were Angus Campbell et al., *The American
Voter* (Detroit, Michigan: John Wiley and Son, 1960); Seymour M. Lipset, *Political
Man* (New York: Doubleday, 1960); and Eugene Burdick and Arthur J. Brodbeck,
eds., *American Voting Behavior* (Glencoe, Ill.: Free Press, 1960), most especially the

classical democracy was essentially a moral system of individual advancement and fulfillment, the pluralists begin with institutions and from that point advance to values.

Basic Beliefs

The major tenet of pluralist theory is that society is a structure of associations. In the struggle for power, which the pluralist believes to be the fundamental description of politics, organized groups are the basic elements. They organize for the security and self-expression of their members. The pluralists are not saying simply that we have a pluralist society; they are contending that the process of *group competition for power* is the essence of political society.

To the charge that the individual has been lost somewhere in this quagmire, the pluralists reply that groups exist to fulfill the needs of the individuals, and the government reacts to the competing desires of individuals by responding to the competing demands of interest groups. Even the electoral process is seen as a ratification of a coalition of interested groups and not a majority winning over a minority.

If certain conditions are met, certain rules of the game followed, then the result of all this group conflict will be what the pluralist terms a condition of equilibrium, a temporary balance of power among contending groups. This is as close as the pluralists come to postulating anything remotely resembling the public interest, for in a democratic society, they argue, this condition of equilibrium constitutes justice or the common good. While there is hardly universal agreement on this point among the pluralists, the underlying premise of this assertion is that the ethical, or moral, validity of public policy and the social and political value structure which permeates such policy is not subject to empirical proof.[14] The public interest is defined only in terms of the *process* by which it is reached and not by its content.

What are the rules of the pluralist process? First, all groups must be assured free access to the centers of decision making, to the legislatures, bureaucracy, courts, and so forth. On this point the pluralists often laud the wisdom of the conservatives' scheme of

articles by Talcott Parsons, "Voting and the Equilibrium of the American Political System," and Eugene Burdick, "Political Theory and Voting Studies."

[14]See, for example, Thomas L. Thorson, *The Logic of Democracy* (New York: Holt, Rinehart and Winston, 1962), pp. 138–39.

separation of powers because it affords many points of access and thus insures the possiblity that avenues will remain open to all groups. They support, too, the liberal belief in procedural freedoms of speech and association, since they are crucial to the creation and functioning of those groups.

Second, for the pluralist system to maintain equilibrium, the number and variety of groups must remain relatively high. There is, of course, no magic number or mix, but the feeling is that sheer number and diversity will help to restrain the demands of any one group. Coupled with this requirement of a large number of groups is the insistence that they remain nonideological in the strict sense of the word, that is, nondoctrinaire or flexible in their demands. The contention here is that in a pluralist setting, groups can not really afford to be inflexible, for one of the unwritten rules of pluralist politics is that all participants must be willing to bargain, negotiate, and compromise.

A third condition that will help in maintaining social stability is the fact that no single group will account for all of the interests of any one individual, except perhaps for those that are on the so-called lunatic fringe. Overlapping group membership and potentially conflicting group goals will mean that groups have less hold on their members; and group leaders will be less insistent on members' obedience and more willing to compromise in their negotiations. But multiple membership in organized groups is not sufficient to prevent the possibility of ideological stalemate. After all, there is little overlap in the membership of the American Medical Association and the United Auto Workers.

A crucial element of the pluralist theory, then, is recognition of the presence of unorganized or potential interests which are actually numerical majorities and may become the base from which future organized interest groups emanate. With this potential threat in mind, the pluralist maintains that organized interest will recognize the possible serious consequences if these submerged interests were to become organized and, therefore, must give to them a minimum amount of recognition. This will once again lessen the possibility of irreconcilable conflict.

Operating under these basic conditions the pluralist contends that democracy will work and, in fact, given the reality of the political world, could not succeed under any other set of circumstances. Government plays an especially significant role in this kind of system. It must serve as an overseer and regulator of the competition between groups, providing the arena for debate, keeping the system open, and ensuring that bargaining and compromise, so essential to the effective maintenance of the pluralist system, occur.

Liberal, Conservative, and Pluralist Theories Compared

The liberal theory of democracy and its two variants, the conservative Federalist and pluralist models, do not by any means exhaust the many possibilities of democratic theory. The three theories discussed do represent major alternatives by which we have attempted to justify the distribution of power in the American political system. It should be apparent that the liberal Jeffersonian and conservative Federalist models differ sharply from the pluralist theory. The Jeffersonians, as we have seen, hoped that men would be rational in their pursuit of the public good, while the Federalists believed that majorities tend to be created by the pursuit of economic gain and wished for a more responsible minority to rule or at best the establishment of additional safeguards against the tyranny of the majority.

The pluralist model describes a situation in which public policies result from neither a limited aristocracy nor a rational majority seeking out the public interest but rather from compromise between various organized minorities. The pluralists are willing to take human nature as they find it, egocentric and group oriented, and their theory is *essentially* descriptive in this sense. But pluralism has its normative adherents also. There are many who believe it expresses a valued ideal. They contend that because the theory reflects a more realistic appraisal of politics in general and human nature in particular, it is the only feasible alternative to coercion and is therefore desirable. Democratic theory is improved by being more faithfully descriptive of the actual political process.

The liberal Jeffersonians react strongly to a system that does not promise any consciously defined direction toward the future. It is their view that pluralism represents the glorification of industrial capitalism and is blind to the problems of the entire body politic. Where, they would ask, are such social ills as environmental blight, poverty, public order, or the cultivation of the arts to be handled if there are no special identifiable social groups which regard these issues as their special interest? The harmonious picture of continually adjusting groups is aimless and not at all consistent with the Jeffersonian faith in a responsive system which reflects the will of the majority and which enables citizens to hold rulers accountable for the decisions they make.

The conservative Federalists react just as strongly to the pluralist variant because it undermines their belief in the necessity and capacity for leadership or statesmanship in the political system. Conciliation and compromise of group interests as a basis for decision making encourages human beings, in the conservatives' eyes, to follow only their egocentric impulses. The group and group self-interest are insufficient replacements for the traditional ordering device of the community.

The most vigorous critics of the pluralist model, however, are those who argue that the pluralists' concern for equilibrium is really an ideological attachment to preservation of the status quo. Indeed, this attachment includes the desire, the critics contend, to preserve certain elite groups and interests in society. As E. E. Schattschneider put it, "The flaw in the pluralist heaven is that the heavenly chorus sings with a strong upper-class accent."[15]

Critics such as Herbert Marcuse join the earlier school of "pluralist skeptics" such as C. Wright Mills and Henry Kariel in stressing the essentially one-dimensional character of pluralistic politics.[16] There are groups which lack organization, or the persistence, or the resources, or the legitimacy to participate even marginally in the balancing process. A number of concerns of potential interest to many or all segments of society are not carried by the interest groups to centers of decision making. (To take a classic example, the proponents of gun control lack cohesive support, while the opponents have those resources necessary to defeat it.) These critics of pluralism echo the desires of both the liberals and conservatives that political and social problems must be formulated in a context other than the battleground of competing self-interests.

Conclusion

Liberal democracy possesses a remarkably dynamic character and insists on the human potential in each of us, thereby expressing

[15]E. E. Schattschneider, *The Semi-Sovereign People* (New York: Holt, Rinehart and Winston, 1960), p. 35. For an instructive comparison of pluralism and classical democracy, see Frank Marini, "John Locke and the Revision of Classical Democratic Theory," *Western Political Quarterly* 22 (March 1969), pp. 5–18.

[16]Herbert Marcuse, *One-Dimensional Man* (Boston: Beacon Press, 1964); C. Wright Mills, *The Power Elite* (New York: Oxford University Press, 1959); and Henry Kariel, *The Decline of American Pluralism* (Stanford, Calif.: Stanford University Press, 1961).

a hope that has the possibility for being more than a benign dream. Whether this possibility is actualized turns, in large measure, on the thrust of the American political culture.

With which of the democratic models does contemporary American culture harmonize to the greatest extent? Is the culture primarily geared to populist and majoritarian values and hence supportive of Jeffersonian possibilities? If so it will emphasize human capability and rationality and—because of this—support a measure of equality among citizens. Futhermore, there will be some stress on the role of government in furthering the dignity of man and the possibilities of human happiness. If the culture is more oriented toward the Federalist model, it will treat humans as frail and unequal and will therefore tend to legitimize the need for rule by elites, the "better sort" of citizens. The natural right of property will be elevated to a level on par with, if not above, other personal rights, and this version of American values will be firmly reinforced by symbolic and mythological devices. Still another possibility is that we will find the culture generally inclining to neither majoritarianism nor elitism. Are there, as the pluralist model requires, values and elements furthering the right and potentiality of egocentric, group-oriented individuals to organize in a generally democratic and uninhibited fashion so as to secure just representation of their common goals in the political system? The kind of democracy we have in these last decades of the twentieth century will depend in large part on the orientation of the American political culture.

III

American Political Culture:
Foundations of Consciousness

> *It would seem very much to be the case that man does not think alone, not even the philosopher; but that his thought, however solitary and rarefied it may appear in his more complex cerebrations, does take root in the soil of his culture and his group.*
> William Barrett, *Philosophy in the Twentieth Century*

> *Americans . . . do not see the political relevance of their unhappiness.* Ira Katznelson and Mark Kesselman,
> *The Politics of Power*

> *There's so much talk about the system. And so little understanding. . . . To understand structured reality requires an understanding of the value source from which it's derived.* Robert M. Pirsig, *Zen and the Art of Motorcycle Maintenance*

In 1813 Thomas Jefferson wrote to John Adams that he was very proud to have led the fight in Virginia to provide public education and to abolish entails and primogeniture. These reforms would, he noted, "raise the mass of people to the high ground of moral respectability" and would create a policy where "everyone, by his property or his satisfactory situation, is interested in the support of law and order." Furthermore, "such men may safely and advantageously reserve to themselves a wholesome control over their public affairs and a high degree of freedom."[1]

Jefferson was applying the sentiments of the Declaration of Independence, which is committed to more than the abstract right to the pursuit of happiness. A government should provide security and follow principles conducive to human development. If it fails, "it is the right of the People to alter or to abolish it, and to institute a new Government, laying its Foundation on such Principles, and organizing its Power in such Form, as to them shall seem most likely to effect their Safety and Happiness." Five years after the Declaration,

---

[1]Thomas Jefferson, "A Letter to John Adams," in *The Few and Many*, ed. Thomas Dye and Harmon Ziegler (Belmont, Calif.: Duxbury Press, 1972), pp. 21–22.

the Articles of Confederation sought to "secure and perpetuate mutual friendship and intercourse among people," echoing Paine's belief that to regain paradise a person need only "hold out to his neighbor the hearty hand of friendship."[2]

That these founding documents, which commit the new nation and its government to policies promoting "happiness and friendship," appear foolishly utopian to our age tells us a great deal. It also raises a host of questions about Americans' expectations, awareness, and feelings about their government and political system—questions, that is, about political consciousness.

Several major elements or components comprise American political culture and shape this consciousness.

First, there is an ideology that encompasses what a society thinks about politics and is articulated by various symbols. Second, there is always a broader philosophical view of what a people think about the world, and also how they seek to know it. Third, the predominant social perspective of a people and the way they envision mankind are very important to political consciousness. To what degree do populist, elitist, or pluralist factors dominate in these fundamental ideological and symbolic, metaphysical and epistemological, and psychological and sociological elements of the American political culture?

To a large extent Americans incline to a collective political consciousness. For what James D. Barber says of presidents is true of all whom they govern. "The President is not some shapeless organism in a flood of novelties, but a man with a memory in a system with a history."[3] So are we all. And Americans' parallel political memories are closely related to their shared culture system. Recognizing the importance of political culture to political consciousness and ultimately to political behavior is not to presume to have deciphered the mystery of human individuality. There are many incalculable and inexplicable individual eccentricities influencing human behavior, and these in turn add to the culture. Thus, the political culture is the "product of both the collective history of a political system and the life histories of the members of that system."[4]

[2]Quoted in Norman Jacobsen, "Political Science and Political Education," *American Political Science Review* 57 (September 1963), p. 564.

[3]James D. Barber, *Presidential Character*, 2nd ed. (Englewood Cliffs, N.J.: Prentice-Hall, 1977), p. 14.

[4]Lucien W. Pye, "Political Culture," *International Encyclopedia of Social Science*, Vol. 12, p. 218.

Theodore Roszak wrote, "As long as politics does not call the culture into question, or culture the politics, people may pay little attention to this metaphysical and psychic dimension of political life."[5] This dimension is never absent, but "it may only vibrate in the background like a groundtone so constant that it is only perceived in silence."[6] In sum, because cultural factors are important to political consciousness, and because political consciousness is crucial to political behavior, an examination of culture and consciousness is of the utmost importance in determining which variant of American democracy will be actualized.

IDEOLOGICAL AND SYMBOLIC FOUNDATIONS

Studies of the American political culture have dealt almost exclusively with the ideological and symbolic foundations. This may be inevitable in a century called the age of ideology. The function of ideology and symbols is clear enough. Kenneth Dolbeare remarked that "*ideology* is first communicated to people, then internalized by them, and finally drawn upon by leaders to *explain* and *justify* their actions or *marshal support* for their policies."[7] Symbols are quite simply the means by which the ideology is communicated.

It may seem paradoxical to describe as highly ideological a people who see themselves as nonphilosophical and pragmatic realists, but so they are nevertheless. Few nations have engaged in a celebration of basic values and institutions as lavish as the United States Bicentennial. Second, only a very few other modern nations have engaged in efforts to export values and politics as intense as those of the United States—by means of aid, military support, and other aspects of American foreign policy. Then, too, in Indochina the United States was ultimately the lone spear-carrier for the capitalist West against the competing ideology of Marxism. There are, admittedly, many reasons for these phenomena, but their basic impulse derives from the strong hold on the American psyche of national beliefs and identity as protected by prescribed rules and epitomized by certain symbols.

Many commentators have found America's ideological and sym-

---

[5]Theodore Roszak, *Where the Wasteland Ends* (New York: Anchor Books, 1973), p. xviii.
[6]Ibid.
[7]Kenneth M. Dolbeare, *Political Change in the United States* (New York: McGraw-Hill, 1974), pp. 91–92.

bolic components to be beyond question, which is the ultimate attainment of an ideology. Hofstadter believes the American experience has been essentially based on the common socioeconomic beliefs of free enterprise, competition, and individualism which, along with the stable political system to which they are joined, have made for a beneficent and therefore unquestioned state of affairs.[8] Louis Hartz argues that because of our peculiar nonfeudal origins, we have no experience with class struggles over ideology. Since there was never a well-defined aristocracy to be overthrown, along with its ideological and symbolic justifications, we do not think of prevailing beliefs and symbols as constituting an ideology. And since these appurtenances have stood firm during a period of American geopolitical and economic success for the middle class, they go unexamined.[9] Tocqueville believed that no real revolution in ideas ever occurred in America. As a result the formalistic, conservative, and traditionalist aspects of the dominant culture persevere, with little criticism.[10] Perhaps Boorstin revealed best of all the ultimate subsconscious power of American ideology. While vigorously claiming to have no ideology, America operates in his view, on a "mood of giveness and a sense of the promised land," which provides our consensus.[11] Finally, Daniel Bell prematurely announced, as the 1960s began, that the age of ideology had ended. "There is today a rough consensus among intellectuals on political issues: the acceptance of a Welfare State; the desirability of decentralized power; a system of mixed economy and political pluralism."[12] The emphasis shifts to politics as consensus rather than to politics as conflict.

Unfortunately for Bell, his timing could not have been worse. The proclaimed politics of consensus, was to be severely challenged by several political movements as repressive to differing degrees and in distinct yet often parallel ways. All of the challenges—those of Black Power, Radical Right, New Left and counterculture, and feminist groups—peaked in their power in the brief eight-year span

[8]Richard Hofstadter, *The American Political Tradition and the Men Who Made It* (New York: Alfred A. Knopf, 1949).

[9]Louis Hartz, *The Liberal Tradition in America* (New York: Harcourt, Brace and World, 1955).

[10]Alexis de Tocqueville, *Democracy in America*, trans. Henry Reeves, 2 vols. (New York: Simon and Schuster, 1964).

[11]Daniel Boorstin, *The Genius of American Politics* (Chicago: University of Chicago Press, 1953).

[12]Daniel Bell, *The End of Ideology*, rev. ed. (New York: Free Press, 1965), p. 397.

between Johnson's inauguration in 1965 and the start of Nixon's second term in 1973. Devine believes that at such times, as in the Civil War period and Great Depression, there may be a temporary weakening of the dominant values and moderation of the power of the ideological and symbolic elements, but they persevere.[13] An observer has only to consider the last decade to realize how fully the recent challenges of Radical Right and Left, militant blacks and feminists, were turned back. Centrist to conservative politics once more reign supreme. The years immediately after the Bicentennial saw trust increase, although slowly, in the political and governmental institutions and values they serve.[14] Thus, ironically we find, as one analyst wrote in late 1977, that "American society, which is demographically the most diverse among Western industralized nations, is at the same time [still] the least amenable to ideological variety." Whereas other Western industrial nations have alternative ideological orientations, "the conceptual preconditions of politically viable American ideology have thus far not allowed the American people a comparable variety of choices.[15]

The implications of this hegemony of persistent ideological values and powerful symbols are many and far-reaching. This is so for domestic policy, campaign styles, and public debate, as well as for foreign policy. I am concerned here, however, with the impact on individual political consciousness and behavioral inclinations. It is likely that any nation which lacks ideological variety and choices will find that its political ideology and symbols concretely and formally vie against the development of the critical, capable, par-

[13]Donald J. Devine, *The Political Culture of the United States* (New York: Little, Brown, 1972), p. 182.

[14]This is revealed in two national surveys conducted during the close of 1977. The Louis Harris organization surveyed 1,498 adults and the University of Michigan's Institute for Social Research polled 3,300 high school seniors. Both samples were asked to indicate whether they believed major public institutions were doing a "good" job, "very good" job, or "not so good" a job. Of sixteen institutions tested in the Harris survey, fifteen had risen in public confidence since 1976. Nevertheless, the Supreme Court, presidency, and Congress still ranked far below their ratings before Indochina and Watergate, with 31 percent, 26 percent, and 15 percent, respectively. Of potentially long-term significance in the Michigan survey was the sharp drop in the level of suspicion and cynicism among seniors as compared with their immediate predecessors. See "Confidence in Institutions Up Strongly," *Washington Post*, January 5, 1979, pp. 1, 8.

[15]Robert A. Heineman, "Ideological Inflexibility and the Human Condition: A Reappraisal of the Liberal View of the Need for Authority" (Paper delivered at the annual meeting of the Southern Political Science Association, New Orleans, La., November 4-7, 1977), pp. 17–18.

ticipatory citizen envisioned by Jefferson. Indeed, to the degree that American political beliefs are elevated as powerful, unquestioned abstractions with a power and force divorced from reality, they may create a blind loyalty, diminished awareness, and subordinate consciousness on the part of the silent majority. This has the gravest implications, for as Anderson notes, "if we can understand unawareness, we can understand political repression."[16]

Let us turn to a brief analysis of the actual content, nature, and function of two key elements of American ideology, the national identity and national beliefs mentioned by Devine.[17]

I Am an American

"I am an American" is the first and foremost political lesson learned by children. Indeed, this almost unbreakable emotional identification with the nation is apparently much stronger in the United States than in many other industrial nations. National identification is clearly waning in such nations as Britain, Canada, Belgium, Spain, and Yugoslavia. In these countries subnational groups—Scots and Welsh, the French in Quebec, the Flemish in Belgium, the Basques and the Serbs—demand and sometimes win greater autonomy and self-determination. One author believes that this internal devolution of the nation-state is a key characteristic of our time.[18] Groups are struggling for their language, customs, self-rule, and way of life, so that their particular traditions and consciousness will not be subordinated to some monolithic, abstract national culture. In this country, however, even groups relegated to the lowest status and experiencing the harshest discrimination seldom sever their tie to the nation and move to subgroup autonomy of the sort that characterizes the cases mentioned above. The most obvious example is black Americans.[19]

Americans traveling in Europe soon hear astonishment expressed at the speed and thoroughness with which Europeans who emigrate to the United States transfer their loyalty to the new country. Many, if not most, even Americanize their names. Our historic isolation

[16]Walt Anderson, *Politics and the New Humanism* (Pacific Palisades, Calif.: Goodyear Publishing, 1973), p. 55.

[17]Devine, *Political Culture*, p. 182.

[18]James Wolfe, "Constitutional Devolution and Functionalist Community-Building: Inverse Trends in European Politics," *Southern Quarterly* 14 (April 1976), pp. 215–30.

[19]Milton Morris, *The Politics of Black America* (New York: Harper and Row, 1975), pp. 125–30.

from Europe no doubt was conducive to the quick change of identity. The need to create unity from diversity of ethnic groups also made for an insistence on Americanization. In the most heterogeneous nation, where one-sixth of the population are recent—either first or second generation—immigrants from over seventy-five nations, this impulse to unification through assimilation continues. "Integration" and "acceptance" are regarded as the ultimate goals for ethnic groups.[20] We have even devised a symbol for the purpose, and its name tells us much: we see our country as a "melting pot" wherein diverse cultural identities are destroyed as individuals respond to the intense heat of nationalism.

A competing social view that has received greater acceptance in Europe and also in the United States recently emphasizes roots. This is sometimes called the "salad bowl" theory of society: it says that a country is enhanced by the contribution of independent and persistent cultural flavors. When efforts are made to alter American political practices so that they reinforce and recognize ethnic or racial differences, however, it is significant that political elites generally react with alarm. For example, the federal judiciary in 1977 approved redistricting for racial purposes in New York only over the firm objections of Chief Justice Burger. "The device employed by the State of New York and endorsed by the Court today, moves us one step farther away from a truly homogeneous society." This is a "retreat from the ideal of the American 'melting pot.'"[21]

The implications for diminished political awareness and consequent ready acquiescence to the nationalistic policies of political elites are rather clear. A call to national loyalty has been used to gain support for "winning the West,""manifest destiny,""the white man's burden," and the anticommunist "crusade." Indians, Mexicans, and Filipinos know the power of American nationalism. Perhaps the ultimate manifestation to date of this ethnocentricism was the Indochina quagmire in which the American people found themselves as their nation approached its Bicentennial. The nationalistic sloganeering and jingoism which passed for debate about escalation of the Vietnam War made a mockery of the Jeffersonian ideal of policymaking through political dialogue. One has only to recall the emptiness of the Johnson and Nixon proclama-

[20]Malcolm Byrnes, "The Idea of the Nation in Recent Political Thought: A Reassessment" (Paper delivered at the annual meeting of the Louisiana Political Science Association, Baton Rouge, La., March 18-19, 1977).

[21]United Jewish Organizations of Williamsburgh, Inc., v. Carey, 97 S. Ct. 996 (1977).

tions that we were "protecting democracy" or "seeking peace with honor" and the bumper stickers reading "America: Love It or Leave It" or "My Country: Right or Wrong." Further reducing mass awareness of such ethnocentric policies is the scarcity of genuine debates on American foreign policy. When they are in office both major parties insist on "bipartisan" support until a policy failure becomes overwhelmingly evident, as in Indochina in the late 1960s and in Iran a decade later.

Long before today's generation of college students were born, in the 1930s, the country gave birth to a "House Un-American Activities Committee." Surely no European legislator would dare propose an Un-French, Un-Swedish or Un-British activities committee. He would be soundly ridiculed. Such is the conformist potential of our exaggerated nationalism. Hartz sees this basic problem of the young and spectacularly successful American nation not as the "danger of the majority, but what has slumbered unconsciously behind it; the 'Tyranny of Opinion' that Tocqueville saw."[22] Given this American tendency, it is critical that one look not only at the implications of nationalism per se but also at the nature, content, and function of the beliefs at the base of the American political culture.

Liberty Equals Property versus Equality

Four fundamental beliefs are listed by Devine—liberty, equality, property, and religion. Liberty and property are juxtaposed, in the American political culture, with equality. That is, liberty and property are limits imposed on egalitarian action, particularly by government, in the area of economics. Religious values are of self-evident importance, from the time of the Great Awakening in colonial America to the Moral Majority of today. Less obvious is another basic belief, the image of man or the operative psychology of a people. "A psychology operates from an idea of what a human being is, and any such idea inevitably generates propositions about what human societies are, what they should be and how they can be studied. Any psychology, then, is also a political ideology and a scientific methodology."[23] Since the operative American view of human nature reflects the structure and nature of American society, I will analyze them simultaneously as psychological and sociological foundations.

[22]Hartz, *Liberal Tradition*, p. 11.
[23]Anderson, *Politics and the New Humanism*, p. 10.

Belief in private property conferred by nature and hence resistant to public confiscation and use by an artificial government is deeply embedded in our culture: as a result, we seldom realize that this attitude makes us unique in classical and contemporary political life. Rousseau, Marx, Sir Thomas More, and others condemned private property. Aristotle and St. Thomas Aquinas praised the personal, economic, and political benefits of widespread property holding. But all viewed the right to property as "social" in origin. Aristotle insisted that since man was a political animal born and nurtured by his polity, he was obligated to share the production of his property for the common good. The right to property, like education, a job, and even the continuation of life itself, was conferred by one's city-state and was subject to complete regulation. St Thomas would agree but would reinforce this position by asserting one's Chistian obligation to share the fruits of property with one's brother. It is no coincidence that the first powerful theoretical defense of property possession as a natural rather than social right was offered by one of the thinkers whose ideas significantly influenced the American Founding Fathers. This was John Locke.

Locke is often called the philosopher of England's "Glorious Revolution" of 1688 in which the growing propertied middle class, or Whigs, won the right to parliamentary representation. In his thought man is viewed as holding property in a prepolitical state of nature.[24] The logic of "natural law" which governs that existence dictates that one should own only that amount of property whose production can be consumed. To own more would mean spoilage. Man gradually develops a primitive monetary system that permits unlimited accumulation of unspoilable goods—valuable gems, for example—that have exchange value. The tension arising from ensuing divisions of wealth is a major component of the "inconveniences" of the state of nature. With the social contract mankind forms a political society and then a government to deal with these inconveniences; securing the right of private property, along with rights to life and liberty, was a major reason for the social contract. Thus this "natural" right, which was not originally conferred by government, imposes a limit on government.

By the time of the Constitution the "happiness and friendship" of the Declaration and Articles had been replaced by property. The

[24]John Locke, *Second Treatise of Civil Government*, ed. Charles L. Sherman (New York: Appleton-Century-Crofts, 1937).

reason in part was the class conflict raging in postrevolutionary America that was revealed so dramatically in 1786 by Shay's Rebellion. The document emerging from Philadelphia was intended, in the words of James Madison, its chief author, to protect against a "malady," or "rage" for "paper money, for an abolition of debts, for an equal division of property, or for any other improper or wicked object." In fact, property is equated with life and liberty itself in the Constitution. Ensuring that people with unequal talents are free to gain and hold differing amounts of property is the raison d'être of the Union. Protecting "the diversity in the faculties of men, from which the rights of property originate, is . . . the first object of government."[25] This object received concrete support in the fiscal and monetary policies devised by Alexander Hamilton, the first secretary of the treasury. It also dictated many of the decisions orchestrated by our most important chief justice, John Marshall, from 1801 to 1835. Laissez-faire government, Social Darwinism, Horatio Alger myths, and many other doctrines flourished on this belief in property as the capitalist ethos became more embedded in the American consciousness than in that of any other people.

Private property even acquired a religious justification in what was and is predominantly a Protestant people. The Puritans held to a doctrine of predestination, that only God's elect would have immortality. Finite man could never penetrate God's mind and be assured of his destiny. Still, as Weber explains, earthly prosperity might reassure one and his neighbors that his was a chosen life. Thus there was a powerful impulse to the work ethic. This protestant ethic harmonized well with the spirit of capitalism.[26]

In our day the equation of property and liberty as natural rights is a powerful obstacle to equality. This may appear contradictory, since equality as a basic value is often perceived as ranking in importance with liberty and property. To some degree it does; however, there are at least four different dimensions of equality, and America's commitment is not the same in each.

Formal *political* equality finds widespread support. Nearly all limitations on equal political rights have been eliminated. One does not have to pay a poll tax, take a literacy test, hold property for bond elections, or be white, male, and at least twenty-one to be enfran-

---

[25]James Madison, Federalist, No. 10, in *The Federalist*, p. 55.
[26]Max Weber, *The Protestant Ethic and the Spirit of Capitalism*, trans. Talcott Parsons (New York: Charles Scribner's Sons, 1958).

chised to participate in politics. Efforts have also been made to realize *legal* equality. There are no debtors' prisons, garnishment is nearly extinct, and harassment of debtors is now a crime; all the accused who face possible imprisonment have a right to counsel; and there are public and private agencies that offer legal aid for the poor. At present there is a growing attack on the disparity of sentences and on punishment that is more lenient for political and white-collar criminals than for others. We have even made some advances in *social* equality. The institutionalized benefit of equal protection. Antimiscegenation laws are invalid. Homosexuals have gained some standing. No one can be denied the right of contract because of race. Blacks, Chicanos, women, and others of traditionally low status are given more formal rights in education and jobs. Both children and the aged receive greater protection. There is, however, much less agreement on this aspect of equality, as demonstrated by the widespread controversy over the feminist movement, homosexual rights, scatter-site housing, and most of all, the affirmative action, or quota, programs intended to help advance women and nonwhite minorities in the workplace. There is even less agreement on the last dimension of equality, the *economic* one.

Apart from some income transfer payments—food stamps, rent supplements, medicare, welfare benefits, and so forth—which alter the distribution not of wealth but of income, there is virtually no redistributive effort in American political life. The United States spends less of its GNP on social welfare programs than any other industrial capitalist state.[27] Such inclinations are largely screened from ever becoming political demands by the sanctity of property—the ranking of property rights with personal liberty and political freedom. The implications for political power are clear. Of what benefit are formal political rights without the substantive economic means to give them meaning? For example, as the 1980s began it was estimated that a minimum of $400,000 was needed to challenge an incumbent congressman in an election; that figure represented merely the value of incumbent perquisites. One needed at least $2

[27]Ira Katznelson, "Considerations on Social Democracy in the United States," *Comparative Politics* 11 (October 1978), p. 84. Marc F. Plattner, "The Welfare State vs. The Redistributive State," *Public Interest* 55 (Spring 1979), pp. 28–48, notes that even with progressive taxation and social welfare programs, "it would be a serious error to infer that the American polity has ever embraced the idea of income redistribution." As he goes on to point out, there is an immense gulf of principle between the welfare state and the redistributive state."

million to $3 million for most senate or gubernatorial contests. In 1978 one senatorial candidate, Republican Jesse Helms of North Carolina, and one gubernatorial aspirant, Republican Bill Clements of Texas, spent $7.5 million each. Both won. And in 1980 Republican presidential aspirant John Connally spent approximately $12 million in the early primaries. Unlike Helms and Clements, he lost, garnering only one delegate.

This basic contradiction in the political culture between formal legal and political equality, on the one hand, and informal socioeconomic inequality, on the other, leads to some divergence in the attitudes of lower and higher income groups. Whereas elites support formal political equality more than the masses, one major study found that "the reverse is true for the value of economic equality."[28] It is possible to obtain some specific details from local surveys such as that done by the New Orleans Urban League of some 1,300 low-income households in October 1978. Ninety-one percent thought energy costs should be reduced for the poor and elderly; between 71 and 85½ thought food and medicine should not be taxed; 53 percent endorsed rent control; 60 percent thought renters should get the same tax credit as homeowners.[29] A decade earlier a nationwide survey comparing class attitudes on two major issues reached similar conclusions; lower-status workers viewed government efforts to improve living conditions more favorably than other groups (see table 1).[30]

It is hardly surprising to find those with less wealth favoring greater economic equality. Albert Szymanski contends that "as a general rule the lower a social class in the structure of a country the more leftist (that is, in favor of more equality and less privilege) will be its politics." In the United States, where there is no significant leftist party and where cross-pressures on lower-class workers are exerted by multiple forces relating to ethnicity, region, or occupational status, "the correlation between class and political attitudes is far from perfect." Still, on economic issues, as distinct from those relating to law and order, foreign policy, and social or symbolic matters, "even in the United States the lower classes, especially the

[28]Herbert McClosky, "Consensus and Ideology in American Politics," *American Political Science Review* 58 (June 1964), p. 367.

[29]*Times-Picayune* (New Orleans, La.), October 23, 1978.

[30]Cited in Richard Hamilton, *Restraining Myths* (New York: John Wiley, 1975), p. 55.

Table 1.
Percentages of Groups Favoring
Selected Government-assured Benefits, 1968

Issue	Manual workers	Independent businessmen	Independent professionals	Managers & officials	Salaried professionals	Clerical & sales
Federal government guarantees jobs and decent living standards	52	30	29	25	37	29
N =	(311)	(89)	(14)	(83)	(75)	(76)
Federal government guarantees low-cost medical care	71	54	23	52	53	51
N =	(330)	(103)	(13)	(75)	(83)	(79)

Note: The two questions were: In general, some people feel that the government in Washington should see to it that every person has a job and a good standard of living. Others think the government should let each person get ahead on his own. Do you think the government should help?

Some say the government in Washington ought to help people get doctors and hospital care at low cost. Do you think the government should help?

Source: Richard Hamilton, *Restraining Myths: Critical Studies of U.S. Social Structure and Politics* (New York: John Wiley and Sons, 1975), pp. 54–55.

working class, are more leftist than the more privileged ones."[31] Still, as the above data indicate, they are not necessarily socialists, since the center lies farther to the right in the United States than in Sweden or Italy, for example.

Examples of a self-serving commitment by the elite to a limited view of equality abound; the desegregation effort presents one example. Affirmative action, quotas, busing, and other programs that aim to combat discrimination quite clearly do not take from the propertied class and give to the lower class so as to compensate racial minorities, who have endured the harshest deprivation. Instead, such programs force the working-class whites to share the available resources and opportunities with minorities. There resuts what social scientists call a "zero-sum game," wherein one of these

[31]Albert Szymanski, *The Capitalist State and the Politics of Class* (Cambridge, Mass.: Winthrop, 1978), pp. 28–30.

two groups can win only at the expense of the other. This competition inevitably exacerbates racial tension. For example, under a racial quota for admission to professional schools, as Justice Douglas said, a competent "poor Appalachian white, or a second generation Chinese in San Francisco, or some other American whose lineage is so diverse as to defy ethnic labels"[32] would be left out. And as critics have noted of the Supreme Court's 1978 ruling in the case of Alan Bakke, the Harvard minority admissions plan so enthusiastically endorsed by Justice Powell as a model goes even further. It overlooks most low-income *nonwhite* applicants in favor of more well-established brethren. A clearer example of the bifurcated elite view of equality is the fact that whereas the federal judiciary in 1954 decided that the equal protection clause of the Fourteenth Amendment entails a fundamental right to desegregated education, it does not entail, according to a 1973 decision, the right to an equally funded education. In Justice Powell's words, "This Court has never heretofore held that wealth discrimination alone provides an adequate basis for invoking strict scrutiny"[33] of any program for possible constitutional violations.

According to economist Lester Thurow of the Massachusetts Institute of Technology, the United States is second only to France in having the most unequal distribution of wealth of the industrialized world. The nation in third place is far removed.[34] Thus "wealth discrimination," the most important form of discrimination, is rampant. Yet it does not come under scrutiny in the political or governmental system.

METAPHYSICAL AND EPISTEMOLOGICAL FOUNDATIONS

The shape of a society depends not only on ideological and symbolic elements but also on the perceived nature of reality (a matter for metaphysics) and how it may be known (a matter for epistemology). The clearest example in political philosophy of the intimate relationship between these and political life is found in Plato's thought.

Plato believed reality to be embodied in transcendent, eternal, and immutable truths or ideas. The visible world provides only a

---

[32]*De Funis* v. *Odegaard*, 82 Wash. 2d. 11 (1973).

[33]*San Antonio Independent School District* v. *Rodriguez*, 411 U.S. 1 (1973).

[34]Lester C. Thurow, "The Myth of the American Economy," *Newsweek*, February 14, 1977, p. 11.

rough approximation. Only individuals of great intellectual ability, those with gold rather than brass in their makeup, who are trained and tested over their lifetime, are capable of perceiving truth. The rest remain like cave-dwellers, seeing the flickering images of themselves and objects about them reflected by their fire on the stone walls. Only the few who have seen beyond the earthly predicament and images and have perceived eternal truth are equipped to rule. All the rest are to be socialized by a "royal lie or Phoenician tale" to internalize a subordinate consciousness.

The souls of the philosopher-kings strain toward the truth as plants search for light. They do this "without any assistance of sense(s)."[35] It is noteworthy that this half-consciousness blocks appreciation, understanding, and respect for the natural world, which is viewed as merely a crude imitation of eternal wisdom. Those of the lower class who seek knowledge through the senses rather than through pure contemplation are said to hold "opinion" and not knowledge. Thus they are not entitled to a share of power.

In the United States this scheme has largely been reversed. We reject knowledge of the soul, faith, pure contemplation, and mystical insight, often viewing them as belonging to the province of the untutored masses. We predicate our technological and political existence mainly on scientific knowledge of the natural world. Hence our existence becomes dominated by decisions of scientists, engineers, and technocrats. Some would say we are, to a degree, trapped at the bottom of Plato's cave.

The dominant epistemology of the American culture is "*empiricism*—the belief that the world has only tangible reality, that things exist out there and their nature and characteristics may be discovered as facts in themselves."[36]

Empiricist reasoning can be illustrated by the example of a person born with no senses—no sight, hearing, touch, smell, or taste. An empiricistwould deny that such a person could ever know anything: he would be in a bubble. This individual would be truly senseless because the blank white paper, the tabula rasa of the mind, would have no impressions written upon it. If for a moment this individual was exposed to some sensory stimulus, say, a running horse, and was then deprived once more of his senses, he would with his mind construct a simple idea from the qualities of horseness and

[35]Plato, *The Republic*, trans. Benjamin Jowett (New York: Vintage Books, 1955), p. 278.
[36]Dolbeare, *Political Change*, p. 104.

motion which had impressed his senses and would store this idea in the memory. We compile a set of ideas from repeated experiences. The mind sorts the various sensory data, combines them into ideas of objects, tests and corrects them if necessary—accounting for the straight stick that appears bent in the water or the rail tracks which seem to converge—reflects on the relationship of ideas, organizes and stores them, and uses them to frame propositions and assertions. Conduct is predicated on such empirically derived knowledge.[37]

Thus knowledge is the structure of relationships among ideas that we have about objects, or substance, which have made impressions on our senses. We can, in the empiricist's view, know nothing that we have not sensed, nor can we destroy knowledge that we have sensed. The empiricist Locke would ask—by way of supporting this epistemology—whether a blind man has a sense of colors and whether a deaf man has a true, distinct notion of sound. "I would have any one try to fancy any taste, which had never affected his palate; or frame the idea of a scent he had never smelt; and when he can do this, I will also conclude that a blind man hath ideas of colours, and a deaf man true distinct notions of sounds."[38] All people who haven't "taken leave of their senses" are capable of philosophy; therefore this is an egalitarian and democratic epistemology. But no one is assured of certain, perfect knowledge, because we cannot be completely confident that the primary and secondary qualities emanating from an object—from substance—as they have been received and interpreted accurately represent the object. Consequently, this is a moderate epistemology which preaches tolerance and humility. Moderation is particularly critical, for where the mind does not perceive the proper connection between the ideas acccording to reason, "there men's opinions are not the product of judgement, or the consequence of reason, but the effects of chance and hazard, of a mind floating at all adventures, without choice, and without direction."[39] Locke claimed to have found the horizons of everyday, practical knowledge. All individuals are capable of limited, relatively accurate knowledge, but none can claim eternal truth.

[37]This discussion of Locke's empiricism relies heavily upon Newton P. Stallknecht and Robert S. Brambaugh, *The Spirit of Western Philosophy* (New York: David McKay, 1950), pp. 302–12.
[38]John Locke, *An Essay Concerning Human Understanding*, ed. Alexander C. Fraser, 2 vols. (New York: Dover, 1959), 1:146.
[39]Ibid., 2:388.

As Sheldon Wolin notes, this reasoning "confined man to a mid-dling sort of condition, incapable of omniscience or perfection."[40] Or as Locke saw it, here was a "state of mediocrity, which is not capable of extremes." This philosophy, which best suited man's limited possibilities, concentrated on "the twilight of probability" between skeptical despair and proud presumption. And since everyday human conduct should be governed by this cautious philosophy and the "egalitarian epistemology of limits," man must build his politics accordingly. Government and theories of politics must be predicated on the realization that more abstract forms of knowledge—including political knowledge—which are further re-moved from direct sensory experience, depend upon, in Locke's phrase, "various and unknown interests, humours, and capacities of men, and not upon any settled ideas of things."[41] Locke's political philosophy is not always consistent with his epistemology. For example, he would ultimately reify natural rights, particularly of property, as an a priori idea, although it is surely not verifiable by empirical tests. But in general his *Second Treatise* on politics is the "application of the epistemology of the *Essay [On Human Under-standing]* to the field of politics."[42]

It is easy to see how this philosophy was intended both to "promote the advantages of everyday life" and, as Sabine says, to "be a solvent for all kinds of prejudice, in morals and religion, as well as in science."[43] Such epistemology undercuts claims to the infallibility of innate principles or ideas. Locke feared that doc-trines of this sort could be manipulated by ruling elites to take people "off the use of their own reason and judgement and put them on believing and taking upon trust without further examination," and "in this posture of blind credulity, they might be more easily governed."[44]

What if this metaphysics of objective material reality and this epistemology of sensory data were carried to an extreme conclu-sion? What if man fully developed the objective consciousness to shut out subjective, nonverifiable ways of knowing, pursuing a

[40]Sheldon Wolin, *Politics and Vision* (Boston: Little, Brown, 1960), pp. 236–37.

[41]Quoted in Ibid., pp. 296–99.

[42]Dante Germino, *Modern Western Political Thought* (Chicago: Rand McNally, 1972), p. 119.

[43]George H. Sabine, *A History of Political Thought*, 3rd ed. (New York: Holt, Rinehart and Winston, 1961), p. 530.

[44]Locke, *An Essay Concerning Human Understanding*, 1:116.

scientific method to regularize the system of observation, experi-
mentation, and testing of data so as to prevent inconsistency and
developing instruments and technologies to compensate for the
trickery of the senses? What would man be like when nature lay at
the mercy of his manipulative ability? What would happen to the
"moderation" and the "equalitarianism" that caution against the
manipulation of more abstract forms of knowledge such as the
political? Would man still be satisfied with "a middling sort of
condition"? Would he still feel "incapable of omniscience or perfection"? And what if this technologically sophisticated culture found
objective science eroding alternative ways of knowing, such as
religious revelation, mysticism, and contemplation, viewing all
these as disprovable? Would those who were most skilled in this
epistemology of the natural world form a new technoscientific
priesthood, a new and very powerful group of philosopher-kings?
And what would their consciousness and that of their contem-
poraries be like? Two centuries after the classical formulation of
empiricist philosophy and one century before it reached fruition in
the United States, Emerson sensed the possibilities of such
technological half-consciousness: "Empirical science is apt to cloud
the sight, and by the very knowledge of functions and processes to
bereave the student of the manly contemplation of the whole. The
savant becomes unpoetic."[45]

The tumultuous 1960s will be remembered partly as the time in
which the United States became the first nation to cross the divide
to become truly a "technological society." This transformation has
had many undeniably positive implications. Still, a fundamental
flaw, a crack in the foundation of the technological society, contributed to some novel problems of participation, policy, and personality. The advent of the technological age brought with it, maybe even
as its essence, a basic contradiction. The magnification of objective,
material possibilities through man's manipulation of nature and
other men with increasingly sophisticated technologies was accompanied by a "restriction of consciousness," constraint placed
upon creativity, spirit, and passion. Subjectivity, feelings, the soul,
the heart, intuitions, emotions, were all discounted and repressed in
preference to rational, objectively quantifiable data. In sum,
technology represents above all else the preeminence of Apollo, of
the scientific mind, and the denial of Dionysus, of feeling.

[45]Ralph W. Emerson, *The Complete Essays and Other Writings* (New York: Random
House, 1940), p. 36.

In his book, *Zen and the Art of Motorcycle Maintenance*, Pirsig gives a useful description of this imbalance of Apollo and Dionysus. He argues that "we take a handful of sand from the endless landscape of awareness around us and call that handful of sand the world." Life is diminished and sterilized to the exact same degree that this selection is based on the total exclusion of subjective and affective concerns. Pirsig believes we have attained our high level of scientific mastery by an obsessive concentration on the rational elements of life. "It's been necessary since before the time of Socrates to reject the passions, the emotions, in order to free the rational mind for an understanding of nature's order which was as yet unknown." Now, given the level of scientific knowledge, this is no longer necessary. "It is time to [reassimilate] those passions which were originally fled from. The passions, the emotions, the affective domain of man's consciousness, are a part of nature's order, too. *The central part*." This bifurcation, this failure of reason and feeling to coalesce, creates psychic disturbances which are projected into the world. "What's wrong with technology is that it's not connected in any real way with matters of the spirit and of the heart. And so it does blind, ugly things quite by accident and gets hated for that."[46] At least four problems that are relevant to political consciousness flow from this noncoalescence between reason and feeling. They have to do with possible distortions of public policy and political personality and with the undermining of both human will, or initiative, and mass participation.

Many observers have criticized the divergence of intellect and morality in technologically grounded *public policies* of the industrialized nations. On a visit to England just after World War II, the most industrially advanced nation of the time, the Greek author Nikos Kazantzakis wrote: "Theoretical thought has gone bankrupt and has turned into a tool applied for destructive purposes, or an aimless, foolish toy in the hands of the magician."[47] Much more recently, *The Best and the Brightest*, one of the most widely read studies of U.S. policy during the Vietnam War, contends that the gap between reason and feeling explains why the technically superior minds of the time led us into this costly blunder.[48] The dangers of Apollinian excesses, of the abuse of technology, is clearly

    [46]Robert Pirsig, *Zen and the Art of Motorcycle Maintenance* (New York: Bantam Books, 1974), pp. 75, 162, & 287.
    [47]Nikos Kazantzakis, *England* (New York: Simon and Schuster, 1965), p. 8.
    [48]David Halberstam, *The Best and the Brightest* (New York: Random House, 1969).

not peculiar to the United States. Those 300,000 antinuclear protestors who marched in Western Europe in October 1981 testify to the commonality of the problem in the West, as do the families who suffered the chemical destruction in Seveso, Italy, and the alliance between farmers and leftists who fought for more than a dozen years to halt construction of the new international airport in Japan, to take just a few examples. Still, the problem is inevitably more acute in the most technologically advanced country, the United States, and there are some fragmented signs of "conscious" efforts to counteract technologically excessive policies.

The distorted policies created by the repression of feeling and passion are not alone in gaining attention; the distorted personality is doing so as well. Peter Shaffer's *Equus*,[49] loosely based on an actual incident, is a provocative theatrical exposition of this very theme. In a culture that blocks expression of all aberrations in thought and behavior that might be labeled madness, passions, or magic, a young man whose life is dominated by secret worship of a horse inexplicably blinds six horses with a metal spike. His psychiatrist, Dr. Dysert, discovers through his analysis of the young man the concrete relationship between psychic repression of emotion and fantasy, on the one hand, and apathy and violence, on the other. He comes to realize the great degree to which mythology, gods, magic, and color have been banned from life in the name of normalcy and the extent to which existence has become dissonant as a result.

Not only can an undue reliance on technical knowledge lead to bizarre public policies and psychic disturbances, it can also threaten the creative spirit and the will. The existential psychologist Rollo May has defined our curious predicament: the same processes which make modern man so powerful—the development of atomic and other kinds of technical energy—also render us powerless.[50] This is so because man's will is undermined by the impersonal, technical power inherent in automated mass production, international communications and transportation systems, a pharmaceutical industry that can shape our every mood, and so forth. These dissociate us from one another and from nature. The Hegelian-Marxist philosopher Herbert Marcuse believes that the result is a one-dimensional man. The "inner dimension of the mind in which opposition to the status-quo can take place is whittled

[49]Peter Shaffer, *Equus* (New York: Avon Books, 1974).
[50]Rollo May, *Love and Will* (New York: W. W. Norton, 1969).

down."[51] Thus where May sees apathy, Marcuse sees a diminution of the "inner dimension."

The questionable nature of certain excessively technological public policies, the bizarre distortions of the human personality, and repression of the will, all have clear political implications. The exaggerated positivistic empiricism which undergirds our society can lead directly to political disenfranchisement. All political decisions are predicated on qualitative value judgments. And all collective decisions affecting human life are inherently political. For this reason Jefferson and other liberal democrats believed that people deserved to be consulted and were capable of articulating their needs and values in the decision-making process we know as politics. Unfortunately, in America at present, many important decisions are not made in any kind of intimate or even indirect consultation with the people. They are relegated to experts who have mastered a particular technology.

One of the most important decisions of the contemporary era confronting the American government is the question of nuclear weaponry. yet not only is the public frequently excluded entirely from such policy decisions, but even elected representatives are often given only a symbolic role. This is because the fundamental moral, normative questions are obscured by debates over tonnage, numbers, MIRVs, payload, first and second strike capability, and other even more complex minutiae of nuclear technology that only the experts understand. An example would be the issue of whether or not to produce a neutron bomb. In his January 1978 television special, Henry Kissinger, the dominant foreign policy figure of the 1970s stated, "I see the neutron bomb as a technical question." Similarly, although to a lesser degree, on economic decisions the American people and their elected representatives are bombarded with data on GNP, per capita income, balance of trade payments, inflation rates, unemployment rates, capital spending, labor productivity, reserve rates, leading economic indicators,and so on ad infinitum. This barrage of facts obscures the possibility that elites at the Federal Reserve, Wall Street, the major corporations, and the major banks may be powerful enough to impose their economic values on the American people.

The power of the scientific, quantitative approach is so en-

[51]Herbert Marcuse, *One-Dimensional Man* (London: Routledge and Kegan Paul, 1964), p. 243.

trenched that we could not even debate racism, our most critical moral issue, on a moral basis. When the federal judiciary finally moved to attack discrimination, it felt the need to justify its ground-breaking decision in the Brown case with a panoply of "scientific" sociological and psychological data. Later, busing for purposes of desegregation was authorized not on moral grounds but because a scientific study, the first Coleman Report in the 1960s, supposedly demonstrated that blacks placed in classrooms with whites performed better. Common sense tells us that this "myth of whiteness" is not valid. When busing drove large numbers of whites from the schools, there was a second Coleman Report in 1976, contending that the earlier one had been misinterpreted and that busing was exerting a counterproductive effect on integration. In this fashion we move from a valid and necessary science to "scientism," the ideological use of science.

These are but a few examples of the manner in which scientism as a basis for political decisions excludes moral concerns from technical expertise and, worse, precludes public discussions of both.

PSYCHOLOGICAL AND SOCIOLOGICAL FOUNDATIONS

The last great cultural pillar supporting the edifice of the American political system consists of interrelated psychological and sociological elements. It is no less important than the other aspects of the political culture.

An operative psychology of human capability can open up many possibilities. The reverse is also true: "The most important single limiting factor is the idea which any human society has about what the possibilities of human development really are."[52] Of equal significance are the social structure and consciousness of a people. The structure of roles, socioeconomic and status categories, class relations, and so forth directly affects one's awareness and behavioral inclinations. So does a people's idea of that social structure, which may or may not be accurate. Whether a society is perceived as equal or unequal, repressive or developmental, just or unjust, tolerant or racist and sexist, affluent or poor, pluralist or conformist, or open or closed will incline the observer in a particular direction. He will be more supportive of change or of the status quo.

[52]Anderson, *Politics and the New Humanism*, p. 143.

When endeavoring to grasp the psychological and sociological foundations of American political consciousness, we must keep two points in mind. First, it is not possible to (dis)prove a theory of human nature, to say whether it is right or wrong. It is only possible to identify which of the major alternative psychologies dominates the American perspective and to clarify its implications for American political consciousness and behavioral inclinations. Second, one must be careful to distinguish the nature and impact of objective social conditions from the subjective social consciousness predominant in the American political culture. We begin by looking for the operative human image in contemporary America.

As one analyst notes, "Basically, psychologists tend to hold to one of three dominant views of the nature of man"—the Freudian, the behaviorist, and the humanist. The former is pessimistic. It sees man as dominated by deep internal, animalistic, and irremovable aggression and hostility which a civilization must repress. Behaviorists see man as without a "nature." He is totally shaped by external stimuli in the environment. Humanists believe that man can exercise will and reason to transcend and control these internal and external determinants. In humanistic psychology, often termed a "third force" in the field, the Freudian fear and behaviorist denial of human nature are, respectively, reversed and rejected.[53]

Government and politics have always been based on just such assessments of human potential and limitations. In Periclean Greece participatory democracy flourished—at least for the citizen class—in part because there was great faith in the rationality of man. In Calvin's Geneva a very authoritarian, puritanical politics was built upon a religious view of the inherent corruptibility of man. Both these societies' views of man were represented in their most important form of expression. In Greece art and philosophy offered an optimistic vision of man. In Geneva, a literal reading and preaching of biblical doctrine described man as conceived in depravity, partaking of original sin, and corrupted by base desires. What single enterprise, activity, or form of communication most pervades American society and hence might be viewed as the most significant expression of the human image? The answer is obviously television.

Approximately 98 percent of American homes have a television

[53]Anne B. Freedman and P. B. Freedman, *The Psychology of Political Control* (New York: St. Martin's Press, 1975), pp. 5, 12.

set, and one-half of them have two that are in use six to seven hours a day. By the time people reach the age of eighteen they have watched an average of 18,000 hours of television, a figure that acquires significance when we realize that people attend an average of only 12,000 hours of school by that time. It is not possible to prove that the human image coming over the airwaves is created by the American people as a whole, for they do not control television, as we will see in a later chapter. But none would deny that the televised image is tied to a broad cultural perspective. Former Commissioner Nicholas Johnson of the Federal Communications Commission (FCC) asserted in May 1976 that "television is an extension of our consciousness." Is the televised image of man more akin to the humanistic psychology of Jefferson which underlies his majoritarian political theory, or to the Federalist psychology which provides the basis for the elite bias?

The answer is as clear as it is discomforting. Morning programming is dominated by game shows which project blatant materialistic greed; afternoons offer soap opera involving various sorts of depravity; and nighttime television sketches an image of sit-com inanity or crime show brutality. Interspersed throughout, commercials present vacuous housewives, a drug-dependent people, and those who define life by material possessions and sexual conquests. Last and of increasing significance are violent competitive sports, particularly football and hockey.

This representation of man by America's most popular art form is reinforced by its social science, which is patterned after physical science. As we shall see in chapter 7, the masses are scientifically proven to be apolitical by choice and have authoritarian personality traits, low support for democratic norms, a fear of equality, and a great deal of inconsistency between abstract beliefs and positions on specific issues. This summary description leads some social scientists to conclude, with Herbert McClosky, that it "is the articulate class rather than the public who serve as the major repositories of the public consciousness and as the carriers of the creed. Responsibility for keeping the system going, hence, falls most heavily upon them."[54] Peter Bachrach has coined the term "neo-federalism" to describe this perspective.[55] Thus, ironically we are brought full

[54]McClosky, "Consensus and Ideology," p. 377.
[55]Peter Bachrach, *The Theory of Democratic Elitism: A Critique* (Boston: Little, Brown, 1967).

circle back to the origins of the American political culture, to the Federalist psychology.

Norman Jacobsen describes the competition in the formative era between what we would today call humanistic thought, identified with Jefferson and Paine, and Freudian and/or behaviorist thought, identified with Adams, Hamilton, and Madison. "The exponents of the latter view, having put their opponents to rout, assumed the responsibility for organizing the government and politics of the country." All their psychological, social, economic, and political theories were woven into the fabric of our culture. The Federalists "erected institutions designed to train generations of citizens to prefer certain goods and conduct over others." This political education[56] is seen as the supreme function of the Constitution.

The most important question about the constitutional system concerns the psychology and anticipated behavioral predispositions upon which it is predicated and the extent to which it influences citizens and officials to the expected behavior patterns. It is not possible to break into the circular relationship of individual behavior and institutionalized psychology and expectations to distinguish cause and effect, although many try. But the critical reciprocity of individual behavior and powerful institutional rewards and sanctions for educating us to prefer certain goods and conduct must be taken into account. As I noted in chapter 1, it is not possible to decipher the inner mystery that determines the movements of the individual, but one can readily see which goods and conduct are encouraged by a system such as the Federalist.

As noted in chapter 2 the Federalist psychology undergirding the system supposes man to be dominated by ineradicable natural tendencies that are predatory and antisocial. To block all outlets for those by removing potential sources of conflict such as property would be repressive. So a system of regulating mutual and conflicting interests is devised. One group of constitutents and their officials is pitted against another group in "antagonistic cooperation" within a fragmented system. Competition and ambition are rewarded. Materialistic attainment and self-interest are encouraged by the system as most in keeping with human nature. Speculations about a higher "public" interest and the public-spirited citizen are derided as foolish constructs of "theoretic" politicians.[57] One au-

---

[56]Jacobsen, "Political Science," p. 566.
[57]Madison, Federalist No. 10, in *The Federalist*, p. 58.

thor says, "Self-interest is the system's lifeblood as much as love is the ideal family's."[58] Another supports this interpretation. "We are structured not for cooperative acts but for private ones; we are given a form of government that calls not for the best in people but only for the minimum in them."[59]

If a governmental system upholds competition rather than cooperation, material acquisition rather than moral development, and self-interest rather than the public interest as the natural principles of human behavior, rewarding those most adept at advancing their ambition, greed, and selfishness, that system will, logically, encourage the development of these very traits: "Madison's constitutional system not only allows for private satisfaction; it depends absolutely on the participants in the system pursuing their private satisfaction." If people "fail in that, should any significant proportion of them succumb, for example to the spirit of charity and self-sacrifice, then the system would collapse."[60]

This systemic bias is partially the source of the oft-heard remark among Americans that by the time good people reach a position in government where they can do good, they have apparently had to sell out. The system seems to compel them by its sanctions and rewards to become more selfish and less altruistic and cooperative. The public strongly senses this. Polls consistently indicate that most parents do not wish their children to go into politics. The noble profession of politics, as Aristotle described it, is historically condemned for citizens and officials alike in American political culture. This systemic psychology may induce many truly noble spirits to opt out of American politics so as not to be corrupted or sullied. Such a situation would leave the field to those least resistant to the systemic rewards and sanctions that encourage selfish goods and conduct.

If the foregoing is correct, we may be "living a self-fulfilling prophecy." That is, "by founding a government geared to selfishness, we can maintain it only by being selfish. By participating within the structure, we are acting out Madison's belief that we are unworthy."[61] The bizarre human portrait drawn by television and the materialistic, self-centered, and confused people portrayed by

[58]H. Mark Roelofs, *Ideology and Myth in American Politics* (Boston: Little, Brown, 1976), p. 105.
[59]David Schuman, *A Preface to Politics* (Lexington, Mass.: D. C. Heath, 1977), p. 28.
[60]Roelofs, *Ideology and Myth*, p. 105.
[61]Schuman, *Preface to Politics*, p. 28.

our social science vindicate the Federalist psychology. Hence the circle is closed. Still, it is not only the political system that encourages ambition, competition, and self-interest. Society at large exerts a similar effect.

The dominant psychology of competitive, acquistive beings conjoins with the scientific epistemology described in the last section to produce a particular type of society in America. It is materialistic, oriented to competition for wealth, status, and power. Production and consumption of material goods are the fundamental social activities. Indeed, production, advertising, and distribution systems are so pervasive and highly developed that we are experiencing some major social transformations.

Societies are traditionally classified by the occupation of the majority. Hence before the industrial revolution we in the United States were an agrarian people. In the post-Civil War era we became an industrial society. By the 1970s, the sophisticated technologies of production and the automation of industry had reduced the need for manufacturing workers and for unskilled labor. Today only a minority of the work force is involved in industrial production. The others are in service jobs or are—several million of them—unemployed. We have yet to devise a suitable descriptive term for this change, so we call ourselves simply a postindustrial society. Daniel Bell, who announced this development in the late 1950s remarked: "What is common to all sociological thought today is the sense of a profound transformation in industrial societies." Many see in the new "structural and social combinations—the new science-based technology, the change in sectors of the economy, the shifts in the occupational systems and the like"[62]—the major source of all other shifts in society, including the political. Limitations of space preclude comprehensive analysis of the phenomenon; however, it is important to assess some of the implications of the new "structural and social combinations" for the social consciousness and political life of the postindustrial citizen.

The social structure of postindustrialism shows at least four major, politically significant characteristics. First, institutions are of immense scale and are hierarchical. A former presidential press secretary argues that "we have gone from the highly pluralistic

[62]Daniel Bell, *The Coming of Post-Industrial Society* (New York: Basic Books, 1973), pp. 475–76. For a dissent from the interpretation of America as a postindustrial society, see Norman Birnbaum, "Is There A Post-Industrial Revolution?" in *Toward A Critical Sociology* (New York: Oxford University Press, 1969).

society of our ancestors—not completely and perhaps not even three-quarters of the way but still a considerable distance—to a pyramidal structure in which leadership is exercised through institutions which assume that power comes down from the top rather than rises from the bottom."[63] Second, there is tremendous specialization, so that increasingly narrow roles for workers and for the social functions of families, schools, and religion come into being. Theodore Lowi sees this compartmentalization and differentiation as the essence of modern America.[64] Third, there is a high level of structural unemployment as unskilled workers are left behind by the new technologies. Such unemployment plagued all advanced societies in the 1970s. Then, too, there is uprootedness. The labor force follows the movements of jobs and plants of national and multinational corporations.

These traits create new social combinations of people. Everett Ladd labels these groups the "newly established," the "disestablished," and the "nonestablished." The last category consists of "those, like blacks, who have never enjoyed high standing in American society." Women may be part of the same group. They are the least equipped in terms of education, wealth, and skills to keep up with the rapid pace of change. They suffer grievously from structural unemployment. The disestablished are the white, lower-middle, and working class "who have been displaced by some of the primary thrusts of contempory change, who find so many of the styles and values to which they are attached severely challenged."[65] The tax burden for social programs and the burden of value changes falls heavily on this group of marginal socioeconomic status. Stagflation, which may be an additional characteristic of postindustrial society, keeps the nonestablished largely on the public dole. Only the wealthy and the highly specialized, high status, secure "brain workers" atop the pyramidal institutions of education, communications, business, and so forth flourish in the automated, scientized postindustrial society.

Although a majority, the disestablished and nonestablished are politically subordinate.

---

[63]George Reedy, *The Presidency in Flux* (New York: Columbia University Press, 1973), p. 43.
[64]Theodore J. Lowi, *The End of Liberalism* (New York: W. W. Norton, 1969).
[65]Everett C. Ladd, Jr., *American Political Parties* (New York: W. W. Norton, 1970), p. 274.

The various movements of the disestablished and the nonestablished fail partly because they confront at some point the opposition of the establishment and its extensive resources—its command of the major institutions; including the media of communications, business corporation, the executive branch of the national government, the education enterprise—but also because they cannot work together.[66]

They cannot work together for historical reasons and because the "social consciousness" of their similar conditions, their parallel economic and class interests, is restricted by several means.

Due to its skill, resources, and position, the dominant political class is able to define the political agenda. It substitutes social, status, and symbolic issues for class-based ones. Drug laws, abortion, ecology, feminist and racial questions, alternative life-styles, and similar issues become the stuff of politics. The two subordinate groups conflict in these areas, "with the establishment looking on, protecting its own interests, occasionally siding with" one or the other.[67]

A fully developed class consciousness of the real social structure and social combinations is also inhibited by appeals to the ideology and symbols of the political culture. Perhaps the single most significant reason why the white majority, and the working class in particular, do not support black political aspirations is because this majority perceives the system as basically democratic.[68] That is, reality is seen as corresponding fairly well with the democratic ideology of the political culture. Another reason why many fail to perceive the difference between ideological justifications of the system and the unequal nature of postindustrialism involves the timidity and establishment bias of social theorists. Ralf Dahrendorf believes that they have failed to utilize the concepts of European sociology properly—power, class, violence, and the like—which would facilitate a more accurate social consciousness.[69]

In addition to a symbolic political agenda and a potent ideological and symbolic justification, the substitution of material goals and values for political ones further blocks the consciousness which is a prerequisite to a majority coalition. Consumption is the essen-

[66]Ibid., pp. 274–75.
[67]Ibid., p. 274.
[68]Morris, *Politics of Black America*, pp. 49–69.
[69]Ralf Dahrendorf, "The American Self-Image: Missing Traits and Their Prospects," in *Up the Mainstream*, ed. Herbert Reid (New York: David McKay, 1974), pp. 11–25.

tial principle of society. Thus communications, production, and transportation are fully geared to perpetuating and expanding the value of consumption. To the degree that material possessions define the good life and most citizens have at least some hope of attaining it, then political activity is much less important. When the tantalizing ideal of consumption weakens, class politics quickly emerges. Stark evidence to support this assertion is provided by the Great Depression, which was the high point of working-class solidarity in the United States. Marcuse sees this materialistic consumption as the most important of the "new forms of social control."[70]

Last, the stratification in postindustrial society is rationalized on the basis of Madisonian psychology. If people have less property, less status, less prestige and power, then it must be because they are of "diverse talents." As Jimmy Carter told poor women being denied access to medicaid funds for abortions, "life isn't fair."

Conclusion

The unfair distribution of wealth and power has political roots deep within the American political culture, which does not harmonize with the populist, majoritarian model of democracy articulated by Jefferson. Nor is the sociocultural base of American politics supportive of pluralist politics. Rather, in the contemporary representation of man, the operative image of society, and the fundamental philosophical orientation, in symbolic manipulation, ideological emphases, and the emerging social structures of postindustrialism, one finds a cultural bias that is clearly elitist in tone and content. Only when people's sensibilities pierce the system's legitimizing value constructs do they see the growing concentration of power in the new social structures and combinations. Then they become more critical of the institutions and leaders over which they have little control. There is a growing rift between Jeffersonian democratic expectations and the sociopolitical structure with its legitimizing social values. "Claims for individual participation and the inherent unresponsiveness of an advanced technological society . . . create profound dissatisfaction with societal performance."[71] But the dissatisfied silent majority of working-class

[70]Marcuse, *One-Dimensional Man*, p. 1.

[71]Everett Carl Ladd, Jr., and Charles D. Hadley, *Transformations of the American Party System* (New York: W. W. Norton, 1975), p. 208.

Americans—disestablished and nonestablished—as yet have found no way to forge an effective coalition. They must build upon a new political consciousness, the foundation of which I shall outline in the conclusion of this book. Before I do so, however, I will consider how the powerful tripartite ideological and symbolic, metaphysical and epistemological, and psychological and sociological components of the American political culture are perpetuated through the process of political socialization.

Part Two

Political Socialization and American Democracy

IV

Political Socialization 1:
Establishing American Political Consciousness

*By what means then, are we to move men's hearts and
bring them to love their fatherland, and its laws? Dare I
say? Through the games they play as children, through
institutions that, though a superficial man would deem
them pointless, develop habits that abide and attachments
that nothing can dissolve.*

Rousseau, *The Government of Poland*

*There are bounded interrelationships within any system
which are responsible for the system's existence, cohesion
and integration. There are various agents in any society,
such as the family, church, school, peer groups, which are
part of a socialization process through which cultural
norms are acquired. This acculturation and acquistion is
a social-psychological phenomenon.*

S. A. Kirkpatrick and L. A. Pettit,
The Social Psychology of Political Life

"Civilization," in the words of the late author James Jones, "is
control. *Self*-control, finally."[1] *Political* self-control is learned
through the internalization of cultural values such as those
analyzed in chapter 3, which are enshrined in a society's mythology,
embodied in social rituals and law, and protected and passed on by
institutions. This is a much less costly and more stable way to
maintain the regime, which is the universal goal of all ruling elites,
than coercion or even satisfying the demands of citizens and power
groupings would be. Recognition of its efficacy is as old as Western
political thought. The first work of that tradition, Plato's *Republic*,
described how the people of his fictional state would be led to accept
the notion that a few philosopher-kings would rule, a larger minority would be guardians, and the masses would be workers. They
would be told that "the earth, their mother, sent them up; and so,
their country being their mother and also their nurse . . . , her
citizens they are to regard as children of the earth and their own

---

[1] James Jones, *The Merry Month of May* (New York: Delacorte Press, 1970), p. 271.

brothers."[2] Thus politics would be grounded in consciousness. Education, law, economics, and art were all designed by Plato to perpetuate his unequal scheme of things.

Since the democratic revolutions of the seventeenth and eighteenth century placed limits on governments' power to coerce belief and invested majorities in most Western nations with formal rights of governance, the questions relating to the so-called politics within assume first-rank importance. Who controls the institutions by which people are socialized? What is the nature of the learned values, loyalties, and behavioral inclinations? What is the ultimate result of the political socialization process? Rousseau would express appreciation of the need to transmit a "civil religion" in such a way as to keep society from flying apart. John Locke could argue against governmental control of press and religion, which had always been used to enforce a particular belief system, without fearing anarchy, because as one commentator says, Locke knew that society itself would "generate and maintain such a system by a variety of means, formal and informal, from political education to social pressure."[3] The term "political socialization" today describes this entire area.

The philosophical approach to understanding political socialization has been supplemented since World War II in the United States by a more quantitative one. The disciplines of sociology, cultural anthropology, political science, and psychology have produced many behavioral studies on the topic. The ensuing analysis draws from all of these disciplines as well as from the philosophical.

Before turning to an examination of American political socialization, I should reemphasize that although I recognize the importance of sociocultural conditioning, my guiding premise is Socratic—that is, humans are ultimately free. In the final analysis, we are at least possessed of the capability for freedom. There is simply little evidence for the oft-heard suggestion that people are brainwashed, for instance by the social agencies discussed here. Even if people were so malleable, American political socialization is clearly not absolute and one-dimensional. There is a goodly element of natural

    [2]Plato, *The Republic*, trans. Benjamin Jowett (New York: Vintage Books, 1955), pp. 124–25. For an argument that Plato intended to show the impossibility of such an arrangement, see the interpretative essay by Allan Bloom included with his translation of *The Republic* (New York: Basic Books, 1968).
    [3]Dante Germino, *Modern Western Political Thought* (Chicago: Rand McNally, 1972), p. 135.

spontaneity in the human spirit, perhaps some primordial impulse to freedom, which resists control. With the increased leisure time, affluence, and prolonged adolescence of post-WW II America, people have greater opportunities to develop this propensity. Further, the rapid pace of change in a technological age makes difficult the continual updating and reinterpretation of sociopolitical values for coming generations. Social change may outstrip the legitimizing ability of socializing agencies. Finally, to the extent that our society is pluralistic, with an imperfect coordination of elite control over social institutions, then contradictory emphases and shading will be placed on the value structure. Many people, such as the poor, the uneducated, and the urban and rural ghetto dwellers, are still sufficiently remote from the central social agencies that they are imperfectly socialized in the dominant values of the system. Finally, the enormity of the sociopolitical and economic problems of the times mandates a high rate of governmental failure, and this tends to weaken the legitimizing efforts of political socialization.

One additional point needs particular emphasis by way of prefacing our analysis. While the dominant ideas of the political culture (such as those described in chapter 3) as transmitted by political socialization do affect everyone, the material circumstances of people in different social roles, classes, or status affect the degree of individual internalization or rejection. The debate over these two influences goes back in recent history at least as far as the dispute between Marx the materialist and Hegel the idealist.

Marxism takes a materialist position on the formation of political attitudes and motives for political behavior. It rejects the idealist position, current in many sectors of the social sciences, that values, political socialization, and norms are the ultimate explanation of social phenomena. Marxists look beyond the values and attitudes that motivate people to why people believe what they do, and beyond the conscious reasons given for political actions to the structural conditions that determine and direct it.[4]

Albert Szymanski, a Marxist, goes on to organize his fine study on the basis of the correlation between an individual's material condition, or class, and political consciousness. One finds at the other pole idealists like Pirsig, who—from within the Hegelian tradition—writes:

[4]Albert Szymanski, *The Capitalist State and the Politics of Class* (Cambridge, Mass.: Winthrop, 1978), p. 25.

Value, the leading edge of reality, is no longer an irrelevant offshoot of structure. Value is the predecessor of structure. It's the preintellectual awareness that gives rise to it. Our structured reality is preselected on the basis of value, and really to understand structured reality requires an understanding of the value source from which it's derived.[5]

He offers an exciting exploration of the impact of rationalism on Western existence.

Surely the truth falls somewhere between Szymanski's claim that structural conditions determine and direct political beliefs and actions and Pirsig's postion that structured reality is derived from values. Political consciousness is more properly viewed as a result of the interaction of materiality (experience) and mentality (ideas). Wilhelm Reich, one of the first thinkers to synthesize Marx's materialist explanation of consciousness with Freud's depth psychology, offers a useful summary. "Man is subject to the conditions of his existence in a twofold way: directly through the immediate influence of his economic and social position, and indirectly by means of the ideologic structure of the society."[6] These two influences may or may not be harmonious. An example of ideologic structure dovetailing with one's economic and social position would be the case of the top party and government leadership in the Soviet Union, whose place is legitimized by Marxian ideology. Perhaps the top half of the American middle class falls into the second category, with capitalist values serving it at some points and not at others. A historical example of discord between social position and dominant ideology would be the eighteenth-century French peasant confronted with the legitimating concepts of the ancien régime.

All the disintegrative factors of human spontaneity, rapid social change, and imperfect coordination of social agencies, plus the individual's socioeconomic situation, militate against the creation of a social automaton. Nonetheless, within these limits a growing amount of social conditioning goes on daily in our technological society. Initially it takes place in the intimate and historically private environs of the family, which currently finds certain transitions threatening its traditional role. Early and basic socialization is also carried out in the many subgroups in the United States,

[5]Robert M. Pirsig, *Zen and the Art of Motorcycle Maintenance* (New York: Bantam Books, 1974), p. 277.
[6]Wilhelm Reich, *The Mass Psychology of Fascism*, trans. Vincent R. Carfagno (New York: Farrar, Straus and Giroux, 1970), p. 18.

whose impact on members' subjective perceptions, a major component of consciousness, is keyed to the objective conditions of the
group. These primary social agencies, which are less centralized
than other major ones, function to establish, imperfectly and within
the parameters sketched above, key elements of American political
consciousness in each succeeding generation.

To what degree and in what particular fashion does the family
and subgroup experience stimulate the kind of self-awareness and
sense of community in which the integrated, moral political consciousness described in chapter 1 is grounded? Is the experience a
developmental one? Does the family and subgroup socialization
process essentially equip people with the knowledge, skills, and
tools for self-rule? Or is it a repressive experience which generally
cripples, stunts, and inhibits the impulses to democratic citizenship? Do these agencies and the others examined in succeeding
chapters transmit a version of the ideological and symbolic, metaphysical and epistemological, and psychological and sociological
cultural components more compatible with the Madisonian, or
elite, model of American democracy or the Jeffersonian populist
variant? The answers to these questions are critical, for if the
process might be described as "negative democratic socialization,"
inhibiting the sense of self, sense of community, and the impulses to
self-assertion and majority rule, then clearly it will reinforce the
tendency to an elitist politics despite the facade of democratic
legitimacy. Let us first consider political socialization by the
American family.

FAMILY SOCIALIZATION: TRADITION AND TRANSITION

What is the nexus between the American family and political
consciousness? Does the family, which has historically been the
most private social unit, offer the greatest hope for perpetuating
independence and the greatest resistance to political repression and
manipulation of consciousness? Some say yes: "Family socialization serves to perpetuate diversity in social and political viewpoints
and can counteract pressures toward centralized socialization and
homogeneity in political outlooks—goals sometimes sought by regime leaders."[7] Or does the political role of the contemporary

[7]Kenneth Prewitt, Richard E. Dawson, and Karen S. Dawson, *Political Socialization*, 2nd ed. (Boston: Little, Brown, 1977), p. 18.

American family incline toward that of Hobbes's Leviathan, consisting primarily in stabilization and reinforcement of the state? R.A. Chapman describes the Hobbesian theory of political socialization as follows:

> By his own experiences and by virtue of the education received from his parents, the child is made into a social being who is accustomed to and understands political relationships of authority and obedience. The child's mind is to be kept free by the parents from influences prejudicial to the true philosophy's [i.e., regime values] teaching of duty and obedience. . . . What binds a child to the family also binds the family sovereign to the state. . . . Hobbes . . . does not worry about creating a highly active citizenry. It is obvious that he sought to cool men off, to pacify them, to drive them into the waiting arms of whoever might be ruling with the frightening imagery of a state of nature in which there is "continual fear and danger of violent death."[8]

Does the American family similarly "link paranoia with pacification" to produce blind political obedience? The importance of these questions is only overshadowed by the difficulty of arriving at answers.

A decade ago, in *The Politics of the Family*, Laing cited two intrinsic difficulties involved in studying families. First, although families have existed for about 100,000 years, we are individually on earth for barely enough time to assess their impact. The other problem is "that the more smoothly they function the more difficult they are to study."[9] (If the experts are correct, this second difficulty is fast disappearing in the United States.) A growing number of the approximately sixty million American families are in disarray.

Economic pressures, geographic mobility, women's liberation, and the growing importance of other social institutions such as schools and television have made the family increasingly vulnerable. Expectations are that by 1985 the "average" family of husband, nonworking mother, and children will represent only 15 percent of American households. Replacing these will be the one- or two-person household: the single, the widowed, the childless, those whose children have left home early, and unmarried couples.

---

[8]R. A. Chapman, "*Leviathan* Writ Small: Thomas Hobbes on the Family," *American Political Science Review* 69 (March 1975), p. 88. For further discussion, see also Gilbert Meilaender, "A Little Monarchy: Hobbes on the Family," *Thought* 53 (December 1978), pp. 401–15.

[9]R. D. Laing, *The Politics of the Family and Other Essays* (New York: Random House, 1971), pp. 85–86.

The decline of the traditional "nuclear family" is causing enormous concern among religious and academic groups and political figures, not to mention among the families themselves.[10] The National Conference of Catholic Bishops targeted 1980 as "Family Year." Family studies are one of the fastest growing academic areas. Institutes, think tanks, and foundations are expending a good deal of time, energy, and money dissecting the family and proposing ways to put it back together again. For example, the prestigious Carnegie Council on Children funded a $2.5 million study from 1972 to 1977 which issued a report entitled "All Our Children: The American Family Under Pressure." While such studies look at many factors, more and more they come to focus on the political nexus as crucial. Family-government relationships have long been camouflaged by the political culture's restricted perception of the role and impact of politics and government on private life. Yet more and more links between the two institutions are being revealed. A George Washington University Seminar on the family is reported to have "identified 268 programs administered by seventeen Federal departments and agencies that have potential impact on families, plus another 63 that have explicit impact, such as direct aid."[11] Even so, the United States is still the only Western nation that does not have a formal policy to encourage the family as an institution.

Feelings run high on the question of what type of government policy on the family should be enacted or even whether there should be a *formal*, comprehensive program. Both opponents and proponents recognize the implications of this decision for the American family's critical transmission of politically significant norms and behavioral inclinations. One social scientist calls the family "the gatekeeper of social experience," noting, the "family starts with a clean slate. The family has the earliest access to the virgin mind of the young child."[12] Others agree that in the family the child "learns attitudes toward authority, toward others, toward himself, toward a vague community outside, and nation: He learns habits of thought

[10]In a Gallup poll asking the American people to express their views on eight social changes, the response indicated a desire for "more emphasis on traditional family ties." There was very little variation among age groups. See "Traditional Values Favored," released June 22, 1978, American Institute of Public Opinion, Princeton, N.J.

[11]*Newsweek*, May 15, 1978, p. 68. See also "How the Government Affects Family Life," *McCalls*, May 1977, pp. 63–64.

[12]Jarol B. Mannheim, *The Politics Within* (Englewood Cliffs, N.J.: Prentice-Hall, 1964), p. 18.

and behavior, independence, conscientiousness, trust."[13] Thus the family experience begins the process of establishing political consciousness. Most families, to the degree they are an instrumental and ideological part of their culture and social system, transmit that culture's general social view, its operative theory of human nature and dominant view of reality and knowledge. Politically "functional" American families, in other words, would transmit the particular mix of American values that we considered in chapter 3. There is broad agreement among researchers that the American family historically "plays an important role in the transmission and reinforcement of those widely shared and highly simplistic beliefs comprising much of what might be labelled the American political culture," including nationalistic sentiment, positive evaluations of political institutions and authority figures, and respect for constituted authority.[14] It inculcates respect for the basic ethos of American society.

Several caveats must quickly be added to this generally accurate account of the historically supportive socializing role played by most American families. First, because formal "politics does not occupy a very central role in the lives of most American families,"[15] there is "considerable slack in the value acquisition process."[16] Effects associated with the life cycle instability of attitudes also make less than clear the correspondence between parents' opinions and children's, although partisanship is transmitted in roughly six to eight cases. A second limit on family political homogeneity is imposed by the existence of countervailing social institutions which vie with parents for the child's attention. The importance of the family varies with that of other agencies. Suffice it to say that no parent or child in our technological society needs instruction in the power of television, schools, workplace, or government. A third limit on continuous linear family socialization is the different sociohistorical experience of parent and child. A depression or war

[13]Robert E. Lane and David O. Sears, *Public Opinion* (Englewood Cliffs, N.J.: Prentice-Hall, 1964), p. 18.

[14]Robert Weissberg, *Political Learning, Political Choice, and Democratic Citizenship* (Englewood Cliffs, N.J.: Prentice-Hall, 1974), pp. 151–52.

[15]Robert S. Sigel, *Learning about Politics: A Reader in Political Socialization* (New York: Random House, 1970), p. 104.

[16]M. Kent Jennings and Richard G. Niemi, "The Transmission of Political Values from Parent to Child," in *The Social Psychology of Political Life*, eds. Samuel A. Kirkpatrick and Lawrence K. Pettit (Belmont, Calif.: Duxbury Press, 1972), p. 176.

or other crisis can cause discord between older and younger generations, with the event itself defining groups. Last, social class and
ethnicity affect family socialization, as many researchers failed to
realize before the disruptions of the mid-1960s and early 1970s. As
one researcher found, "The widespread alienation that characterizes the disreputable poor manifests itself in the abandonment of
the goals of the social system, and in the commitment either to the
goals of the self-system or those of the counterculture (the culture of
poverty)," or to both.[17] While this study dealt with nonpolitical
goals of the social system, the implications for questioning political
ones are similar. We will look at such subgroup socialization in the
next section.

Haphazard political teaching in the family, influential competing
social institutions, and generational dissonance due to crisis experiences all contribute to the growing confusion over exactly what
the politically significant norms and consciousness transmitted by
the family process will be on the other end of the transition from the
traditional nuclear family to the multifold family types of the
future. The competing theories and groups of what one might call
"reform liberals, conservatives, and radicals," seeking to "save" the
family, debate not only whether their particular theories and proposals will do that, but also what are the implications of the theories
and proposals for who controls and shapes the emerging family
types. Who will have the greatest influence on their socialization
function if and when various types of reforms are adopted?

The fierceness of this debate was dramatically demonstrated by
the controversy which erupted over one major effort of reform
liberals to provide some activist government role in the family,
in this instance primarily middle-class ones, with the Mondale-
Brademas Child and Family Services Act of 1975. This proposal,
which was immediately killed by massive conservative opposition,
would have provided day-care services, recreational, educational,
and health programs for children. Participation in the program
would have been voluntary, and parents would have composed
one-half of the membership of local councils that would set policy
for the program. The bill stated clearly that nothing in the act would
alter or interfere in any way with the rights and responsibilities of

---

[17]Sandro Segre, "Family Stability, Social Classes, and Values in Traditional and
Industrial Societies," *Journal of Marriage and the Family* 37 (May 1975), p. 434.

parents. A pamphlet with a distorted version of the bill was circulated by fundamentalist churches, in conservative school organizations, and by right-wing political groups. It was headed REARING CHILDREN BY THE GOVERNMENT OR BY PARENTS? It included inaccurate quotations from the *Congressional Record*; one read: "As a matter of the child's right, the government shall exert control over the family because we have recognized that the child is not the care of the parents but the care of the State." Reform liberals were quickly confronted with the reality that middle-class America, or at least certain vocal and conservative elements of the same, did not want the government any more involved with its family life than it presently is. Noted conservative author and lecturer Russell Kirk, in a major address on the family and the state, attacked the "baby-bin" bill, saying, "a congeries of educationists, politicians, and 'social reform' lobbyists clearly have become eager to reduce the functions of the family and enlarge those of the nation-state." He went on to say that "any such grand design would require the imparting of a civil religion by the agencies of the state: but the ambitious reformers generally are silent on that point."[18]

If liberals are unduly insensitive to what Kirk calls the dangers of "compulsory collectivism" and government supervision of the family through bureaucratically administered programs—and the whole welfare structure created by reform liberalism is ample evidence of the ills of this—then conservatives, who essentially want no formal family policy, are equally insensitive in the matter of families' vulnerability to manipulation by private, nongovernmental power. Kirk contends that "the more the family is denied opportunity to function in its customary ways, the more the political apparatus assumes direction and control over what once were private or familial concerns."[19] Could it be more correct to say that private institutions, particularly in communications and economic areas, are equally supplanting family functions? This is true for many Americans and particularly for the bottom one-fifth of families who receive only some 5 percent of all family income.[20] All those who must scramble for economic survival must often ignore family and parental obligations. The middle-class mind-set that

[18]Russell Kirk, "Little Platoon We Belong to in Society," *Vital Speeches* 34 (January 15, 1978), p. 201.

[19]Ibid., p. 203.

[20]Benjamin A. Okner, "Distributional Aspects of Tax Reform during the Past Fifteen Years," *National Tax Journal* 33 (March 1979), pp. 10–17.

involves conservative fear of governmental intervention in the family and was so well demonstrated in the furor over the Mondale-Brademas Act also ignores the fact that poor families have always been subject to government supervision, even to the extent of searches of the home without a warrant. (The Supreme Court ratified this practice in 1971 for families receiving various types of welfare in *Wyman* v *James*.) Furthermore, the reader of the opening chapter of *The Autobiography of Malcolm X,* entitled "Nightmare," or of part 1 of Anne Moody's *Coming of Age in Mississippi*, cannot fail to realize the intimate role governments at all levels have historically played in the lives of poor families of low status. This dual danger of government or private control of families gives rise to the radicals' desire to provide the wherewithal for extreme family independence.

While the eleven-member Carnegie Council on Children presented its goal of supporting more family independence as very traditional and even conservative, it did concede that the means it proposed to this end were rather radical: (1) government should guarantee every family head a job; (2) there should be a minimum income level for all families of at least one-half of the nation's median income; (3) a tax credit of $6,000 should be given a family of four; (4) a policy of looking to institutions for child care should be only a last resort.[21] These measures would redistribute family income to some extent, offsetting the effect of poverty on families which has been identified by the report as the single most destructive element of family life. It would, in the council's view, provide basic economic security, reduce the dependence of families on other institutions, and give to the families greater decision-making authority.

Quite clearly the radical solution would give government plus economic and educational institutions less leverage to affect the values, interpersonal relations, and ideological and behavioral inclinations of what has been variously termed the family drama, system, or psychosocial interior. Because of the threat to these powerful institutions and the well-placed interests they represent, and because the proposals conflict dramatically with major cul-

---

[21]Pamela G. Hollie, "Study Urges a U.S. Family Policy," *New York Times*, September 12, 1977. For an account of how other industrial democracies approach this matter, see Alfred Kahn and S. Kamerman, *Not for the Poor Alone: European Social Services* (Philadelphia: Temple University Press, 1975).

tural values such as property rights, limited government, and self-reliance, the proposals had no real chance of being enacted.

There is no doubt that the family continues to be the dominant carrier and/or teacher of cultural values. The form that this cultural transmission takes will depend, to a large extent, on how successful the family will be in coping with the changes in its character discussed above. Social historian Christopher Lasch argues in his book *Haven in A Heartless World: The Family Besieged*[22] that declining family independence means a wholesale loss of individual autonomy and a shift of power from the individual to society and the state. Only time and future events will tell whether this specter of an increasingly subordinate sociopolitical role for the family does indeed loom on the horizon. The power of the family will, however, always be subject to the ever-increasing influence of subgroup associations.

SUBGROUP SOCIALIZATION: OBJECTIVE CONDITIONS AND SUBJECTIVE PERCEPTIONS

"Get off my case," responds one of Trudeau's "Doonesbury" characters to an older sibling who is scolding him for taking up smoking. "At my age, I need all the acceptance I can get!" "Acceptance?" says the older brother "But there's not a peer within miles!" Rejoinder: "[I'm] practicin'. There's a gang I want to join in the fall."

Peers need be neither visible nor within miles to induce "practicin'" of attitudes and behavioral patterns in any of us, and some of them may even violate family precepts. Nor are such attitudes found merely among the young, for at no age are humans insular. We need group acceptance, gained through internalization of relevant group norms, "values, and hierarchies of values, plus behavioral expectations, frequently unwritten but by no means unimportant in obtaining group objectives and minimizing intragroup conflict." Thus subgroups, particularly the biologically

---

[22]Christopher Lasch, *Haven in a Heartless World: The Family Besieged* (New York: Basic Books, 1977). Other useful studies on this theme are: Richard Sennett, *The Uses of Disorder* (New York: Alfred A. Knopf, 1970), and *The Fall of Public Man* (New York: Random House, 1974); Eli Zaretsky, *Capitalism, the Family, and Personal Life* (New York: Harper and Row, 1976); and Stuart Ewen, *Captains of Consciousness* (New York: McGraw-Hill, 1976).

grounded ones of sex and race, are a major factor affecting political consciousness, although "one must avoid the danger of overestimating the evidence of the influence of group norms."[23]

Postindustrialism has been harsh on traditional group bonds, as it has on the family, so undermining regional, ethnic, and other group identities that we became a mass society. The new technologies of production, transportation, and communications, and the mobility and homogenization seemed to bring the melting pot to a permanent boil. Such analyses, however, clearly underestimate the individual's need for group relations. Indeed—as the middle-class encounter movement demonstrates—people will even form artificial groups and quickly engage in intimate sharing of atomized egos to compensate for postindustrial isolation and alienation. More significantly, the 1970s saw the resurgence of what promises to be an ongoing emphasis on ethnicity and other dimensions of groupness. And the politics of the time found that group demands and negotiations were one of its characteristic features. Reinforcement comes in the responses of governmental institutions and society itself to these group impulses. Thus subgroup socialization, particularly that of the most ineradicable identities, such as sex and race, will remain of considerable importance in the foreseeable future, even in the face of the tendencies to replace primary group identity with the synthetic mass-produced labels of occupation, consumer, or audience for the media.

Group influence on political attitudes and behavior may be viewed as good or bad, depending on how one looks at the phenomenon. Critics believe that tight, insular group bonds only perpetuate such attitudes as intolerance, bigotry, and fear, plus economic and status-related anxiety, all of which lead to social conflict. Still, those who believe in the need for conscious group identity see it as a prerequisite for political action. A Penobscot Indian woman was widely quoted by the press in 1978 as saying that even if her tribe and the Passamaquoddy tribe did not win their historic legal claim to two-thirds of Maine, the struggle gave them a sense of their ethnic identity. In effect, it contributed significantly to the emergence of their political consciousness.

While some observers may differ on the desirability of group influence, they ignore its impact at the expense of erroneous in-

[23]Bernard C. Hennessy, *Public Opinion*, 3rd ed. (Belmont, Calif.: Wadsworth Publishing, 1975), pp. 231, 233.

terpretations of public opinion. Greenberg points out that students of political socialization in the 1950s and 1960s consistently and incorrectly "concluded that the American political system is characterized by rather high levels of supportive attitudes and these attitudes are widely and homogeneously distributed."[24] The insurrections and violence from the mid-1960s to the early 1970s exploded the notion that attitudes were homogeneous, and as Greenberg says, the finding was not anticipated by the major studies. Why? Because, as Schley R. Lyons notes, the sample was almost exclusively from one group, "white, middle-class children living in urban, industrial communities."[25] Another reason was that few of the "samplers" were Negroes, Mexicans, or slum dwellers. To realize how overwhelming was the middle-class mind-set during the era of these studies one need only recall that at about the same time the Kennedy administration first "discovered" poverty among minority groups and Appalachian whites.

It is particularly ironic that the significance of subgroup socialization should be so overlooked in the most heterogeneous national population extant. Americans carry some twenty-five to thirty group tags, ranging from the class-related identities of educational attainment, occupation, and income to the biologically grounded labels of sex, race, age, and ethnicity. The last of these usually, but not always, determines one's religion. Some analysts term the class labels "achieved" group identity and the others "ascribed," but as we shall see, the latter may largely predetermine the former.

One might state as a general axiom that in the United States, biological groupings tend to reinforce a positive consciousness, with a desirable self-image, sense of efficacy, and activist or assertive behavioral predispositions to the degree that they correlate with the desirable class-related identities of high education and income and occupation compatible with high status. The nexus of biology and class is, in this view, a most important one. Those who are so fortunate as to be a member of the dominant race, sex, and ethnic group, main-line religion, and upper-class or upper-middle-class status are socialized to anticipate power. In the fifth and final volume of *Children of Crisis*, entitled *Privileged Ones*, Robert Coles finds that virtually all upper-class families transmit to their chil-

[24]Edward Greenberg, ed.,*Political Socialization* (New York: Atherton Press, 1970), p. 8.
[25]Schley R. Lyons, "Socialization of Ghetto Children," *Journal of Politics* 32 (May 1970), p. 289.

dren a class-bound sense of entitlement. Integrated into the psychology of their children is an overpowering sense of self and belief in the rightness of the privilege and authority of their dominant class. One boy explains: "If my father weren't a grower and didn't have migrants, then they wouldn't have anything to do."[26]

In contrast are persons who suffer under conditions where their sex and race correlate closely over time with undesirable class characteristics. Robert Weissberg says flatly: "Though the data are limited, it is nevertheless clear that lower-class children, black children, and young females are socialized to be handicapped in the political struggle."[27] For an understanding of the impact of subgroup socialization in America it is necessary to consider carefully the possible adverse effects on women and blacks, the subordinate sex and racial groups, of the constraints placed on them as individuals as a result of their biological group identity.

The nation entered its third century with women comprising 51.6 percent of its 213,137,000 people, or 109,337,000 persons.[28] There were 5.6 million more women than men because women outlive men by an average of 8.5 years. This majority labors under some exceedingly distressing class constraints in education and to an even greater extent in income and occupation. While women above eighteen had slightly more education than the general population, in 1978 approximately 3.6 million men were enrolled full time in college, as opposed to 3.2 million women. For every 100 men with a degree between the ages of twenty-five and twenty-nine, only 77 women had one. The dramatic surge of part-time female students, 2.5 million as compared with 2.1 million males in 1978, promises to change this ratio. Most often women who do earn a degree are discouraged from studies which lead to occupations producing wealth and power. Kate Millett attributes this channeling of people to the definition of a " 'feminine' subject matter, assigning the humanities and certain social sciences (at least in their lower or

[26]Excerpted in *Atlantic*, September 1977, p. 54. See also *Privileged Ones: The Well-Off and the Rich in America* (Boston: Little, Brown, 1978).

[27]Weissberg, *Political Learning*, p. 120.

[28]My statistical portrait of women in America was drawn from these sources: Barbara Deckard, *The Women's Movement* (New York: Harper and Row, 1975); Kirsten Amundsen, *A New Look at the Silenced Majority: Women and American Democracy*, 2nd ed. (Englewood Cliffs, N.J.: Prentice-Hall, 1977); the first detailed study by the Census Bureau of the demographic, economic, and social trends among women, released on April 26, 1976; "Women at Work," *Newsweek*, December 6, 1976, pp. 68–81. Also consulted were the very useful statistics compiled by the Women's Bureau of the Labor Department.

marginal branches) to the females—and science and technology, the professions, business and engineering to the male."[29]

In the two decades preceding the Bicentennial, the median individual income differential separating working men from women doubled, with men earning $13,859 versus $8,312 for women in 1976. Overall, women earned about 60 percent of male earnings, or for every $100 a woman earned, a man earned $175. The traditional expectation that income will correlate with education is contradicted by the fact that women with four years of college made 14 percent less per year than men with a high school education. The situation of families headed by women remains particularly stark. Their income was only 47 percent of that of families headed by men, with 33 percent of the former, and only 5 percent of the latter, falling below the poverty level. Alimony, child support, and transfer payments of a tenuous sort alleviate the situation only marginally, as Kirsten Amundsen makes clear.[30]

With regard to occupation, 1976 found 38.6 million women working or seeking employment. One-half of the women workers were in twelve low-paying occupations as secretaries, seamstresses, foodservice workers, and the like. In some of these jobs the workers were more than 90 percent female. Among doctors, dentists, engineers, and scientists women numbered respectively, 6.5, 2.1, 1.2, and 7 percent. They held fewer than 1 percent of all skilled manufacturing jobs. Stanley Aronowitz contends that "the segregation of both black and white women within American manufacturing industry has been even more severe than that of black males."[31] Only 2.2 percent of the jobs in the approximately 450 trades with apprenticeship programs of recruitments were held by women. Even within the same occupations women earned much less: as sales clerks, 38.8 percent of male earnings; as scientists, 76 percent; as engineers, 85 percent; and as secondary school teachers, 81 percent. Finally, men filled approximately 85 percent of all managerial roles, and their dominance increased with the significance of the position.

Compounding the dilemma of women is the low actual value placed on staying home and being a housewife, although to the

[29]Kate Millett, *Sexual Politics* (New York: Avon Books, 1971), p. 42.

[30]Amundsen, *A New Look at the Silenced Majority: Women and American Democracy*, p. 23.

[31]Stanley Aronowitz, *False Promises: The Shaping of Working Class Consciousness* (New York: McGraw-Hill, 1973), p. 206.

spiraling number of single women and those whose incomes are vital to their families, this presents no dilemma at all. As late as 1976 the Department of Labor ranked housework at the bottom on a scale of complexity of 22,000 jobs, with the jobs of restroom attendants and shovelers of poultry offal. And since a commodity economy such as ours places no exchange value on being a housewife, which produces no salable product, women are required to work in their own homes free of charge.

The same caste conditions exist among blacks, who constitute somewhat more than 11 percent of the population, or approximately 25 million people.[32] They, like women, suffer severe constraints in income, occupation, and education. For example, only 58 percent of black seventeen-year-olds are functionally literate, in contrast with 92 percent of whites that age. The doubling of black enrollment in colleges in the first half of the 1970s (blacks are now 10.7 percent of all students) is less important for group power than is the type of studies pursued. More than 60 percent of blacks are attending two-year colleges and vocational schools, and another 20 percent attend historically underfunded black colleges. Some 92 of every 100 medical students are white, as are 95 percent of all law students. Of the 42,000 persons applying for 15,700 medical school openings in 1976, fewer than 1,300 of those accepted were from minority groups.

In terms of occupation and income, the situation at the time of the Bicentennial was even bleaker. One of every three blacks had an income below the poverty level. The figure for whites was one in ten. This was, however, better than in 1966, when 42 percent of blacks

[32]The statistical data on blacks in America were taken from the following: Joel Dreyfus, *The Bakke Case: The Politics of Inequality* (New York: Harcourt Brace Jovanovich, 1979); Milton P. Morris, *The Politics of Black America* (New York: Harper and Row, 1975); "The Social and Economic Status of the Black Population in the United States, 1974" (Washington, D.C.: U.S. Bureau of the Census, 1975); "Social and Economic Profile of Black Mississippians" (Jackson: Mississippi Research and Development Center, May 1977).

Statistics and social relations indicate an increasing gap between the growing "black bourgeoisie," who have made major gains, and the black lower class, which is falling farther and farther behind. The Urban League describes this phenomenon as a "disturbing duality." In 1968 the Kerner Commission said America was moving toward "two societies, one black, one white—separate and unequal." Today it's probably more accurate to say that America is divided into two classes, one comfortable and one not. See, Steve Roberts, "Black Progress and Poverty Are Underlined by Statistics," *New York Times*, February 28, 1978, p. 22. See also Paul Delaney, "Middle-Class Gains Create Tension in Black Community," *New York Times*, February 28, 1978; and Louis H. Bolce III and Susan H. Gray, "Blacks, Whites, and 'Race Politics'," *Public Interest* 54 (Winter 1979), pp. 61–75.

fell below the poverty level. Thirty-six percent of the bottom one-sixth of the socioeconomic scale are black, while only 2 percent of the top one-sixth of the scale are black. Blacks earn a median income that is only 61 percent of that of whites. Black families earn on the average only 58 percent of the median income of white families ($9,560 versus $16,740 in 1976). These figures are even more dramatic in the South, where most blacks live and where state and local governments do least for lower-income groups. Black families in the region receive approximately 56 percent of the income of white families. Mississippi ranks first, with over one-half of its black families below the poverty level, in contrast to about 15 percent of white families. Blacks suffer a consistent national rate of unemployment double that of whites. The level of underemployment is incalculable. In no significant occupation are blacks decently represented. For example, in the late 1970s there was a total of 350,000 lawyers approximately 6,000 of whom were black. Only 3 percent of the medical profession ws black. Trends in these grim statistics for women and blacks revealed mixed progress, and in some instances a marked worsening, in the midst of the economic crises of the 1970s.

What attitudes and behavioral predispositions do we see in these two subordinate groups? Is Weissberg correct? Do they experience the reverse of Coles's "privileged ones" and internalize a negative self-image, subordinate behavioral inclinations, and adherence to the self-legitimizing values of dominant groups? Baldwin believes not; "the American Negro has the great advantage of having never believed the collection of myths to which Americans cling."[33] And one of Faulkner's brilliantly drawn young black characters says, when his young white friend begins to move up and away, leaving him behind, "I ain't ashamed of nobody, not even me."[34] But is this the case? Do blacks, and women, possess sufficient group integrity and the means of mutual reinforcement to resist negative socialization?

Brown v. *Board of Education* emphasized that a racially segregated subordinate group would internalize a sense of inferority. Clark's famous black doll-white doll test, where black children consistently chose a white doll when given a choice, dramatically il-

---

[33]James Baldwin, *The Fire Next Time* (New York: Dial Press, 1963), p. 115.
[34]William Faulkner, "The Fire and the Hearth," in *Go Down, Moses* (New York: Random House, 1973), p. 114.

lustrated this point. Still, there is some evidence that the black liberation movement that followed the Brown case significantly alleviated this situation. One author concluded from a mid-1970s sample of eighty-eight black and ninety-white adolescents in three midwestern cities whose early socialization occurred during the 1960s that "the current generation of young blacks is acquiring more positive self-images than previous generations."[35] They were more likely to blame failure on the system than on themselves. Another recent study concludes "that college educated blacks have broken the chains of self-blame which may have gripped them."[36] But only a fraction of blacks are college-educated. What of the rest? Also, socialization during the last quarter of the century may be greatly different from the dynamic one preceding it. There are some signs of regression in self-concepts.

Joel Aberbach's analysis of the responses of a mixed sample of some eight hundred individuals interviewed in the Detroit area is one of the most provocative efforts to analyze black self-esteem and inclinations to blame the self or the system for low socioeconomic status. He concludes of the large majority of blacks who are not college-educated: "The negative impact of the black experience in the United States on black self-image is much in evidence in the power consciousness of high-school educated blacks who are more likely to blame themselves for unsatisfactory amounts of power than are high-school educated whites." Overall, blacks are more likely than whites to ascribe lack of power to individual failures or inadequacies. Also, they are "more prone to cite [remediable] group weakness as the reason for power dissatisfaction."[37] Perhaps black belief in "the collection of myths" is stronger than Baldwin thought, and maybe there was some feeling of shame in Faulkner's young Henry. Could those forces partially explain the dramatically greater quiescence of black ghettos in the 1970s than in the 1960s?

Assessing women's response to their situation with any degree of assurance is impossible, since the data are so limited. Kate Millett believes that "what little literature the social sciences afford us in this context confirms the presence in women of the expected traits of minority status: group self-hatred and self-rejection, a contempt

[35]William E. Husbary, "Race, Deprivation, and Adolescent Self-Image," *Social Science Quarterly* 56 (June 1975), p. 104.

[36]Joel D. Aberbach, "Power Consciousness: A Comparative Analysis," *American Political Science Review* 71 (April 1977), p. 1555.

[37]Ibid., p. 1559.

both for herself and for her fellows—the result of that continual, however subtle, reiteration of her inferiority which she eventually accepts as a fact."[38] She cites studies indicating that a large majority of female children wished they had been born male, while boys overwhelmingly reject the idea of being a girl as undesirable. Amundsen points to similar evidence, such as the fact that male babies are preferred by parents of both sexes. Millett and Amundsen stress Philip Goldberg's findings about the group feeling of women undergraduates. When asked to assess the same essay, signed in some cases by "John" and in others by "Joan" McKay, the students rated Joan's work more harshly.[39] The women's liberation movement has apparently had only marginal impact on such lack of esteem. Polls of the late 1970s generally found more men than women supporting the ERA.[40]

These bits and pieces of research illustrate the negative cognitive and emotional impact associated with belonging to a subordinate race or sex. Such feelings of inferiority reflect the group's objective conditions in American society. The pressure on all subgroups to reconcile their own particular perspective psychologically with the dominant values is very intense in "normal" times. Nevertheless, the internalized accommodation is always tenuous, so long as the potential exists for rallying subgroup consciousness. The legitimizing veneer of regime values which teach people to blame themselves, not the system, can be stripped away by "abnormal" conditions conducive to group consciousness. The urban black explosions from 1964 to 1968 which included over 300 racial clashes in more than 257 cities with more than 200 dead and 50,000 arrested are conclusive evidence of this phenomenological reality. System elites have often responded to these occurrences of subgroup uprisings among the disadvantaged with calls for law and order. A more insidious, and ultimately more effective, method of "control" is the homogenization of attitudes which destroy the competing subgroup values. "The 'deeper' social laws are implanted, the more 'hard-programmed' or 'pickled' into us, the more like 'natural' laws

[38]Millett, *Sexual Politics*, p. 56.
[39]Ibid.
[40]A Gallup poll released June 16, 1978, just after a demonstration in Washington by some 60,000 supporters of the Equal Rights Amendment and just before a critical House Judiciary Committee vote on extending the ratification period, showed 2–1 support, 58 percent to 31 percent, for the amendment nationwide. Men favored it by 62 percent and women by 54 percent. See "Public Favors ERA Passage," released July 16, 1978, American Institute of Public Opinion, Princeton, N.J.

they come to appear to be. Indeed, if someone breaks such a 'deeply' implanted social law, we are inclined to say that he is 'unnatural.'"[41]

Conclusion

The political socialization carried out by the two primary social agencies, family and subgroup, first establishes political consciousness in America.

Unfortunately, reliable evidence on these two agencies is very difficult to obtain, given the intimate nature of the family and subgroup experience. Still, the large majority of studies conducted by political scientists in the postwar era on the impact of family and subgroups, as well as other agencies, would most likely agree with Dawson and Prewitt: "Political socialization is a developmental process through which the citizen (or potential citizen) matures politically."[42] One classic study of five nations found American political socialization to be largely democratic. In the United States a "civic culture" is transmitted by a complex process that includes training in many social institutions—family, peer group, school, workplace, as well as the political system itself.[43] Allegedly, this creates beliefs and behavioral inclinations supportive of the generally democratic orientations of American politics.

Many racial minorities, feminists, and others benefiting least from establishment values see the process by which these values are inculcated by the family and subgroup, then communicated and perpetuated by other agencies, as largely repressive. Stanley Aronowitz argues that the dominant class controls the means of mental construction through its control of the means of material production. The family, school, the working environment, and other institutions which socialize children comprise the ideological apparatus of the prevailing social and economic system. Through both the interactions that occur daily in these and the overarching ideologies that legitimate them, all these institutions "reproduce . . . the pyramidal configuration of the whole society." The hierarchical authority relations of capitalist society parallel the

[41]Laing, *The Politics of the Family*, p. 9.
[42]Richard E. Dawson and Kenneth Prewitt, *Political Socialization* (Boston: Little, Brown, 1969), p. 17.
[43]Gabriel Almond and Sidney Verba, *Civic Culture* (Boston: Little, Brown, 1965), pp. 366–67.

patterns of "ownership and domination" underlying "the social and technical division of labor in society." Just as commodities are reproduced "within a specific hierarchically arranged matrix of economic institutions," so also to Aronowitz is the labor force itself reproduced by and through the socializing institutions. He rejects the dogmatic Marxist theory that sees all noneconomic institutions merely copying the economic base. To the contrary they are necessary for the "production" of the economic institutions, in Aronowitz's view. Unless the work force was socialized to treat the workplace as a "natural" institution standing above and apart from the creativity and labor of the workers, it "would be necessary to continuously make legitimate to every generation of workers social divisions within the labor process or else to simply control them through force." So the socializing institutions render the open use of force unnecessary. From childhood on, "workers find themselves at the bottom of a pyramidal structure within these institutions." They are thus led to expect that all social institutions will assign them to the same position. Theories about human nature are introduced that elevate this experience to the level of belief. Finally,

the superiority and inferiority ratings of human beings based on the criteria of adaptive intelligence justify the hierarchical organization of labor, the domination of political institutions over individual lives, the tracking system in the schools, and the differential treatment accorded members of a person's family by parents.[44]

On the basis of the information which is available, it appears probable that the apologists, e.g., Dawson and Prewitt, Almond and Verba, are overly complacent, whereas the critics, e.g., Aronowitz, are excessively harsh. In truth, the family has been and continues to be the social agency most apart from the establishment control which radicals fear—with the glaring exception of poor ones. On the other hand, many current cultural and political pressures threaten this autonomy and may render families more vulnerable to manipulation.

Turning to subgroups, one finds that they do possess a clearly demonstrated capacity for independent socialization. Many studies in the late 1950s and early 1960s overlooked this variable and concluded, falsely, that near-universal affection for the system was

[44]Aronowitz, *False Promises*, p. 60.

being established in the hearts and minds of young Americans. Soon after that came a deluge of black urban riots, struggles by American Indians, Mexican-Americans, and other ethnic minorities, and an intense push by feminists for redress of grievances. These demonstrate that a group's "objective conditions" do influence "subjective perceptions" in a fashion that may be quite contrary to the homogenizing and legitimating thrust of dominant social values. Thus the melting pot is not as successful as the radicals allege and the apologists desire. On the other hand, there is some evidence that certain values of the political culture—the virtues of individualistic self-reliance and the Horatio Alger myth of equal opportunity— may lead individuals to blame themselves excessively for low socioeconomic status, even when such status may be overwhelmingly a product of the historical patterns of discrimination experienced by such readily visible subgroups as blacks and women.

V

Political Socialization 2: Communicating American Political Consciousness

> *The socialization of children has largely been transferred from home and school to TV programmers who are un-elected, unnamed and unknown, and who are not subject to collective—not to mention democratic—review.*
>
> George Gerbner, Dean, University of Pennsylvania,
> Annenberg School of Communications

> *[In the United States] communications is the means by which one person relates to another through technological or fabricated devices. It is not a system of actions which, by its inherent structure, builds or "produces" a community or common humanity.*
>
> Marcus Raskin, *Being and Doing*

Man is the only animal, wrote Aristotle in the opening book of *The Politics*, "whom nature has endowed with the gift of speech." While other animals have a verbal ability to express pleasure or pain, speech was intended to distinguish "the expedient and inexpedient, and therefore likewise the just and unjust." Only man has the ability to distinguish between good and evil and justice and injustice "and the association of living beings who have this sense makes a family and a state."[1] For Aristotle this unique linguistic ability, combined with the more fundamental capacity for thought and the resulting tendency to political association, constituted the essence of mankind.

Approximately eighteen hundred years later Thomas Hobbes—Locke's predecessor by several decades—echoed this view.

The most noble and profitable invention of all others was that of SPEECH, consisting of *names* or *appellations* and their connection, whereby men register their thoughts, recall them when they are past, and do declare them one to another for mutual utility for conversation; without which there had

---

[1]Aristotle, *The Politics*, trans. Benjamin Jowett (New York: Random House, The Modern Library, 1943), pp. 54–55.

been among men neither commonwealth nor society nor contract for peace, no more than among lions, bears, or wolves.[2]

Going further than Aristotle, Hobbes also asserted that "there is nothing in the world universal but names." Thus "true and false are attributes of speech, not of things, which simply exist."[3] This nominalist position holds that the labeling and judging of things by authoritative linguistic symbols (as transmitted by dominant media of communications) in a society constitutes the operative reality for a people. Still, as Locke knew, the more abstract and complex, the more removed from simple concrete things our naming and labeling becomes, our categorizing and distinguishing of good and evil, of justice and injustice, the greater the possibility of error and deception. If Aristotle, Hobbes, and like-minded thinkers are even partially correct, then both the connotations, tone and relative descriptive accuracy of verbal and written linguistics are critical for our political consciousness. It is through these that we communicate our collective understanding of the political order.

Language itself constitutes only one-half of the communications process by which men create, to recall Aristotle's words, a political "association of human beings." Equally important for the kind of beliefs and behavioral inclinations shaped within that association is the nature of the channels or media through which the people speak with one another and with their leaders. Political, religious, and other institutional elites have always known this. Their response to the immense communications possibilities opened up by Gutenberg's press in the fifteenth century was generally one of fear and hostility. For example, the hierarchy of the Catholic church has historically sought to ban items which might undermine its value structure and world vision by an index blacklisting threatening books and films. In seventeenth-century England, all printed matter had to have the king's imprimatur before it could be published. In reaction, the eighteenth-century Enlightenment democratic revolutions attempted to guarantee the right to communicate through various printed media. These avenues of communicating were to be relatively secure from governmental prior restraint and were to have major protections from subsequent punishment for publish-

[2]Thomas Hobbes, *Leviathan* (New York: Bobbs-Merrill, 1958), p. 37.

[3]Quoted in Lee McDonald, *Western Political Theory, Part 2: Machiavelli to Burke* (New York: Harcourt Brace Jovanovich, 1968), p. 305.

ing and circulating news. When the Philadelphia convention failed to protect these rights explicitly, the Antifederalists insisted upon them as one condition of ratification. Jefferson left no doubt as to his priorities in an oft-quoted letter to Edward Corrington that was written the same year of the constitutional convention: "Were it left to me to decide whether we should have a government without newspapers, or newspapers without a government, I should not hesitate a moment to prefer the latter."[4] Governments throughout the world have periodically sought—sometimes successfully—to dispense with various media.

With these points in mind we want to ask the same questions about the socialization function of communications—language and television—that were raised in the preceding chapter about families and subgroups. Do they generally transmit a version of the tripartitite cultural components compatible with the Jeffersonian-populist model of American democracy or the other two variants? And through their direct and indirect impact do they function vis-à-vis the individual in a repressive or developmental manner? Do they aid in communicating a humanistic and rational political consciousness with a clear sense of self and sense of others? Who controls them? What specific values dominate the agencies? What interests are served? What is their relationship to one another and the other agencies we examine? Let us begin with a look at language.

LANGUAGE: CONTENT, CODES, AND CATEGORIES

It is significant that the dissident movement of black and student protestors of the 1960s objected, among other things, to the state of the language. One of the first of these protests was the "Free Speech Movement" in Berkeley. Later, in 1970, former Yippie leader and subsequent underground fugitive Abbie Hoffman, speaking at Yale—the veritable heart of the establishment—declared as a first task: "We gotta redefine the fucking language."[5] One commentator, not of this critical persuasion, summed up the reasons behind Hoffman's and other assaults: "This institution—language—was

[4]Quoted in Marvin L. Stone, "Appetite for Mergers: Conglomerates and the Media," *USA Today*, September 1978, p. 10.
[5]Quoted in A. Bartlett Giamatti, "Why Young People Today Can't Write," *National Observer*, April 17, 1976.

perceived as being repressive. It was thought to be the agent for all other repressive codes—legal, political, and cultural." In a phrase, "language impeded freedom,"[6] by reinforcing, as the radical indictment might have phrased it, the elitist, neo-Federalist thrust of the American political culture and diminishing majoritarian possibilities.

Like citizens of all countries, Americans perceive political reality and think about it; describe political things and communicate about them; evaluate policies, parties, and leaders, and choose accordingly, with socially authoritative terms. These have both denotative meaning and, often of more significance, they have "coded" connotative power which imply affective or pejorative judgments. Two writers diagrammed the relationship of language to politics in America in the following way:

> Political and Social Authority
> [is based on]
> Public Rationality and Morality
> [and is based on]

> The System of Language which incorporates the values and conventions of a social and political system, and provide a model or a logic of action.[7]

Put more simply, the politics and the language of any given period are inextricably interrelated. Hence the struggle by regime critics to redefine or replace authoriative terms and reshape the tone and denotative-connotative content of the language seeks alternative values, models, and a different logic of action. As one would expect such attempted reform occasions a reaction.

If Hoffman's verbal salvo opened the struggle in the 1970s over the political content of the language, the decade's final State of the Union address might be viewed as concluding it. In an attempt to link the contemporary American scene in general and his administration in particular to the legitimizing rhetoric of the "founding" generation, Jimmy Carter said:

We are their heirs. And they are sending us a *message* across the centuries. The *words* they made so vivid are now growing faintly indistinct, because

[6]Ibid.
[7]David L. Paletz and William F. Harris, "Four-Letter Threats to Authority," *Journal of Politics* 37 (1975), p. 963.

they are not heard often enough. They are words like *justice, equality, unity, sacrifice, liberty, faith,* and *love.*

Lest there be doubt about the meaning of these seven emotionally powerful terms, Carter added: "These words remind us that the duty of our generation of Americans is to renew our national faith —not focused just against foreign threats but against selfishness, cynicism and apathy."[8] He ended the secular liturgy by claiming to have laid a "new foundation." Carter's speechwriters had obviously not read Orwell's 1946 essay on "Politics and the English Language," which is still the best one on the topic. Orwell had warned that "the invasion of one's mind by ready-made phrases (*lay the foundation, achieve a radical transformation*) can only be prevented if one is constantly on guard against them, and every such phrase anaesthetises a portion of one's [speaker and listener] brain."[9]

It is no surprise that most major regime statements such as the State of the Union address quoted above do abound in anaesthetizing abstract, ideological, and symbolically powerful expressions and phraseology. As Orwell had pointed out, politically orthodox statements of Left or Right, from doctrinaire revolutionaries or from regime leaders, almost always do. We might also consider the fact that in the United States, dissenting "symbolic speech," such as burning draft cards, or the flag, or similar actions, which are a clear challenge to the authoritativeness of regime symbols, is *not* afforded clear constitutional protection by the federal judiciary. Indeed, one can easily make a case for certain trends toward a closed, intolerant, and ideologically restrictive American political language.

Further evidence of the efforts of regime elites to restrict the "terms of political discourse"[10] is the visceral government reaction to the use of obscenity in the heckling of political candidates, demonstrations, or underground pamphleteering or papers. Paletz and Harris interpret dissidents' recourse to these "disruptive" terms as a last-ditch, backs-to-the-wall reversion to a dimly recalled consciousness of no-saying.

[8]"State of the Union Address," *Washington Post*, January 24, 1979.

[9]George Orwell, "Politics and the English Language," in *Orwell's Nineteen Eighty Four: Text, Sources, Criticism*, ed. Irving Howe (New York: Harcourt, Brace and World, 1963), p. 149.

[10]See William Connolly's useful study with that title (Lexington, Mass.: D. C. Heath, 1974).

The public expression of obscenity may provide us with the closest thing we have to a paradigm of defiance of authority's command to obey, when otherwise we may not know how to say we don't want to. Indeed, obscenity may seem to be an inarticulate primitive chant precisely because of the primordial need of the alternative of defiance or disobedience which it serves and which has been socialized out of us in the name of social cohesiveness.[11]

Responses to the sexual imagery often depicted in four-letter words are much less predictable and manageable than responses to such words as those seven in Carter's speech. Fear of this unpredictability may partially explain the judicial energy expended to define obscenity and then prohibit public access to it. In *Miller* v. *California* (1973), Burger likened obscenity to a dangerous drug, conceding that while the sexual revolution has had some healthy benefits, "it does not follow that no regulation of patently offensive 'hardcore' materials is needed or permissible; civilized people do not allow unregulated access to heroin because it is a derivative of medicinal morphine."[12] He goes on to argue that repression of obscenity does not inhibit controversy in economics, politics, literature, and sociopolitical philosophy.

If, as one author believes, language is an internal censor, a "cultural and political guidance system into which values handed down from the past are deposited,"[13] then Carter's efforts to reinforce key terms and Burger's effort to block disruptive ones are strategically sound tactics for maintaining a system of supportive discourse and consciousness. Indeed, "the last thing a society bent on holding to its security . . . gives up is its alleged rationality, the ritual of set thinking and perceptual patterns."[14] This involves not merely explicit ideological and symbolic terminology but also—in a technological society—necessarily a scientific element.

In the immediate pre-World War II era, when there was much concern about demogogic leadership and mass deception through language manipulation, T.S. Eliot wrote that for the maintenance and transmission of a culture "there is no safeguard more reliable than a . . . literary language—not necessarily a scientific language,

[11]Paletz and Harris, "Four-Letter Threats to Authority," pp. 976–77.
[12]*Miller* v. *California*, 413 U.S. 15 (1973).
[13]Claus Mueller, *The Politics of Communication* (New York: Oxford University Press, 1973), pp. 17–18.
[14]Paletz and Harris, "Four-Letter Threats to Authority," p. 975.

but certainly a poetic one."[15] He was speaking of the Welsh language in particular, as used for daily life. A majoritarian democratic culture of the Jeffersonian type does not necessarily require a poetic-literary language but may not be operable nor transmittable on the basis of a highly scientific one.

There are several reasons. First and most obviously, as previously noted, by moving the discussion of public issues from moral, spiritual, political, and human terms—that is, "qualitative" ones —to objective, scientific, and technological or "quantitative" ones, the public will likely be disenfranchised. For example, the seven years of nuclear disarmament "talks" leading to the second Strategic Arms Limitations Agreement (SALT II) were delayed several months in early 1979 by disagreement over something called "telemetry encryption." Such terminology mystifies rather than clarifies issues and excludes rather than invites participation, as it may be intended to do. "Concerning these unknowns," as Theodore Roszak says in another context, "the layman may not even have command of the vocabulary for responsible speculation."[16] In such an event, technocratic experts dominate by default. (It should be pointed out that while jargon is often used to obscure, some technical questions may be difficult to express in everyday language.)

A less obvious but equally important danger to majoritarian democracy arises from the possible adverse impact on policymakers' perceptions and consciousness of adopting an overly scientific vocabulary and related models and perceptual patterns. The Indochina war provides an example. It was gamed and modeled and projected on computers and described and explained on the basis of scientific data—body counts, bomb tonnage, bombing raids, and so forth—plus scientifically sterilized and objectified concepts such as protective reaction strikes, pacification programs, and the like. Not only did this diminish public consciousness of the actual nature of the war, but it may have led many of the war's planners to lose sight of their ideological and even psychological motivations and to see, with their conceptual tunnel vision, a light at the end which was nonexistent. Ultimately, qualitative factors such as the social unity, will, and leadership differences of the opposing sides in that war, which could not be effectively modeled nor articulated in the arcane

[15]T. S. Eliot, *Notes toward a Definition of Culture* (London: Faber and Faber, 1948), p. 57.

[16]Theodore Roszak, *Where the Wasteland Ends* (Garden City, N.Y.: Anchor Books, 1973), p. 237.

computer language, proved decisive over technological might. Many domestic examples of curious omissions of decisive human and moral factors abound in urban planning, economic and monetary policy, and medical and environmental issues. To quote Orwell again; "If thought corrupts language, language can also corrupt thought."[17] Adopting a sterilized, impersonal, objective, and scientized language may lead to similar thought processes.

A last, broader, and more subtle danger of an excessively scientific language not counterbalanced by spiritual, moral, normative and evaluative terms is what Marcuse calls the "closing of the universe of discourse."[18] This means something more, ultimately, than the mere disenfranchisement from specific policy debates discussed above. Jurgen Habermas, who has addressed this, believes that the West is in the midst of a process whereby the terminology and "reified models of the sciences migrate into the sociocultural life-world and gain subjective power over the latter's self-understanding." This "new ideology," as he calls it, "violates an interest" in one of the "fundamental conditions of our cultural existence: language." The interest violated "extends to the maintenance of intersubjectivity of mutual understanding as well as to the creation of communication without domination."[19] In a basic sense, subcultural groups and generations not trained in scientific terminology and models, plus individuals who for whatever reason have failed to grasp them, may no longer be able to talk with or influence those imbued with the new ideology, because they no longer share the same world view. This potential noncommunicability of scientific and nonscientific world visions is illustrated in the now-famous (if fictional?) confrontation between Carlos Castenada, the social scientist, and Don Juan, the Yaqui *brujo*.

The old sorcerer has introduced Castenada to the experience of flight, with the aid of peyote buttons. Afterward the scientist pushes the brujo to explain rationally how this happened.

"Did I take off like a bird?"
"You always ask me questions I cannot answer. . . . What you want to know makes no sense. Birds fly like birds and a man who has taken the devil's weed flies as such."

[17]Orwell, "Politics and the English Language," p. 149.
[18]Herbert Marcuse, *One-Dimensional Man: Studies in the Ideology of Advanced Industrial Society* (Boston: Beacon Press, 1964), p. 84.
[19]Jurgen Habermas, *Toward a Rational Society*, trans. Jeremy J. Shapiro (Boston: Beacon Press, 1970), p. 113.

"Then I didn't really fly, Don Juan. I flew in my imagination. Where was my body?"
"The trouble with you is that you understand things in only one way."
"You see, Don Juan, you and I are differently oriented.

Being true to his world view Castenada tries to pursue the possibility of empirically verifying what happened. He wants to know first what another observer would have seen had he been a witness or, second, whether they should try an experiment.

"If he had simply watched you, he might have seen you flying, or he might not. That depends on the man. . . . If your friends knew about men flying with devil's weed, they would agree."
"Let's put it another way, Don Juan. What I meant to say is that if I had tied myself to a rock with a heavy chain I would have flown just the same because my body had nothing to do with my flying."
"If you tie yourself to a rock, I'm afraid you will have to fly holding the rock with its heavy chain."[20]

To the degree that top-level public and private policymakers, war planners, economists, behavioral scientists, urban planners, energy specialists, and the like do internalize the terminology and "reified models of the sciences," in Habermas's phrase, then it is possible that they become, like Castenada, quite "differently oriented" and "understand things in only one way." (They most assuredly do not fly.) Should this possibility reach fruition, then the basic requirement of a democracy that the citizenry and their decision makers communicate from the same ground, within the same universe, will be lost. Perhaps the growing hostility of the silent but no longer totally passive majority toward policymaking experts and their bureaucratese is a manifestation of this situation.

The third and last question pertaining to the implication of our language for political consciousness is its significance for the population's view of socioeconomic stratification. Political scientist Murray Edelman says flatly, in a book subtitled "Words That Succeed and Policies That Fail," that it is "language and symbols that justify acceptance of inequality and tolerance of chronic social problems." The rich field of study as to how this transpires is as yet largely uncultivated. Edelman is not, it should be emphasized,

[20]Carlos Castenada, *The Teachings of Don Juan: A Yaqui Way of Knowledge* (New York: Ballantine Books, 1968), pp. 130–31.

speaking of the influence of outright political terms, although these are obviously important.

The *fundamental* influence upon political beliefs flow, however, from language that is not perceived as political at all, but nevertheless structures perceptions of status, authority, merit, deviance, and the causes of social problems. Here is a level of politics that conventional political science rarely touches, but one that explains a great deal of the overt political maneuvering and governmental action that focuses public attention.[21]

He and others in this emerging area of study identify at least three major ways in which ordinary language, commonly regarded as apolitical, resonates with socioeconomic inequality. They are: (1) the unequal distribution of language skills and the resources necessary to attain these; (2) the gatekeeper power of verbal tests and measurements, plus the increasing hegemony of the dominant usage; and (3) status quo, system-serving language codes and categorizations.

Next to the lack of economic resources, there are few greater group liabilities than the lack of verbal skills. Yet just as with wealth, those individuals who need language resources the most, the poor, have the least access to them. This diminishes the prospect of acquiring the status, economic resources, and political power to effectuate needed change. It also adversely affects the possibility that individuals will pierce the web of systemic rationalizations and artificially induced needs confronting them to arrive at genuine self-understanding. Absent a certain linguistic competence, any individual may be overwhelmed by the barrage of advertisements, political announcements, and similar efforts aimed at affecting his consciousness. He may be unable, finally, to articulate to himself as well as to others just what his true needs are. "The recognition of certain needs and their relative importance requires cognitive skills and political awareness. Both tend to be limited for large segments of the population."[22] Jesse Jackson preaches the need for rigorous study, including mastering standard English usage, because he knows how vulnerable a subordinate group which lacks this skill is to manipulation.

Giamatti gives us another example of how a lack of verbal skills

[21]Murray Edelman, *Political Language* (New York: Harcourt Brace Jovanovich, 1977), pp. 2, 21.
[22]Mueller, *Politics of Communication*, p. 23.

can handicap individuals. It is possible that some more romantic followers of Hoffman and other protest movement leaders may have been led to think it unnecessary, even counterrevolutionary, to bother with the hard work required to master the language. Of young people who cannot write and either do not know this or do not care, Giamatti says simply, "they have been duped. By thinking that language can be denied . . . , they have of course become blocked and stunted and frustrated—and at the most important level. It is a sad irony."[23]

The socioeconomic dimension of this issue is exacerbated by the gatekeeping function performed in a technological society by a host of tests geared to verbal competence. These are used to admit one into, and upward in, the educational and economic systems, as well as in the growing and powerful public bureaucracy. If they do not develop verbal skills, subordinate socioeconomic groups will find these gates shut, token and temporary racial-ethnic-sexual affirmative action programs notwithstanding.

Compounding this problem is the increasing hegemony exercised by the dominant usage over traditional subcultural variations. The near future promises a homogenized "standard" English. Aronowitz writes, "The appropriation of the production of linguistic forms by mass communications has had a disintegrating effect on the autonomous language of all sectors of the underlying population." The move to uniformity subsumes terms as well as dialects, language structures, and subcultural connotations and meanings. Some examples are Southern dialects, Northern working-class speech, and ethnic language. "All are grist for the popular mills." Still, all these ingredients in the melting pot are not equally strong, and some lose their original flavor. New terms are often invented to replace the transformed, coopted ones. While all subcultures have capitulated to some degree before mass culture, there remains an "impulse toward invention and independence that can be observed every day in the games, language, symbols, that are constantly evolving."[24] The pervasiveness of the mass media bears heavily, however, on this inventiveness.

A third way in which American usage resonates with social stratification is by the kind of system-serving images conjured up

[23]Giamatti, "Why Young People Today Can't Write."

[24]Stanley Aronowitz, *False Promises: The Shaping of Working Class Consciousness* (New York: McGraw-Hill, 1973), pp. 15–16.

through normal everyday categorizations and language codes. As Edelman says, any categorization scheme "is bound to be political" because through it people are ranked; and this determines "degrees of status and influence." This includes "IQ's, psychiatric labels, typologies of talent, skills, or knowledge, employment statuses, criminal statuses, personality types,"[25] and many others, including sexist and racist ones. Old categories may take on new, undesirable meanings. Subordinate groups are subjected to communications phraseology which labels them as follows: "Unskilled," "ill-educated," "functionally illiterate," and probably also "illegitimate," "welfare generation," "living in chronic poverty," suffering high "unemployment," and residing in "ghettos" of similar people with much "deviant" behavior. "Ill," "un," "under," and "non" are the most common prefixes by which we preface our thinking of subordinate (subordinary?) groups. The coded nature of such categorizations and prefixes stimulates at best paternalistic feelings among well-meaning groups not in such conditions. They may evoke among less sympathetic populations a sense of the inevitability and unchangeability of such a situation and perhaps the individual unworthiness of those in such a state. Furthermore, there is an impact on the individuals so classified. "Language also provides the basis for self-reflection and individuation because it enables the individual to reason with himself and perceive, through a dialogue with others, those aspects which set him apart from others."[26] Or as Edelman put it, "language, events, and self-conceptions are a part of the same transaction, mutually determining one another's meanings."[27]

This typological stamping carries powerful portents of negative "self-conception," of individuals perceiving as highly unworthy that "which sets one apart." Such social categorization may be analogous to branding, with the brand seared deep within the individual's consciousness. Compare also these ill-sounding human categories with the fine-sounding terminology used to name and identify the organs and policies of the socioeconomic and political system which are supposed to respond to the needs of such groups. "Health and Human Services" and "Full Employment and Balanced Budget Act of 1978," or "Social Security," financed by "con-

---

[25]Edelman, *Political Language*, p. 62.
[26]Mueller, *Politics of Communication*, p. 14.
[27]Edelman, *Political Language*, p. 4.

tributions." Or compare the powerful, evocative terms used to rationalize the stratified socioeconomic system: "free enterprise," "personal independence," "private property," "individualism," "liberty," "competition of the marketplace," "self-reliance," "upward mobility," "opportunity," and similar ones. Marx had called such terms used to justify inequality "brave words," undergirding a culture which he saw as "for the enormous majority, a mere training to act as a machine."[28] Thus, in addition to the linkage of American usage to explicitly political matters, as in Carter's speech, there is also a clear relationship of class, language, and consciousness.

MASS COMMUNICATION: TELEVISION

In that previously cited letter to Corrington, Thomas Jefferson added two qualifications to his support of an unfettered press: "But I should mean that every man should receive those papers, and he should be capable of reading them." Present-day Jeffersonians are of mixed feelings regarding the present state of the former requirement, since only some 15 percent of the population regularly receive newspapers. But virtually everyone has access to some public information via the television in their homes, from which two-thirds get the bulk of their news. This includes a majority of college-educated Americans. It is true, on the other hand, that probably only 20-25 percent "watch" the news on any consistent basis. Radio and intellectual magazines have similarly lost audiences. Many books receive their greatest public from their television showing, and many more people view the electronic news-magazines than read printed ones. This is not to deny the dominant influence of key newspapers and magazines on elite consciousness. For example, the ambitious and then relatively unknown governor of Georgia was well-advised back in 1972 that if he wished to influence elite opinion, he should read, on a daily basis, the *Washington Post*, the *New York Times*, and the *Wall Street Journal*, as well as cultivate editors of the most influential magazines, *Harpers* and *Atlantic*, many of whom are native Southerners. The now-famous campaign planning memo from Hamilton Jordan and others to Carter also said, "Stories in *The New York Times* and *Washington*

---

[28]Karl Marx and Friedrich Engels, *The Communist Manifesto*, in *The Marx-Engels Reader*, ed. Robert C. Tucker (New York: W. W. Norton, 1972), pp. 348–49.

Post . . . have to be carefully planned and planted." Because of limitations of space and the fact that my primary concern here is with the sociocultural influences on mass consciousness, I will not enter into an analysis of print media. I will focus exclusively on network television, beginning with analysis of its content, then—at more length—of its structure and its impact.

Network television content is comprised, as we all know, of news and public affairs programs, daytime drama, talk and game shows, sports, movies, sit-coms, and other prime-time entertainment programming plus—last but certainly not least—commercial advertisements (and at election time, political ones). These commercials and the entertainment programs they support constitute the large bulk of television items. This is particularly true in the heavy-viewing, high-profit slots of prime time, where few if any public affairs and news programs are to be found consistently.

By the age of eighteen, the average American is estimated to have seen 350,000 commercials. One study describes them as the best thing on television in terms of production costs and quality. Such commercials are "psychological war for the hearts and minds of the people." They teach the "important illusions of our culture . . . , the superficial markings of our nation, the tags of our tribe."[29] The entertainment programs paid for by these advertisements attempt, logically, to convey compatible lessons. A network vice president writes: "Program makers are supposed to devise and produce shows that will attract mass audiences without unduly offending these audiences or too deeply moving them emotionally. Such ruffling, it is thought, will interfere with their ability to receive, recall, and respond to the commercial messages." He advised that the basic premise is that the "cool fire" is to be "used mostly as a stroking distraction . . . , a massage, a 'there, there,' a need, an addiction, a psychic fortress—a friend."[30] One individual, Fred Silverman, was so successful in shaping this type of entertainment that he became a top executive at all three networks in turn, receiving a salary from NBC, his third network, in excess of $1 million annually (until he was fired in the summer of 1981).

[29]Jon Price, *The Best Thing on TV: Commercials* (New York: Viking Press, 1979), quoted in Richard Reeves, "On Political Books," *Washington Monthly*, September 1978, pp. 55–56.

[30]Bob Shanks, *The Cool Fire: How to Make It on Television* (New York: W. W. Norton, 1976), quoted in review by Jeff Greenfield, *New York Times Book Review*, May 2, 1976, p. 8.

The socioeconomic and political significance of this escapist programming is often underestimated. Indeed, in all likelihood, if we consider "the impact of television on political attitudes, entertainment far outweighs news in importance."[31] This is probably true if for no other reason than that entertainment constitutes such a dominant share of television viewing, much more than news and public affairs. One authority notes the interrelation between all the components of television programming: "One of the fascinating things about telelvision is the continual overlapping of everything. Drama is inevitably propaganda, it is also advertising. It is continually selling a way of life [which was Aristotle's phrase for a constitution], or patterns of consumption."[32]

The "way of life" depicted in this video world is not, to borrow a phrase from America's poet of democracy, one of democratic vistas in the populist sense. In its normal design (as distinguished from the intrusion of spontaneous events, discussed below), television projects the *neo-Federalist* value structure, the technological world view associated with modern-day science, and the human image and social consciousness of the dominant elitist cultural variant with less deviation than is the case with any of the six socializing agencies discussed herein. Materialist possessions are equated with liberation and status (not to mention sexual potency, which Madison failed to mention). Private enterprise, depicted usually in small-scale and always in human terms, keeps a generally noble America strong, while government is much less efficient and trustworthy. The irrefutable workability, and hence truth, of space-age science is demonstrated in prime-time moonwalks, the miracles of advanced medical technology, the swiftness and smoothness of computer-designed automobiles. Humans are, with few exceptions, highly competitive economic beings and, lamentably, subject to infinitely varied forms of corruption and baseness. Last, society is largely middle class and devoid of any significant systemically grounded suffering or conflict, although much individual suffering is caused by corrupt individuals.

The accuracy of this summation of the "normal" content of television can be tested by simply viewing one of those 118 million plus sets in use four to six hours a day. If it is found to be a fair

[31]Ira Katznelson and Mark Kesselman, *The Politics of Power* (New York: Harcourt Brace Jovanovich, 1975), p. 377.

[32]Erik Barnouw, quoted in *Television as a Social Force*, eds. Douglass Cater and Richard Adler (New York: Praeger, 1975), p. 8.

description, then the obvious question is, why does American television "normally" reproduce so consistently the dominant cultural variant? The answer to this has to do, in the United States as in all countries which have television, with who controls the system.

The identity of the group that controls programming and access to the air—whether viewers, owners, government, or advertisers, or some particular mix of these four—will shape the medium and thereby prefigure its impact. "For the architecture of information is quite different when diverse economic classes and social collectivities feed into the information flow, from the information architecture that is created by their exclusion."[33] A quick glance about the world finds many different systems of control and access. In Britain the two public channels of the British Broadcasting Corporation (BBC) are run by a public board, with the system financially dependent upon government appropriations and annual fees paid by viewers. The one independently owned channel, ITV, receives revenue from advertisers, whose influence is minimized by the fact they are barred from sponsoring particular programs. Viewers in France finance the government owned and operated network with fees, and there is no commercial television and little advertising. Japan has a mixed public-private system, with both sectors having roughly the same number of stations. As in England, tax monies and viewer fees support the public channel. Soviet television is completely owned and operated by the government.

The institutionalized interrelationship of the four sectors—viewers, owners, government, and advertisers—in the United States may be distinguished from all these other systems, Network owners, the people they hire to operate television, and the corporate advertisers exercise far more control than the other two parties. Government does have some impact through its ownership and operation of the Public Broadcasting System (PBS) and through the licensing and regulatory authority of the Federal Communications Commission.

The FCC ostensibly upholds legislative statutes intended to insure that the airways are in service of the public interest. All too often, however, this "independent" regulatory agency serves the interest of owners and advertisers, primarily by staffing itself with industry personnel. Common Cause found, for example, that from

[33]Richard Bunce, *Television in the Corporate Interest* (New York: Praeger, 1976), p. 138.

1971 to 1975, "51 percent (or 19) out of the 37 senior officials at the Federal Communications Commission who had been hired . . . came from private enterprises regulated by the FCC."[34] The second largest group of appointments come from legal firms who specialize in the field, which gives them more of a community of interests with the regulated enterprises than with the public. Also, large numbers of commissioners and their top aides go directly back into the industry upon leaving the FCC. Thus "the F.C.C. has viewed its institutional role as that of protecting stability in the communications industry."[35] This is reinforced by the fact that "at least a few years ago, a working majority of members of Congress were tied either directly, or through law firms, to broadcast interests."[36] Thus the government sector is often coopted, or neutralized, or maybe sometimes intimidated, by the two dominant groups in the control structure.

The viewer sector itself is virtually powerless to enter as an independent group with affirmative decision-making power into the process of determining what will be the content of television and what purposes will guide utilization of the public airways. Indeed, few viewers could even conceive of such a role. Reflecting on the adverse implications of this statement, Richard Bunce concludes that "left to the inclinations of the Federal Communications Commission, and to the control of private business, our communications resources will not soon, if ever, be used to facilitate a communications democracy."[37]

The Communications Act of 1934 was intended to promote "a communications democracy" in the oncoming television age by providing, among other things, for local station ownership. Diversity and local accountability were the goals of this key statute. A decade later the Justice Department forced the Radio Corporation of America (RCA) to divest itself of one of its Red and Blue networks (the latter became ABC) so as to promote diversity at the network level. Later the FCC placed limits on the amount of stock a business

[34]"Common Cause Study Finds Conflicts of Interest in U.S. Agencies," *Washington Post*, October 21, 1976.

[35]Marcus Raskin, "The Dream Colony," in *Television Today: The End of Communications and the Death of Community*, ed. Richard L. Stavinis (Washington, D.C.: Communication Service Corporation, for the Institute for Policy Studies, 1969), p. 20.

[36]Jeff Greenfield, "TV is Not the World," *Columbia Journalism Review* 57 (May/June 1978), p. 34. My analysis has greatly profited from this article.

[37]Bunce, *Television in the Corporate Interest*, pp. 134, 140.

or individual could hold in a broadcasting company. Yet a recent study concludes that ownership of American media in general, and broadcast media in particular, has now been largely concentrated in the hands of a few large corporate conglomerates,[38] and local accountability is more myth than reality. "RCA (which owns NBC), CBS and ABC rank 31st, 102nd, and 170th, respectively, on the *Fortune* 500 list of the largest industrial corporations."[39] They are extensively involved in ownership of publishing houses, magazines, theaters, and—most importantly for our discussion—key urban television affiliates. "Each of the three networks own five V.H.F. stations, all three own stations in New York, Los Angeles, and Chicago." This gives instant control by the suppliers of programming of "over a quarter of the American viewing population."[40] In addition, they are linked through corporate ties to "nine broadcasting giants which own 4/5ths of the commercial V.H.F. stations in the five largest markets."[41] Consequently, over 90 percent of all programming originates with the networks (although this was declining as the 1980s unfolded for a host of reasons.) This includes news items. As one executive puts it, "in almost all cases, the networks only air news programs that are produced by our own news departments.

All of this means that the three networks plus those corporate interests that pay each of them over $6 billion annually for advertising as of 1978 (with an unknown amount going to their affiliates and the interrelated urban broadcasting giants), have a clear monopoly on American television. The unique nature of the medium exacerbates this situation.

There is no way around the advertiser-sponsored (or corporation-underwritten), network-supplied access to national television. There is no off-Broadway, no small publishing house, no off-beat newspaper or magazine, no independent film maker who every once in a while breaks through the cultural mainstram to have an important national voice. What TV concentrates, in a way no other medium ever could hope to do, is access. Whether you want to talk politics, or sell a new product, or sing a new song, or make children laugh or think, either you get the approval of NBC, CBS,

[38]Peter L. Brosnan, "Who Owns the Networks?" *Nation*, November 25, 1978, p. 560.
[39]Stone, "Appetite for Mergers: Conglomerates and the Media," p. 12.
[40]Greenfield, "TV is Not the World," p. 34.
[41]Fred W. Friendly, "McGraw-Hill and a Free Press," *Wall Street Journal*, January 26, 1979.

ABC or PBS, or to a substantial extent you don't do it on nationwide television.[42]

As with education, wealth, language, and status, "communications inequalities are power inequalities."[43]

If one asks who owns the networks, the answer appears to be a few major banks. "At least five (Chase Manhattan, Prudential, Chemical Bank, Citibank and Banker's Trust) . . . hold 15 percent of ABC, 12 percent of CBS, and 8 percent of RCA/NBC." (As recently as 1973 the Rockefeller-controlled Chase Manhattan owned 14 percent of CBS stock outright.) Normally 7 percent to 10 percent of voting stock confers control over a corporation upon the group possessing it, except family-held entities with large concentrations of stock. A few years ago a critical publication on the media by the Trilateral Commission, an influential elite organization, called for "significant measures" to "restore an appropriate balance between the press, the government, and other institutions in society" in the "broader interests of society and government."[44] The most influential member of the Trilateral Commission at that time was David Rockefeller, an executive officer of Chase Manhattan Bank. Many leaders have been recruited from the Trilateral Commission, for example, Henry Kissinger and Jimmy Carter. Given this overlap of concentrated ownership with influential elite associations and links to decision makers, it is at least possible that such a mix of control might confer a contemporary corporate imprimatur much like the king's imprimatur of old. Fortunately, the worst possibilities for such control are significantly reduced in number and degree, at least in the area of current events, if not where documentaries, entertainment, or economic and political advertising are concerned, by the very spontaneity of the medium.

Because it is engaged in animated (and therefore constantly shifting) depiction of an ever-changing scene, American television fails to present a consistent, completely designed "normal" landscape whose "cultural illusions, national markings, and tribal tags" reflect the consensus-oriented, elitist, neo-Federalist cultural variant. The subject world is often unavoidably disrupted by the intrusion of undesigned programs—that is, real events. The drama-

[42]Greenfield, "TV is Not the World," pp. 32–34.
[43]Bunce, *Television in the Corporate Interest*, p. 135.
[44]Brosnan, "Who Owns the Networks?" pp. 577–79.

tic immediacy of the medium means that it cannot help but project, on the occasion when they are highlighted, some of the less visible and more disturbing nooks and crannies of our real political world. Over the last couple of decades televised events have included several political assassinations, extensive urban riots, poverty, an unsuccessful and bloody war, visibly unsafe streets, deceit at the highest levels of government, looting and pillaging by some 20,000 people during a brownout in America's largest city, and suffering and deformities caused by industrial waste. Members of the Trilateral Commission, like many people, criticize the messenger for carrying these disturbing messages.

It is true that the networks do not seek out subjects suggestive of endemic distress, although they do readily cover sensational individual failures such as the sexual peccadilloes and financial corruption of political leaders. "Among all the news media, television engages least in investigative reporting. . . . They [the networks] employ fewer reporters for investigative purposes than a large daily newspaper."[45] And the networks are usually slow to provide critical analysis of deep-seated systemic malfunctions, such as the Vietnam War or Watergate. The former received very uncritical treatment from the networks in the early years, when print journalists such as David Halberstam were battling government in an effort to present an other than official version of that experience. For example, CBS news executive Fred Friendly publicly rebuked the network and resigned because it would not cover the initial congressional hearings on Vietnam in 1966. And Watergate was investigated by print rather than electronic journalists until the story broke, while the early congressional hearings were covered originally by PBS, with first spot coverage and then rotating network coverage, until the full dimensions of the tale became known.

One analyst points out that the "structure of TV news renders its contents far more completely within the practical, day-to-day discretionary control of the TV news executive than is the case with the newspapers, the content of which is by comparison more powerfully influenced by events, sources, and other external or uncontrollable factors."[46] Which concerns of the TV news executives produce essentially indistinguishable presentations on all three

[45]Katznelson and Kesselman, *The Politics of Power*, p. 374.
[46]Paul H. Weaver, "Newspaper News and Television News," in *Television as a Cultural Force*, Douglass Cater and Richard Adler (New York: Praeger, 1976) p. 87.

networks? They are: (1) to maintain an audience; (2) to cut unnecessary news costs; (3) to avoid controversy that might offend the affiliates (and sponsors); and (4) to present "balanced" stories so as not to violate the FCC "fairness" doctrine.[47]

Costly, controversial, in-depth investigations of issues such as inequities in the tax structure, the distribution of wealth, comparative health statistics, and longevity rates of subordinate versus dominant groups, and the power of multinationals—all of which relate to the system—are apparently ruled out by such criteria. When the news organizations act courageously, as CBS did, for example, in presenting "The Selling of the Pentagon" in 1971, or NBC did in analyzing the status of Florida migrants in 1970, they are quickly brought into line. Congress conducted a vigorous set of hearings on the CBS program, threatening to send to jail some news executives who refused to turn over unused film, and Coca-Cola, which owned the citrus-fruit farm highlighted by NBC, withdrew its ads for 1971.[48] Always in the background is the possibility—recall the position of the Trilateral Commission—that "bottom-line responsibility to stockholders becomes a form of censorhip."[49]

What difference does it make what is or is not on television? How concretely do the images, messages, values, role models, and behavioral patterns depicted by "designed" programming and those revealed by televising contemporary "current events" affect American political consciousness? Television is such an omnipresent, inviting, and easy target that far too often omnipotent, usually undesirable, power over public attitudes is attributed to it. Still, the burgeoning mass of statistical psychological and social science findings tends to reveal, as one carefully stated "catalogue of media

[47]Michael J. Robinson, "American Political Legitimacy in an Era of Electronic Journalism: Reflections of the Evening News," in *Television as a Cultural Force*, p. 112. These concerns may vitiate in-depth analysis of controversial socioeconomic or deep-seated systemic problems, but they do not prevent, in Robinson's view, the generally liberal electronic journalists from criticism of political officials. Robinson is well known for analyses of the proclivity of television newspeople to criticism of government and politicians. In Robinson's view this bias affects particularly the "inadvertent audience" and produces "video malaise." See, for example, his "Public Affairs Television and the Growth of Political Malaise: The Case of 'The Selling of the Pentagon,' " *American Political Science Review* 70 (June 1976), pp. 409–35. Analysts like Greenfield, cited above, believe that Robinson is incorrectly interpreting the people's understandable disillusionment, caused by real political incompetence and failures, as a reaction to the transmitters of information.
[48]Katznelson and Kesselman, *The Politics of Power*, p. 372.
[49]Brosnan, "Who Owns the Networks?" p. 578.

effects on attitude change" says, that "actual conversion is small, but there is considerable modifying, crystallization, and reinforcement effect."[50] The ability of television to "convert" views is limited by viewer intelligence, peer-group counterpressures, competing systems of communications, and other "mediating factors." More important, as the dean of American political journalists Joseph Kraft explains, it is primarily limited by experience. "One of the few things we know about public opinion is that it grows from experience. People develop views when something happens to them. The more acute the happening—the more it makes us pay in money or blood—the more strongly held the view. Which is why wars and depression breed such powerful feelings."[51] Television is the easiest available experience, providing passive entertainment requiring minimal exertion—which is why so many people choose it for forty hours a week over education, additional work, interacting with their family, or other complex and demanding activities. It is also the most superficial experience, hence it seldom if ever "originates" values, attitudes, or powerful feelings; and in this sense as an agent of socialization it can only reinforce, at least among adults.

Even in the absence of extensive converting power, television is a major dependent, or secondary, force acting on consciousness through its reinforcement ability. Corporate decision makers would not spend, as they did, $600,000 for each of the twenty-two minutes of advertising time on the January 1981, Superbowl broadcast if there was doubt as to television's effectiveness at presenting desirable images and stimulating particular responses. Neither would the major-party presidential candidates spend over one-half their available campaign funds on television if they distrusted its utility.

The single most important impact of the normal content of television, this cool fire which portrays important illusions of our culture, may well be to reinforce what Michael Parenti labels "center extremism (albeit with a tilt to the right)" within "the appearance of heterodoxy."[52] The entertainment and advertising (economic and political) are unequivocally hostile to other than centrist values. By omitting or condemning values of the socialist

[50]James C. Strouse, *The Mass Media, Public Opinion, and Public Policy Analysis* (Columbus, Ohio: Charles E. Merrill, 1975), p. 203.

[51]Joseph Kraft, "Carter, 'Dear Abby' Hour Spikes Myths," *Times-Picayune* (New Orleans, La.), March 9, 1977.

[52]Michael Parenti, *Power and the Powerless* (New York: St. Martin's Press, 1978); see chapter 4 in particular.

Left, particularly, and of the Radical Right, and portraying so resolutely the neo-Federalist values of the center, television exaggerates and reinforces them. Thus viewers get—in a nonlinear sense—extremism. The process works just as effectively in public affairs programming through the FCC "equal time" and fairness provisions.

Requiring nonpreferential, balanced presentation of views within what is metaphorically termed the "marketplace of ideas" mandates centrism. It is as if noncentrist views are, by definition, invalid. Kenneth Dolbeare points out two key fallacies of this operative economic metaphor. One is the obvious one that the market in political ideas is not free at all, no more than is the economic market which serves as the model. Decades of socialization and legitimacy, to say nothing of the surrounding political consciousness, support only the dominant belief system of the society. Thus the whole analogy is a facade that serves only to cloak perpetuation of a single set of ideas.

The other problem is that accepting the analogy's relativistic premise "isolates those who are already powerless, when their only chance is to be united. It provides a 'legitimate' ground on which to mobilize support against those who claim to have a morally and socially justifiable alternative to the status-quo."[53] Hence overtly unbiased, fair presentation and equal treatment serve the purpose of the dogmatic center. Marxist thinker Herbert Marcuse sees this enforced neutralization of noncentrist critiques as hidden censorship. "Effective dissent is blocked where it could finally emerge: in the formation of opinion, in information and communication, in speech and assembly."[54] This process can result in toleration of the intolerable: in so-called objective and balanced discussions of such things as the possibility of using nuclear weaponry, "kid-vid" violence and advertising, of the definition of appropriate domestic intelligence gathering by federal agencies, of the functionality of economic stratification, and so on. "Balanced" treatment of these legitimizes them to a substantial degree. On the other side of the political spectrum, a prominent non-Marxist like Catholic theologian Michael Novak also attacks the rigid, quasi-liberal modernity

[53]Kenneth Dolbeare, *Political Change in the United States* (New York: McGraw-Hill, 1974), pp. 107–8.
[54]Herbert Marcuse, *"Repressive Tolerance,"* in Herbert Marcuse, Barrington Moore, and Robert Paul Wolff, *A Critique of Pure Tolerance* (Boston: Beacon Press, 1965), p. 95.

of American television: "The present system is effectively a form of social control." Run by college-educated Americans, fewer than 10 percent of the populace, it serves, in his view, "the two mammoth institutions of modern life: the state and the great corporation." Small-scale institutions such as the family, neighborhood, and subnational governments, plus localistic values—all so dear to Novak—are undermined by the permissive "educated class's fantasies about the fantasies of the population."[55]

Ultimately television's impact on political consciousness is a contradictory one. On the minus side, it does tend to delimit consciousness as described above. Television also—as many critics charge—undeniably reinforces culturally based propensities to violence, the narcissistic ideology of materialistic consumption for self-aggrandizement, and racial and sexual sterotypes. For example, the United States Civil Rights Commission reported that in 1978 women comprised only 27.7 percent of the prime-time dramatic characters, and among the ten roles they most commonly played, none involved a professional or managerial occupation of the sort that pays well. It is small wonder that groups like the National Citizens Commitee for Broadcasting, the National Parent-Teacher Association, consumer groups, feminist and minority organizations, and untold numbers of people working locally fight vigorously to compel the sponsors, networks, owners, and their protector, the FCC, to reform the medium. They have had some success since 1966, when they won the right to enter as FCC license renewal proceedings "parties in interest." Still, so long as these efforts leave control over the public airways almost exclusively in the hands of private interests who benefit from a noncontroversial, one-dimensional medium, it is unlikely that the video world of American television will ever be a marketplace of ideas. It may not even be a shopping basket. Cable television (some facilities for which have two-way transmission capacity, satellite reception systems, and similar technological innovations) is unlikely to change this state of affairs if the present structure remains intact. As Bunce says, "The potential for mass communication in the sense of mass participation in the communication process, under the present control structure, will likely remain some future promise forever."[56]

[55]Michael Novak, "Television Shapes the Soul," in *Television as a Cultural Force*, pp. 18–19.

[56]Bunce, *Television in the Corporate Interest*, p. 4.

On a more positive note, television has an unparalleled capacity to project instantly the spontaneous eruptions of our real political world nationwide and thereby impress them vividly on political consciousness. This unavoidable role, which contradicts so dramatically the socially legitimizing efforts of normal programming, is the saving grace of the medium as it is presently constituted.

Many critics overestimate the impact of corporate television. They forget that "the first generation of television viewers turned into the most raucous, dissident, anti-corporate generation this nation had ever seen; . . . the young men and women of Berkeley and Columbia and Jackson State." Marie Winn, for example, sees the very process of television watching as inherently devitalizing to the human spirit. And Jerry Mander offers "four arguments for the elimination of television."[57] They echo concerns expressed just before that first television generation grew up to join together in the 1960s student movement by critics who included Paul Goodman. Terry, a character in one of his novels, was described as follows:

There was something worse than his emptiness. He was not empty but crammed. It was that he regarded the detritus of our culture, the world of TV or Hollywood or even the advertising, as if that were the normal, lively world. He did not have enough common sense, or confidence in himself, to look directly at the street. If a scene was on the TV and had that official warrant and interpretation, he had the courage to think that it was real; otherwise he doubted it.[58]

As in 1962, so in the 1980s people rightly worry that the abstract, institutionalized perceptions, pictures, interpretations, and rationalizations of the TV world may supplant the personalized and intimately concrete understanding of one's authentic experiential odyssey. Howard Beale, the "mad prophet" of the airways in Paddy Chayefsky's 1977 movie *Network*, plaintively admonished his audience, "You're beginning to think the tube is reality and your own lives aren't real." And James Baldwin once noted, speaking of movies, that "the language of the camera is the language of our dreams." Maybe, but the small dreams of the (hollow) television tube and human reality are not the same. In another place, Baldwin advised his nephew in a famous letter to "trust your experience."[59]

[57]Greenfield, "TV is Not the World," p. 32.
[58]Paul Goodman, *Making Do* (New York: Macmillian, 1963), pp. 74–75.
[59]James Baldwin, *The Devil Finds Work*, quoted in review by Orde Combs, *New York Times Book Review*, May 2, 1976, p. 6.

As the television age evolves, Americans' capacity to distinguish experience from television and to rely on the former becomes critically important. If as the 1980s unfold the population is relatively quiet, it is more likely because the times are complex and a multiplicity of issues cross-pressure citizens than because television has collectively hypnotized or indoctrinated them. When and if war or economic depression or some other deep-seated experience affects citizens either personally or through television, it is likely that they will stir, the soothing, escapist, bland, centrist, socially legitimizing illusions of the unreal, abnormal world of "normal" American television notwithstanding.

Conclusion

The relationship of American language patterns and television to the dominant neo-Federalist political culture is much clearer than was the case with the family and subgroup. Indeed, the ideosymbolic, scientific-technological, and socioeconomic content of American usage may be more tightly aligned with that elite cultural variant than any other agency. If this is so, then proponents of either reformist or radical change have their work cut out for them. For it appears undeniable that "language is," as Marx and Engels wrote, "as old as consciousness, language is practical consciousness."[60] It seems indisputable that our linguistic "guidance system" is more and more dominated by regime, scientific, and economic elites. The specifically political as well as conceptual and social-psychological content which they inject into the language becomes a major influence on individual and societal perception of problems and conception of alternatives. As one anthropologist who has studied the role of events versus human will in various societies notes: "To change the world in a conscious way one must first have a conscious understanding of what the world is like. Lack of such understanding is a dismal portent."[61] Until and unless linguistic resources are more evenly distributed, onerous codes and categories identified and eliminated, moral and qualitative concepts revitalized, and constraints on ideosymbolic alternatives removed, the portent for American political consciousness is not a positive one.

Turning from language to television, one finds an elite control

[60]Quoted in Mueller, *Politics of Communication* p. 19.
    [61]Marvin Harris, *Cannibals and Kings: The Origins of Culture* (New York: Random House, 1977), p. 194.

structure, banal entertainment programming, unrelieved economic and political huckstering and a rigidly centrist approach to
public affairs. The medium tends, in itś normal operation, to de-
politicize and to deflect attention away from basic issues such as
the distribution of wealth or other major systemic matters. Still,
because of the spontaneous nature of television, this depoliticiz-
ing role is offset by the unavoidable broadcasting of such "ab-
normalities" as political corruption, racial crises, and other such
events. In this regard, television is a major vehicle stimulating po-
liticization, if sporadically. These and other facts of the politics of
television have occasioned such debate by citizen's groups, political
figures, organizations like the Trilateral Commission, and industry
and regulatory personnel, that Congress saw fit to begin reexamin-
ing government policy on the medium near the end of the 1970s.
Congressmen Lionel Van Deerlin (a Democrat from California) and
Louis Frey (a Republican from Florida) introduced, in 1978, a major
reform bill, the Communications Act, which would almost entirely
deregulate radio broadcasting and would partially deregulate television. According to one study of the issue, "industry spokesmen
have been generally favorable to the proposal. . . . Citizen groups,
however, have been upset." Whether this bill passes and alters the
status quo or whether the system as presently constituted continues, all affected parties recognize that "there is no way to separate
the mass media system from the larger social system."[62]

[62]Larry Rothstein, *New Direction in Mass Communications Policy: Implications for Citizen Education and Participation* (Washington, D.C.: U.S. Department of Health, Education, and Welfare, 1978), pp. 7, 22.

VI

Political Socialization 3: Perpetuating
American Political Consciousness

Love, work and knowledge are the well-springs of our life.
Wilhelm Reich, *The Mass Psychology of Fascism*

*Of all the safeguards that we hear spoken of as helping
to maintain constitutional continuity the most important
. . . is education, that is, educating citizens for the way of
living that belongs to the consitution in each case.*
Aristotle, *The Politics*

*The economic health of the nation has a more direct
impact on the daily lives of Americans than any other
aspect of our national life.*
Public Research Corporation survey for U.S.
Department of Labor,1978

In the second edition of the most widely used introductory text on
political socialization, Dawson and Prewitt note that while most
scholars initially assumed that early political learning is crucial in
determining adult political outlooks and behavior, recently some
have wondered how crucial the early years really are."[1] At least two
significant changes have occurred, leading to a reexamination of the
overemphasis in some of the first studies on the permanency of
preadolescent and/or preadult socialization in families and subgroups.

The first change impelling us to take a closer look at secondary
agencies has been the expansion and transformation of certain
formerly decentralized, small-scale social institutions into interrelated and centralized national behemoths, which occurred during
the period when America was becoming a technological society. For
example, vast changes in the shape and functioning of America's
enormous educational system, which in 1978 involved some 60
million people and well over $155 billion, greatly influence how we
understand our world, how we relate to one another as a people,
what we discuss, and how we disperse information. The technol-

---

[1]Kenneth Prewitt, Richard Dawson and Karen S. Dawson, *Political Socialization*,
2nd ed. (Boston: Little, Brown, 1977), p. 74.

117

ogical age has also brought ever greater interdependence in the economic sphere of life. Now, national economic concerns intrude throughout the farthest regions of the country. Hence the political consciousness of the generation of citizens studying and working in contemporary, large-scale America is inevitably affected to at least as great a degree by schooling and economics as by family, subgroup, and communications. Neither of these two agencies loomed so important for earlier generations.

A second development of significance has to do with the environmental stress placed on attitudes learned in youth by a lifetime of kaleidoscopic sociopolitical experience. As we enter the last decades of the century, the chaotic, already fast pace of life seems to accelerate, presenting new situations which can destabilize old attitudes. An increasingly large proportion of the population now reach old age, which is defined as a period later in life than heretofore, so that the possibility of attitude destablization becomes greater. Thus it becomes less and less feasible to assume the automatic primacy of beliefs and behavioral predispositions learned in the family and subgroup and transmitted through communications channels—assumptions made by early socialization studies under the influence, first, of psychological views about early childhood personality development and, second, of sociological views regarding the unshakable influence of primary agencies. As a result we must examine the effect of other institutional influences, such as schooling and the economic workplace, on political consciousness.

By focusing last on these agencies I do not mean to imply that others, left·unexamined, lack importance. Political events, the government itself, religion, aging, the marketplace, and other institutions, experiences, and group associations condition beliefs and behavioral inclinations in a significant fashion throughout the course of one's life. None of these, however, has so significant a long-term impact on American political consciousness. None is so important in the perpetuation of the dominant values of American political consciousness.

SCHOOLING AND SOCIALIZATION: STRUCTURE, PROCESS, AND CONTENT

The several meanings of "educate" include: (1) to foster the growth or expansion of knowledge, wisdom, desirable qualities of mind or character, physical health, or general competence; (2) to train by formal instruction and supervised practice in a trade, skill, or profession; (3) to condition or persuade to feel, believe, or react in a particular way by providing with often selective information or knowledge, that is, to make willing to accept.[2] These developmental, instrumental and conditioning functions which are present in all educational systems to varying degrees, may clash. Liberal democratic theorists like John Stuart Mill, Jefferson, and John Dewey would subordinate the latter two to the developmental function. Economic elites and their allies in politics and other institutions tend to favor the instrumental role of education, while the conditioning function receives the greatest stress by authoritarian regimes. The degree of emphasis placed on these by national educational systems has long been recognized as one of the most important political questions to be examined in any society.

Aristotle emphasized that education is of fundamental importance in developing the distinctive human abilities of reason and speech and in providing the training for various crafts and jobs. But he was eminently clear in saying that the most important purpose of education was in creating the proper citizenry for a city-state, that is, "educating citizens for the way of living that belongs to the constitution in each case." Individuals have to be trained and have their habits formed for their polity. To Aristotle the constitution and way of living of a people were one and the same, involving all the relationships, values, and meanings of a political culture. Transmission of such information cannot be left simply to parents, who teach it only partially, or to subgroups, who do so selectively. Educational oversight must be a "public concern, not a private affair . . . , each man separately bringing up his own children and teaching them just what he thinks they ought to learn."[3]

One observer of the American educational system describes its "legitimating myths" in very Aristotelian terms: the anthropological traditions have emphasized a function of primitive rituals and initiation ceremonies assumed by modern educational systems. Rites of passage serve to induct people into membership status in society, and in the process of creating members by symbolically redefining them, they also affirm the social reality of society and its

[2]*Webster's Third New International Dictionary* (Springfield, Mass.: G. and C. Merriam Co., 1966).
[3]Aristotle, *The Politics*, trans. T. A. Sinclair (Baltimore, Md.: Penguin Books 1962), pp. 215–16, 299.

central values.[4] Another analyst also sees the extremely traumatic experience of leaving the home and entering the large, expensive, and powerful American educational system as a rite of initiation. Borrowing from Camus, Collins views the individual entering the school as a stranger. He is an egocentric outsider who has moved heretofore in the subjective, warm, personal, informal and largely private and loving domain of home and peers. Now he confronts this impersonal institution, the school. The school's major purpose is not to teach him the three R's. Schooling aims first of all to socialize the child to the objective world, Collins notes, by which he means the world of political life. Drawing on the work of sociologists Berger and Luckman, Collins sees schools as employing several techniques, including intimidation, mystification, and manipulation of prestige symbols.[5]

The school's initiation, habituation, and induction of the young stranger to the objective way of life in his or her political society proceeds in all countries. In no other industrial democracy, however, does schooling carry greater socioeconomic and political implications for the student's future than in the United States. As Seymour Martin Lipset explains, in Europe and Israel, as in Britain, "the socialist parties and labor movements placed greater emphasis on collectivist measures to lift up the economic level of the bottom, than on opening the door to a race for the top" through education. The social democracies of these countries have always spent far less on education and have never had, proportionally, a school population the size of that in the United States. Furthermore, their educational systems have almost always been less egalitarian than ours. The very rigorous European lycees or gymnasia, which Israel copied, weed out students at a much earlier age than American common schools. Also, a much higher percentage of Americans than of citizens in any European country have secured higher education. To advance their future Americans must consume as much education as possible, for while the United States has devoted more resources to education as the road to success than any other country and has distributed the access to education more equally, Americans spend disproportionately less than the social democ-

[4]David H. Kamens, "Legitimating Myths and Educational Organization: The Relationship between Organization Ideology and Formal Structure," *American Sociological Review* 32 (April 1977), p. 210.
[5]Clinton Collins, "The Multiple Realities of Schooling," *Intellect* 102 (May 1974), p. 532.

racies on social welfare, old age pensions, medical services, unemployment benefits, public housing, and so forth.

This fact implies to the national citizenry of the social democracies a recognition that forces other than individual ability and initiative are primarily responsible for a person's socioeconomic attainment. For this reason and also because these countries have values and "leftist parties which stress the extent to which the economic system blocks opportunity for the lowly, *failure to be successful is not as strongly perceived as personal failure*."[6] Thus there is much less pressure on these European students than on their American counterparts to internalize the standards, assessments, values, explanations, and relationships of the objective history which their educational systems initiate and habituate them to. Consequently the initimidation, mystification, and manipulation of prestige symbols by which schooling enforces the rites of initiation everywhere are further strengthened by an even more powerful force in the United States—the recognition of necessity.

What is the nature of that experience of the young American "stranger" being initiated into his society by the school? Does the experience of schooling cripple or facilitate democratic impulses in this individual? Does it condition a willingness to accept things as they are, or does it lead to dreams and inclinations toward things as they should be? Is it primarily an instrumental and individualistic experience or a developmental and communitarian one? In real life few teachers and students have grappled with these dilemmas more brilliantly than Phaedrus and his students in Pirsig's aforementioned *Zen and the Art of Motorcycle Maintenance,* subtitled *An Inquiry into Values*.

In Pirsig's tale, Phaedrus, with an IQ of 170, found himself teaching rhetoric in a Montana teaching college in the late 1950s. "At a teaching college you teach and teach . . . until your mind grows dull and your creativity vanishes and you become an automaton saying the same dull things over and over to endless waves of innocent students who lose respect." The political environment of the school was a very difficult one.

The state of Montana at this time was undergoing an outbreak of ultra-right-wing politics. . . . A nationally known professor from the University of Montana at Missoula was prohibited from speaking on campus on the

[6]Seymour Martin Lipset, "Education and Equality: Israel and the United States Compared," *Society* 11 (March 1974), pp. 56–66.

grounds that it would stir up trouble. Professors were told that all public statements must be cleared through the college public-relations office before they could be made. Academic standards were demolished. . . The legislature had passed a law fining the college eight thousand dollars for every student who failed.[7]

In addition to these problems, the governor had supplied a list of fifty "subersives" on Montana faculties to a national police agency. As part of his vendetta against the college president, a political enemy, funds were cut.

One day, in the midst of this deadening situation, Sarah, an elderly teacher near retirement, passed by Phaedrus's office and remarked, "I hope you are teaching Quality to your students." Phaedrus looked and, finding no Quality in this educational experi- ence, sought it for himself and set his students on the same quest. To help in the search he abolished grades and rigid goals and refused to define Quality for the students. He believed these things "forced students to conform to artificial forms that destroyed their own creativity." Phaedrus wished his students "to become creative by deciding for themselves what was good writing instead of asking him all the time. The real purpose of withholding the grades was to force them to look within themselves, the only place they would ever get a really right answer." This effort at a nongraded, non- authoritarian educational experience created great anxiety. Many students found the situation "Kafkaesque . . . they saw they were to be punished for failure to do something but no one would tell them what they were supposed to do. They looked within themselves and saw nothing and looked at Phaedrus and saw nothing and just sat there helpless, not knowing what to do. The vacuum was deadly. One girl suffered a nervous breakdown." But soon the better, more interested students relaxed, became friendly and less competitive, and turned in superb work. The traditional end of term evaluations found the students who normally earned A's favoring the system by two to one and the B-C students evenly split. But the largest cohort, the students who traditionally earned D's or F's were unanimously opposed, as were the administration and the overwhelming major- ity of the faculty.

Phaedrus dropped the effort the next term, drawing this conclu-

[7]Robert M. Pirsig, *Zen and the Art of Motorcycle Maintenance* (New York: Bantam Books, 1974), p. 140.

sion: "The student's biggest problem was a slave mentality which had been built into him by years of carrot-and-whip grading, a mule mentality which said, 'If you don't whip me, I won't work.' He didn't get whipped." A complementary mentality existed among most of the faculty and the administration. Phaedrus believed that "the 'system' or 'society' or whatever you want to call it, is best served not by mules but by free men." He had sought to provide an educational "environment in which that mule can turn into a free man."[8]

John Holt, Ivan Illich, Jonathan Kozol, Joel Spring, and other educational critics blast real-life American schooling for producing, as Pirsig contended, a slave mentality. Unlike him, however, they fear that this is exactly what best serves the society as we know it. Spring's analysis is representative of this critical perspective. He charges American schooling with creating "institutional dependence," which alienates "man's ability to act or create his own social being." The competitive principle, in his view, rewards imitation, selfishness, and aggression, rather than originality, cooperation, and compassion. Social adjustment, control, and adaptation of people to technocratic imperatives is perceived as the key educational function. A particular style of middle-class values is imposed as schools affirm existing social structures. The goals and results of teaching are assessed in terms of behavioral objectives which reflect the idea that education should teach only that which can be measured. Education becomes, as in Skinner's *Walden Two*, "the essential form of control," yet the subterfuges of educational progress, choice, reform, and freedom lead students to feel free. In actuality, personalities are manipulated and molded for smooth incorporation into the institutional organization."[9] Students are prepared to accept political and economic subordination and their critical role as consumers.

To accurately assess the degree to which the American educational system reflects Pirsig's and Spring's account and suffers the antidemocratic liabilities alleged by the critics is an awesome task. Still, even a cursory examination of the structure, process, and content of American schooling for its political implications reveals some disturbing features. Structurally one finds much evidence of a

[8]Ibid., pp. 140–234. This experience is described.
[9]Joel H. Spring, *Education and the Rise of the Corporate State* (Boston: Beacon Press, 1972), pp. 149–172.

trend to bureaucratization and centralized control, which is a break with past practice. Since *Brown* v. *Board of Education*,[10] the federal courts, the Department of Education, and other agencies intimately involved with overseeing desegregation have usurped much of the power of local boards—for the best of reasons, it should be added. This reached its zenith in Judge Garrity's takeover of South Boston High, where he not only transferred pupils, teachers, and administrators but reportedly decided from the bench one day whether the school needed more tennis balls. Money, law, political power, and the threat or actual use of force give these appointed federal elites their authority over the schools. Unless events or opposition derails the process, more centralization will come about.

At the state level, university accountability is increasingly enforced through the combined authority of system administrators and state boards which were energized by the campus unrest of the 1960s to exercise more control of dissident students and teachers. Master plans for higher education swept the country in the 1970s, bringing the same consolidation and centralization to higher education that court orders and edicts from the Department of Health, Education and Welfare brought to public schools. Frank Erwin, a businessman and former chairman of the regents of the University of Texas, is quoted as saying bluntly that faculty and students have nothing to do with governing the university: "Authority comes from the top." During peaceful periods some government by faculty is permissible "because there's no reason not to give it to them."[11] At the public school level moves to teacher accountability, cost efficiency, performance contracting, and performance-based recertification bring the classroom more and more under the control of system administrators. It is possible, as one educator fears, "that much of the decision-making authority of the professional educator will be taken from him and placed in the hands of noneducators."[12] Occupational projections of the Bureau of Labor Statistics indicate that nonteachers in the system will experience a dramatic increase. While the demand for secondary teachers through 1985 will actually drop by 8.1 percent and that for elementary teachers will grow only by 12.8 percent, the jobs available for elementary and secon-

[10]*Brown* v. *Board of Education of Topeka, Kansas,* 347 U.S. 483 (1954).

[11]Quoted in Michael Parenti, *Power and the Powerless* (New York: St. Martin's Press, 1978), p. 135.

[12]Richard W. Morshead, "The Clash of Hidden Ideologies in Contemporary Education," *Education Digest* 40 (November 1975), pp. 18–19.

dary administrators will jump by 33.7 percent. College administrators are predicted to increase by a whopping 81.3 percent, while college and university teachers will decline by 2.1 percent.

Turning to the educational process itself, one finds all too often regimentation and harsh and perhaps unfair competition. The sanctions, rewards, and deprivations of schooling may indeed encourage, as Pirsig feared, not initiative and creativity, but submission and imitation, while the standards and measurements used to rank people and performance remain quantitative rather than qualitative. The two metaphors that reappear in the critical literature on the educational process are the school as factory or prison. Since the American school and factory system developed jointly, there is no doubt that the latter influenced the former. One observer notes, "The conservative notion of the ways schools should function is largely patterned after the classical model of the factory."[13] The factory system of mass-producing students through assembly-line procedures reached its apex in the megauniversity. Still, the prison analogy raises the most disturbing questions.

The metaphor of school as prison increasingly pervades the literature. A decade ago a Carnegie Corporation study concluded that public schools are "intolerably oppressive and joyless," preoccupied "with order and control." Schools and prisons, the report added, share "stultifying rules, the lack of privacy, the authoritarianism, the abuse of power."[14] Political scientist Harmon Zeigler, who has studied American schools extensively, says flatly: "Public schools approach 'total institutions': they resemble prisons or mental hospitals." He describes the school as "one of the most arbitrary and anti-democratic institutions known to man."[15]

Two other authors have listed the similarities between schools and prisons: (1) both usually have drab, fortresslike exteriors, ringed by insurmountable fences, and identical interior rooms with long hallways; (2) they smell alike; (3) both have regimented codes of obedience and behavior; (4) both have a wide range of sanctions, including corporal punishment by the schools in all but two states and capital punishment in most prisons; (5) interpersonal relations are rigidly structured with separate facilities and grandiose symbols of power accruing to the dominant group and powerlessness

[13]Ibid., p. 18.

[14]Quoted in Parenti, *Power and the Powerless*, pp. 117–18.

[15]Thomas R. Dye and L. Harmon Zeigler, *The Irony of Democracy*, 2nd ed. (Belmont, Calif.: Duxbury Press, 1972), pp. 380–81.

characterizing the subordinate group in each, (6) both schools and prisons operate using the same psychology—behavior modification.[16] "Most education departments are awash with behavior mod . . . [using] reinforcement techniques to make students shape up."[17] School socialization in the "context of behavioral psychology . . . becomes a process of encouraging personalities that fit into the model" desired by the system. Deviants, that is, those who do not follow the rules, are "socially maladjusted. For the future functioning of the educational system and the mental health of the students social adaptation must take place"[18]—and the same holds true for prison populations. One compelling educational tool—and one of the most significant—Pirsig calls "carrot-and-whip grading," which is based on competitive tests.

Competition, the fundamental operative principle of American education is drawn from our capitalistic economy and the attendant individualistic culture. Success or failure at any of the innumerable (con)tests that students confront carries the gravest implications. There has been an explosion of tests in the educational process, from the "normal" ones in the classroom to IQ tests, often administered during the second grade, to tests which track students into academic, vocational, and general fields of study, such as college placement tests, graduate record examinations, and law school aptitude tests. The latest fad is "minimum-competency" tests, used to decide grade promotion or graduation in approximately three-dozen states. National testing is a very lucrative, mysterious (to students and parents alike), and authoritative means of pitting people against one another and ranking them as to the outcome.

Some groups bear a heavier share of the burden of this testing. A genetic endowment theory of race has been expounded by Arthur Jensen of Harvard, as well as others, predicated on IQ tests. Jensen believes that about 80 percent of IQ is inherited, and since blacks on the average perform more poorly on the tests than whites, blacks must be, so the argument goes, genetically inferior.[19] The grave implications of the prevalent ranking of people by test scores are

[16]Craig Haney and Philip G. Zimbardo, "The Blackboard Penitentiary: It's Tough to Tell a High School from a Prison," *Psychology Today* 9 (June 1975), pp. 26ff.

[17]Walt Anderson, *Politics and the New Humanism* (Pacific Palisades, Calif.: Goodyear Publishing, 1973), p. 129.

[18]Spring, *Education and the Rise of the Corporate State*, p. 170.

[19]A useful discussion of this issue can be found in Richard Hernstein, "I.Q.," *Atlantic*, September 1971, pp. 43–58.

clear. Many important factors other than ability may affect test performance. They include the home environment, cultural factors, teachers' expectations, and students' attitudes. A former U.S. commissioner of education maintains that the back-to-basics movement combined with minimum-competency testing has "overtones of racism,"[20] if special additional services for less fortunate children are not provided.

Highlighting the politically significant content of American schooling is manipulation of regime symbols, plus substantive instruction in government and economics that is often so selective as to smack of propaganda. Perhaps the most blatant example is the enormous volume of material distributed by the Federal Bureau of Investigation during the Cold War years for classes on communism. One such piece by J. Edgar Hoover read, "In communist lands, schools are centers for indoctrination—that is, to make boys and girls into better communists." It continues: "Teachers are not interested in making the pupils better citizens, able to think for themselves, but train them to be mouthpieces of the state." Maps were distributed showing the "Communist Empire" in sinister black. There were explanations of the "tools of subversion" and "espionage targets," and instructions as to what students "can do to fight communism," as well as an admonition that "patriotism is everybody's job." Copies of Hoover's ghost-written *Masters of Deceit* and *A Study of Communism* were often utilized in class. Finally, since propagandists always lack subtlety and a sense of irony, students were advised to "attack bigotry and prejudice" and avoid "hysteria, witch hunts, and vigilantism," although they were to "report any information about espionage, sabotage, and subversive activities."[21]

Détente brought about some curriculum adjustment, although courses on communism are still taught. The current trend is toward courses on consumer economics, free enterprise, and the virtues of the capitalist system, as well as vocational or career education intended to teach skills and habits for occupational roles. Arizona apparently touched off the national wave of such courses by initiating in 1971 the requirement that every student take a semester course in the "essentials and benefits of the free enterprise system."

[20]Harold Howe II addressing the National Conference on Achievement Testing and Basic Skills sponsored by the Department of Health, Education, and Welfare. See *New York Times*, March 3, 1978.
[21]Materials in possession of the author.

Superintendent of Public Instruction Weldon P. Shofstall drew up the discussion guide for class use.[22]

Planned Economy	*Free Market*
Minimum-wage laws are essential and desirable.	Minimum-wage laws always contribute to unemployment.
Launch a government war on poverty and you decrease the number of poor people.	Subsidizing the poor tends to increase their number.
Socialism encourages coercive collectivism.	The Free Market encourages free and responsible individuals.
The workers should have special rights under the law.	Everybody should be equal only before the law. Free enterprise depends upon a highly ethical moral system in order to function.
Collectivism (all for one and one for all) as a way of life represents the failure of men and women to adhere to a highly ethical moral system.	Collectivism as a way of life is a manifestation of the abyss into which men sink when not motivated by the pursuit of truth and justice.
Human life has no essential value as such—is not sacred.	All human life has essential value —is sacred.
Man created God.	God created Man.
Atheism is basic in a viable economic system.	Theism is basic in a viable economic system.
Public works, such as Gateway Arch, Urban Renewal, or Moon Shots are paid for with tax money; therefore, they are desirable and free to the public.	Public works are paid for by mandatory taxes representing a portion of your labor and mine.

[22]Joseph Stocker, "Brainwashing the Classrooms," *Nation*, February 6, 1973, p. 76.

In addition, many business groups have ready access to the classroom. For example, by the late 1970s the U.S. Chamber of Commerce had distributed its "Economics for Young Americans," a kit containing filmstrips, scripts, ditto sheets, and teachers' guides, to schools in Ohio, Illinois, Maryland, and Louisiana. Even some conservatives are embarrassed by such overt efforts to make the public schools, in Hoover's phrase, "centers for indoctrination."

The sponsor of the Arizona bill justified the legislation on the grounds that "a youngster will have some foundation to stand on when he does come up against professors that are collectivists or socialists."[23] For some reason state legislators in particular tend to view political scientists as insufficiently appreciative of the system. This is curious, since political scientists depend on the system as much if not more than any other professional group and are, given the current academic surplus, particularly vulnerable. One need only scan the major texts in American government to discount the notion that courses are collectivist or socialist in orientation.

Vocational tracking by counselors, often starting at the junior high level, emphasis in high school on career and trade skills, and behavioral training and premature emphasis on professionalism at the university level characterized the educational beginnings of America's third century. This was a reaction both to the economic recessions of the 1970s and to the disturbances in humanities departments of colleges and high schools in the late 1960s. Early 1978 saw Congress pass the Career Incentive Education Act providing federal funds, to be matched by the states, to "instruct more teachers in the career information they should be transmitting, to bring expert advice into the classrooms, and to take students out to work situations where they can learn conditions for themselves."[24] At the college level, business and science enrollments and funding boomed, while the liberal arts, particularly the more "impractical" ones like languages, suffered. Instrumentalism dominated administrators and many students and faculty. These developments are often implemented under the guise of progressive reform which raises a major concern not so much "that a conservative educational ideology might come to dominate American Schools, but that

---

[23]Ibid., p. 653.
[24]Marvin Stone, "Putting Youth on Course," *U.S. News and World Report*, February 6, 1978, p. 76.

such a policy . . . [might] be accepted unknowingly, without debate or rational examination."[25]

Not surprisingly, the structure, process, and content of the American educational rite we have described stimulates counter-rituals among the young strangers. The most dramatic of these is vandalism, termed "ritual desecration" by H. L. Nieburg. "Day and night, the schools of America suffer befoulment, overturned furniture, splashed paint in classrooms, and broken doors and toilet seats in the johns." He cites British sociologist Stanley Cohen's assessment of the ritual significance of seemingly meaningless property destruction. "It is a political judgment."[26] This judgment is most damning in the big city schools, where 10 percent of the public school population, some 5 million children, matriculate. In these schools, fled by the middle class, where funds shrink as the already inequitable property tax base erodes, performance is three to five years behind the national average. The high school dropout rate is approximately twice the national average of 25 percent. "Their hallways are awash with drugs and violence. [In 1976] cases of aggravated assault in schools topped 150,000, and vandalism cost school districts an estimated $600 million."[27]

Vandalism may be viewed as aimed at destroying the system, but dropping out, drugs, assaults, and other crimes against one's peers are more in the vein of self-destruction. Lipset explained how America places more stress than the European-Israeli social democracies on the long-shot opportunity for the top through education, and we touched on the irrationality and bias of the legitimizing device of competitive testing to define the merits of one's effort. The competitive mythology serves to shroud the fact that some aspects of failure are impersonal in origin and induces the individual to assume responsibility, with the gravest psychological consequences. Aronowitz says schools "serve to impress upon the child that his failure to climb the occupational ladder or rise beyond his parents' social class is a function of his own lack of intelligence or effort."[28] Kenneth Clark said of the psychic fate of the inner-city students,

[25]Morshead, "The Clash of Hidden Ideologies," p. 19.
[26]H. L. Nieburg, *Culture Storm: Politics and the Ritual Order* (New York: St. Martin's Press, 1973), p. 133.
[27]"Big City Schools: Can They Be Saved?" *Newsweek*, September 12, 1977, p. 62.
[28]Stanley Aronowitz, *False Promises: The Shaping of Working Class Consciousness* (New York: McGraw-Hill, 1973), p. 81.

"Their schools are brainwashing them into a sense of inferiority."[29]

All this contributes to self-destructive behavior. Lipset explained:

Flowing from the assumption that failure in a highly competitive system is highly painful, is "anomic behavior," withdrawal from the effort to succeed by engaging in forms of ruleless hedonistic activities frowned on by the conventional work-a-day-world. This takes the form of alcoholism, and more recently, of drugs, as well as other forms of deviant behavior. Traditionally, such behavior was found more typically among the "failures," the very poor, the lumpenproletariat, the oppressed ethnic-racial minorities.

He goes on to describe the spread of anticompetitive ideologies among elite offspring in the late 1960s as evidence that "the pain, the psychic anxiety, involved in the competitive system may be becoming too much even for many who are seemingly privileged."[30] Time has outstripped this analysis, however, for there was little evidence of the anticompetitive counterculture and commune mentality among elite offspring a decade or more later. It is more likely that Clark is correct in seeing psychic pain and self-destruction pervading the poorer inner-city schools. Edgar Litt commented, "Much of our education is 'class-confirming' and instills different self-images appropriate for different career roles in a stratified capitalistic system."[31]

Two well-known radical economists concluded from their in-depth study of American education that the true function of our schools and colleges is not to reform the system but to reinforce it by reproducing the inequalities that sustain it and the attitudes which legitimate it.[32] Another study suggests that this function is being fulfilled all too well. The author says that below-average performance of blacks on nationwide tests reflects not "stupidity, not a failure of genes and not the result of poor encouragement by parents. Rather, it is a functional adaptation to reality." American Indians, Mexican-Americans, Puerto Ricans, and black children "pick up discouraging yet quite realistic messages about the com-

[29]*Newsweek*, September 12, 1971, pp. 64–67. See also "Black Youth: A Lost Generation?" *Newsweek*, August 7, 1978, pp. 22–34.

[30]Lipset, "Education and Equality," p. 61.

[31]Edgar Litt, "Liberty above Equality: The Counterreformation in High Education Policy," *American Behavioral Scientist* 17 (March/April 1974), p. 552.

[32]Samuel Bowles and Herbert Gintis, *Schooling In Capitalist America* (New York: Basic Books, 1976).

paratively poor payoff that education is likely to have for them."[33]
Internalizing such messages mandates failure, which contributes to
deviant behavior and reinforces the social reality leading to such
lessons. Jesse Jackson's EXCEL gospel is aimed squarely at breaking
this vicious, self-fulfilling class-race prophecy of despair and self-
destruction. Without systemic change to increase the opportunity
for success, however, self-help rhetoric may only further convince
the individual that he must shoulder the burden of failure alone.

WORKPLACE: STRUCTURE, PROCESS, AND CONTENT

We now come to the final political socialization agency to be
examined—the workplace. By considering the workplace last I do
not mean to imply that its impact is less than that of other institutionalized settings. Whereas the family is the first institution one
encounters, however, the workplace is generally the last to be
confronted and experienced in a self-conscious way. Curiously
enough, while there is much public concern about the potential
influence of such agencies as the media and the schools there is
generally less recognition paid to the manner in which labor activity—which occupies enormous amounts of time and energy—
and economic life in general affect politically significant beliefs and
behavioral inclinations. Political journalist Samuel Lubell writes
that "how our economy is managed has become the shaping force of
the future."[34] A survey done by Public Research Corporation for the
U.S. Department of Labor and released in September 1978 concluded that the economic health of the nation has a more direct
impact on the daily lives of Americans than any other aspect of our
national life.[35]

As a preeminent social activity, economics involves a great deal of
human energy. It is of critical importance to all members of every
society. Devotees of the two major theories of how best to organize
modern economics each stress first and foremost the personal and
political benefits of one or the other form of economic organization.

[33]John U. Ogby, "Minority Education and Caste: The American System in Cross-
Cultural Perspective," Carnegie Council on Children Study, 1978, quoted in New York
Times, March 12, 1978.
[34]Samuel Lubell, The Future While It Happened (New York: W. W. Norton, 1973), p.
128.
[35]Albert H. and Susan D. Cantril, "Unemployment, Government, and the American People," A National Opinion Survey by Public Research Corp. (U.S. Department
of Labor, 1978).

Proponents of socialism claim that as private ownership of the means of production permits the wealthy to dominate the workplace, exploitation of man by man inevitably occurs. Consequently alienation and a false consciousness will come to characterize the human personality under capitalism. Socialize ownership and you get, in Marx's words, an "association" wherein the free development of each is the condition for the free development of all. This is a prerequisite, for the socialists, to personal and political self-determination. "A *being* only considers himself independent when he stands on his own feet; and he only stands on his own feet when he owes his *existence* to himself. A man who lives by the grace of another regards himself as a dependent being."[36]

From Adam Smith's *Wealth of Nations* in 1776 to William S. Simon's *A Time For Truth* in 1978 to Ronald Reagan's economic advisers, capitalist thinkers have emphasized that rather than being a threat, private enterprise is essential to liberty and human self-development. Socialized ownership presents, to the capitalists, an inevitable specter of tyranny. The mobility conferred by freedom of contract in the private workplace (plus the free choice of the open marketplace)[37] builds independent and assertive human beings, in the view of someone like Simon. Thus we find that both sets of theorists stress principally the developmental implications of socialism or capitalism rather than merely the benefits of economic efficiency and productivity.

While the American economy is in reality mixed with both private ownership and an extensive amount of governmental regulation, of the economies of the developed world it is the most free from public ownership of the means of production, or socialism. This means that even with the regulation that does exist, the workplace is less subject to governmental or public authority than its counterpart in England, Sweden, or other industrial nations.

If Lubell and the Labor Department study are correct, then the functioning of America's mixed but predominantly capitalist system is of crucial importance to political consciousness. This is particularly true of the workplace. Indeed, the length of time

[36]Karl Marx, *Economic and Philosophic Manuscripts of 1844*, in *The Marx-Engels Reader*, ed. Robert C. Tucker (New York: W. W. Norton, 1972), p. 77.

[37]For an excellent introduction to studies of the impact of the marketplace, with references to the major works on the topic, see Robert E. Lane, "Autonomy, Felicity, Futility: the Effects of the Market Economy on Political Personality," *Journal of Politics* 40 (February 1978), pp. 2–24.

humans spend working and the fact that work is the major way humans interact with the physical world led Freud to the conclusion that work is one of the two most important aspects of life (the other was love). Perhaps the 100 million Americans in the labor force who spend some 10,000 days on the job would agree with such a high estimation of the significance of work. This work experience usually constitutes about forty hours a week for forty years or more of an American's existence. Furthermore, the hours and years spent in the workplace occur during the peak years of life, when one is enjoying the highest use of human faculties. No other activity so occupies the waking hours of adult America.

Because of the inordinate amount of time spent on this consuming human activity, there is one school of thought which attaches unparalleled shaping power to work. Our art has often articulated this persepective. For example, in Martin Scorsese's movie of 1976, *Taxi Driver*, the Wizard tells the main character, Travis: "Man takes a job, you know. That job becomes what he is. You do a thing and that's what you are. You become the job, a taxi driver, a lawyer, a doctor. You, you got no choice anway." Travis is unconvinced: "That's the dumbest thing I ever heard." The Wizard responds: "Whaddya'want? I'm no Bertrand Russell. I'm just a taxi driver!" This concern that individuals might, over time, *become what they do* arose in the American consciousness with the origins of the industrial revolution. The working population was transformed: 80 percent self-employed in 1880 became only 31 percent self-employed by 1900. Today, 80 percent are wage and salary workers. The single most powerful artistic depiction of the adverse possibilities of placing individuals in stultifying jobs appeared precisely at midpoint between agrarian and industrial America, in the 1850s. We refer to Melville's "Bartleby, the Scrivener: A Story of Wall Street."[38]

Scriveners were law-copyists employed primarily by legal firms. Bartleby, by the account of his Wall Street employer, "was a scrivener the strangest I ever saw or heard of." He was assigned a tiny, enclosed corner in which to carry out his tedious task of laboriously copying legal documents. His employer "resolved to assign Bartleby a corner . . . and placed his desk close up to a small side-window." Originally, this had permitted a "lateral view of certain grimy back-yards and bricks." Even this view had been

[38]Herman Melville, "Bartleby, the Scrivener," in *The Shorter Novels of Herman Melville* (Greenwich, Conn.: Fawcett Publications, 1956), pp. 114–47.

finally eliminated by buildings, and by Bartleby's time there was a wall three feet from the window. Only a feeble light filtered in. The lawyer placed a tall folding screen about the small corner to "entirely isolate Bartleby from my sight, though not remove him from my voice." The employer, who was not an unkindly man, expected his employees to comply instantly with his commands. Yet whenever he asked Bartleby to come from behind his screen to perform certain tasks the repeated response was "I prefer not to." This quiet yet firm resistance to authority caused enormous exasperation, which was intensified when it was discovered that Bartleby lived in the office. Upon being told that he was fired and must leave the premises, Bartleby responded, "I would prefer not to" and refused to leave. Finally, in desperation the employer changed offices, abandoning Bartleby, who was arrested for trespassing in the office of the new tenant and was placed in the infamous Tombs prison of New York. He refused to eat or talk, and when his former employer—haunted by conscience—went to visit Bartleby he found him dead, "his knees drawn up, and lying on his side, his head touching the cold stones." Upon trying to find out something of Bartleby before he was a scrivener, the former employer stumbled upon a strange rumor.

Bartleby had been a subordinate clerk in the Dead Letter Office at Washington, from which he had suddenly been removed by a change in Administration. When I think over this rumor I cannot adequately express the emotions which seize me. Dead letters! Does it not sound like dead men? Conceive a man by nature and misfortune prone to a pallid hopelessness; can any business seem more fitted to heighten it than of continually handling these dead letters, and assorting them for the flames! For by the cartload they are annually burned. Sometimes from out the folded paper the pale clerk takes a ring;—the finger it was meant for, perhaps, moulders in the grave; a bank-note sent in swiftest charity;—he whom it would relieve, nor eats, nor hungers any more; pardon for those who died despairing; hope for those who died unhoping; good tiding for those who died stifled by unrelieved calamities. On errands of life, these letters speed to death.
Ah Bartleby! Ah humanity![39]

As a dead letter clerk, Bartleby suffered the ultimate penalty of a job whose content was a source of unrelieved despair. He then

---

[39]Ibid., pp. 114, 120, 121, 146, 147.

stepped into a highly authoritarian structure and a work process of minute and deadening specialization and isolation. Melville's closing cry indicates his concern for the future of a society embarking on a system of industrial production where the work experience might parallel Bartleby's. Should he be even remotely prescient, and should Scorsese's Wizard be onto something, then the structure within which individuals work, the process of that labor experience and the content of the job are extremely significant to the consciousness of Americans.

With regard to the structure of the workplace, the most important question to be addressed is—who owns it? Adam Smith, whose role in capitalist theory parallels Marx's in socialist thought, defended his new capitalist economics in the midst of the eighteenth-century transition from a British political economy where aristocrats and the giant merchant families of the Empire benefited extensively from state favors. He stressed that freeing individuals to take economic initiative would not only expand gross economic output but would also make for a more stable population and country. In this, after a fashion, he echoed Aristotle, who believed that private ownership of possessions creates character and the virtues of generosity and hospitality. It also makes for social peace and fewer quarrels as people attend to their business. (One should add quickly that Aristotle, unlike Smith, who viewed the right of property ownership as purely social and not natural in origin, opposed an economy wherein wealth was accumulated for its own sake and believed in one's social obligation to share some measure of what one produced with others.) The middle-class society with widespread ownership of the means of production was, to Aristotle, the best possible society: "Only can the government ever be stable where the middle class exceeds one or both of the others."[40] Looking at the distribution of ownership of the tools and factories constituting the American workplace today, one finds a situation far different from either Aristotle's best society or Smith's idea of capitalism.

One way of approaching the issue of who owns America is to calculate the net worth of the population. Some economists and political scientists estimate that 50 percent of Americans have no savings, 20-30 percent have liquid assets less than $1,000 and 10-15 percent owe more than they own. The approximately 140 percent

[40]Aristotle, *The Politics*, trans. Benjamin Jowett (New York: Random House, The Modern Library, 1943), p. 194.

increase in consumer debts in the 1970s further reduced the worth of many Americans. It is probable that the assests of those whose net worth ranges upward to several thousand dollars are invested in a house, pension, or insurance hence are not translatable into e-conomic authority over the workplace.[41]

The findings above are paralleled by other studies.[42] Government figures indicate that 1 percent of the people own close to 25 percent of all wealth in America. William Connolly finds that the top 10 percent own 56 percent of all wealth, and 20 percent own 77 percent. The top 10 percent hold also about 75 percent of all savings, while 2 percent hold nearly all public bonds and 80-90 percent of all corporate bonds. In advanced capitalist economies it is, of course, stocks through which ownership of the workplace is principally held. Only one family in six own any stock at all, which is less than 10 percent of the population. And one-tenth of all stockholders own 81 percent of all stock. Connolly and several others who have looked at this carefully also find that 1.5 percent of Americans own approx-imately 51.1 percent of the value of all corporate stock, while 2.5 percent own some 67 percent. Thus one commentator contends: "A small group of Americans, probably numbering in the ten of thousands, collectively owns blocks of stock large enough to control many large corporations. . . . The means of production are con-trolled by a group no larger than the population of a small town."[43]

These figures on the concentration of ownership raise serious questions about the applicability of the middle-class model to the American economy. We are not a nation with widely dispersed possession of the means of production; rather, some 80 percent of Americans are wage and salary workers with little or no financial

[41]James D. Smith, Steven D. Franklin, and Douglas A. Wion, "Distribution of Financial Assets," quoted in *Newsweek*, April 7, 1975, p. 64. See also James D. Smith, ed., *The Personal Distribution of Income and Wealth*, Studies in Income and Wealth, No. 39, National Bureau of Economic Research (New York: Columbia University Press, 1975); Lester C. Thurow, *The Zero-Sum Society: Distribution and the Possibilities for Economic Change* (New York: Basic Books, 1980); and David Harrop, *America's Paychecks: Who Makes What*, (New York: Facts on File, 1980).

[42]U.S. Bureau of the Census, *Statistical Abstract of the United States, 1977* (Wash-ington, D.C., 1978) p. 464; Michael H. Best and William E. Connolly, *The Politicized Economy* (Lexington, Mass.: D.C. Heath, 1976), pp. 75–76; Albert Szymanski, *The Capitalist State and the Politics of Class* (Cambridge, Mass.: Winthrop,1978, p. 34; Edward S. Greenberg, *The American Political System: A Radical Approach* (Cambridge, Mass: Winthrop, 1977), pp. 121–22; Michael Parenti, *Democracy for the Few* (New York: St. Martins Press, 1974), p. 14; Ira Katznelson and Mark Kesselman, *The Politics of Power* (New York; Harcourt Brace Jovanovich, 1975), pp. 49–52.

[43]Katznelson and Kesselman, *The Politics of Power*, p. 52.

independence. Two percent of Americans, on the other hand, may genuinely be called upper-class elites, while the remaining 18 percent or so compose a growing managerial stratum. Still, the possibly adverse impact of such concentration can be avoided if the process by which the workplace is organized and operated is such as to permit contemporary workers—unlike Bartleby—to experience their laboring hours in a democratic manner. This process is our next concern.

In terms of the habituation of adult Americans to self-rule or the reverse, the single most important thing may be the degree to which industrial democracy characterizes the organization of the American workplace. The major vehicle for this possibility is, of course, unionization. One government-convened study in 1977 of "the role of the workplace in citizen education" had the following to say about unions:

> There are close to 200 national and international organizations classified as unions, and more than 65,000 locals, state councils, and regional organizations. . . . Unions provide opportunities for citizen education in two ways: (1) through participation in industrial citizenship, i.e., activities and responsibilities associated with the workplace; and (2) through specific educational and other programs designed to enhance the citizenship skill of labor members.[44]

The right to unionize did not come easily in America. In fact, of all the advanced Western societies the United States had the bloodiest struggle over this and other workers' rights in the industrializing period at the turn of the century. "For years both the police and the National Guard served the *status quo* as the main bulwark of free enterprise in upholding the antiunion philosophy of employers and government. . . . The years between 1870 and 1935 were filled with violent strikes and riots."[45] In 1935 the National Labor Relations, or Wagner, Act gave statutory protection to the right to unionize. Subsequent amendments plus additional legislation have expanded on that basic right. Twenty years after the Wagner Act union membership peaked at 33.2 percent of all nonagricultural workers. In the twenty years following that high point it declined,

[44]"Examining the Role of the Workplace in Citizen Education," U.S. Department of Health, Education, and Welfare, Publication No. (OE) 78–07004 (1978), p. 2.
[45]Lynne B. Iglitzin, *Violent Conflict in American Society* (San Francisco: Chandler Publishing, 1972), p. 111.

because of a host of factors, to some 24 percent. Union membership has eroded since then.

There is no doubt that unionization greatly improved the lot of American workers. This is particularly true for salary and job security. Still, even the briefest examination of the labor union movement in America today reveals that its approach to what that government study called "industrial citizenship, i.e., activities and responsibilities associated with the workplace," is more timid and conservative than is the case in any other Western democracy. Even many Third World union movements pursue worker participation in decision making to a much greater degree. This situation led Sam Brown, former antiwar student leader and then Carter appointee to head ACTION, to tell a State Department Forum in the summer of 1977: "We know that workplace democracy is a concept ill-developed in American society. It is another of the places where we stand to learn from Jamaica, from Tanzania, from Cuba, from Yugoslavia. . . . "[46] Major labor leaders themselves disclaim interest in worker control. Lane Kirkland, president of the American Federation of Labor and Congress of Industrial Organizations (AFL-CIO) commented: "Management is singularly fortunate in this country. Its role and status is not under serious attack by any ideology espoused by labor. The American worker is uniquely free of class consciousness."[47] This is indeed something of a singular situation, for in European countries workers serve as full-fledged members of the boards, which actually run the companies there. This has been the case, for example, since 1951, in West Germany.

If one attempts to determine why democratizing the workplace is not a major goal of American labor unions, there are a host of possible explanations. One has to do with divisions within the work force which inhibit workers' solidarity. All the ethnic, racial, and religious divisions in America, plus the sexual and regional ones, are overlaid in the technological political economy with an enormous variety of occupational differentiation. Further, American

[46]Sam Brown, "Foreign Policy in the Third World," transcript of forum (Washington, D.C.: U.S. Department of State, August 3, 1977). Three useful general studies are: David Jenkins, *Job Power: Blue and White Collar Democracy* (Baltimore Md.: Penguin Press, 1974); Daniel Zwerdling, *Workplace Democracy* (New York: Harper and Row, 1978); and Martin Carnoy and Derek Shearer, *Economic Democracy* (New York: M. E. Sharpe, 1980).

[47]Quoted in A. H. Raskin. "It Isn't Labor's Day," *Nation*, September 9, 1978, pp. 200–01. The classic study of this phenomenon is C. Wright Mills, *White Collar: The American Middle Class* (New York: Oxford University Press, 1951).

labor is not an independent political force but is aligned—perhaps of necessity in our two-party system— with the major parties. Still another factor is the cultural stress on the rights attached to private property and the conceptualization of society as competitive, individualistic, and imbued with potential upward social mobility. When these are combined with the legitimating thrust of other socialization agencies, there is produced a sociopsychological separation of workplace democracy from political democracy within the fragmented work force. And one more major explanation is offered to explain this interesting phenomenon.

If dollar valuation, rather than worker control, comes to be the preeminent standard for judging the workplace within a societal context of heated consumption, and members of "big labor"— particularly the key unions—are successful in extracting high wage settlements and hence increasing worker ability to consume, then self-determination in the workplace is of much lesser concern. George Meany, the late president of the AFL-CIO, explained:

Labor, to some extent, has become middle-class. When you have no property, you don't have anything, you have nothing to lose by these radical actions. But when you become a person who has a home and has property, to some extent you become conservative. And I would say to that extent, labor has become conservative.[48]

A conservative, middle-class (in income, not wealth) component of key unions forgoing possible working control for huge salary increases and greater job security characterizes the American labor movement today. Aronowitz, who spent his life in the union movement and in the plants, says: "The person has become nothing more than another commodity that is exchanged like all other economic goods."[49]

It is not only the structure and process of the work experience that is important. Recall that for Bartleby it was the content of his job that so affected him. Valued at approximately $3.0 trillion, American production comprises far more goods and services than any other society in the world, so that America is often labeled a consumers' paradise. But there are some who contend that if one looks closely at the components of this gross economic output, there

[48]Quoted in Everett C. Ladd, Jr., with Charles D. Hadley, *Transformations of the American Party System* (New York: W. W. Norton, 1975), p. 195.

[49]Aronowitz, *False Promises*, p. 15.

is much evidence that America, rather than being a paradise, is embarked on a gigantic scientific-industrial death trip. Given the enormous variety of products issuing from the American work-place, it is really not possible to confidently label it as either a manifestation of Eros, that is, life-enhancing, or Thanatos, a death wish. Still, one can identify some prominent elements of our indus-trial production that do present parallels to Bartleby's job with dead letters. For instance, along with some other advanced societies, America is piling up nuclear waste which will be live for thousands of years, without having any idea of how to detoxify it or store it safely. These present grave dangers to our own and sub-sequent generations. Another clear example of life-denying com-ponents of our production which comes readily to mind is weap-onry, of which the United States is the largest producer and seller in the world. Also, the introduction into the environment of countless new chemicals each year, certain ones of which inevitably prove to be carcinogenic or have other adverse effects is certainly life-threatening, as is the spread of other environmental pollutants. Yet another example is automobiles of questionable safety, some of which will reach speeds in excess of 100 miles per hour. The multibillion-dollar pharmaceutical industry turns out an exceed-ingly high volume of powerful drugs, new and old, some of which— if not used with great care—can present grave dangers. Production of tobacco, a proven health threat, is subsidized by the federal government at an annual cost exceeding $100 million.

These and other unfortunate products of our economic system are major factors in 45,000 to 50,000 automobile deaths annually, approximately 60,000 deaths from industrial pollution per year, untold hundreds of thousands of deaths attributable to smoking, such bizarre things as more deaths by Darvon than by heroin some years, environmentally caused genetic defects, and the highest cancer rate in the world. It is a significant comment on our sociopolitical conciousness that all too few Americans regard as political the question of *what* is produced. The government counts equally, in computing GNP, such things as the manufacturing of a nuclear missile and the building of a hospital.

How does one assess the impact on workers' political conscious-ness of spending 10,000 days in a workplace owned by someone else, organized and run by managerial personnel, and—for some at least—producing things of clear or possible danger to human exis-tence? It is not an easy task. One way involves measuring the degree of job satisfaction or frustration, either of which might lead to political behavior—supportive in the first instance and critical in the latter case. Still, it is not only highly presumptuous to assume that this exceedingly personal and complex experience can be quantified, but—because of the possible wording of the questions, the interplay of questioner and worker, the increased manipulative sophistication of management science or industrial psychology, and other things—this can be a very misleading exercise. What happens most often is that the particular mix of these factors plus economic fluctuations produces confusing findings. The apologists tend to focus on studies measuring high job satisfaction, while the critics do the reverse. For example, one particularly complacent "public opinion" text stresses that the post-World War II Gallup job survey—asking, "On the whole, would you say you are satisfied or dissatisfied with the work you do?"—have found "impressively high percentages of job satisfaction."[50] On the other hand, the "Quality of Employment Survey" released by the University of Michigan's Survey Research Center in the spring of 1979 reported significant declines in job satisfaction between 1973 and 1977. [51] Young workers, blacks, the semiskilled, blue-collar workers, and those employed in manufacturing—all of whom are more likely not to own their workplace, run it, or determine its content—reported lowest satisfaction. The self-employed reported the highest level of satisfaction.

A more interesting and probably more productive approach to the question of job satisfaction was that used by Studs Terkel. He simply went about the country conducting oral interviews or, as he subtitled his book, letting "People Talk about What They Do All Day and How They Feel about What They Do." He found that although many people consider their job worthwhile, more felt the reverse. Restlessness and frustration on the job were determined by "daily circumstances, an *awareness* of being hurt, and an inordinate hunger for 'another way.'" He concluded that "perhaps it is time the 'work ethic' was redefined and its idea reclaimed from the banal men who invoke it. In a world of cybernetics, of an almost runaway technology, things are increasingly making things. It is for our

[50]Harry Holloway and John George, *Public Opinion* (New York: St. Martin's Press, 1979), p. 157.
[51]Robert Quinn and Graham L. Staines, "1977 Quality of Employment Survey: Descriptive Statistics, with Comparative Data from the 1969–70 and the 1972–73 Surveys" (Ann Arbor, Mich.: Institute for Social Research, 1979).

species, it would seem, to go on to other matters. Human matters." Dissatisfaction was expressed extensively and openly to Terkel. As he put it,"The desperation is unquiet."[52]

When combined with anxieties about status and the economic situation plus an inadequate education, desperation resulting from job frustration can lead to authoritarian political inclinations. A large volume of social science studies have concluded that an antidemocratic "working-class authoritarianism"[53] is widespread in the United States and is reflected in a desire for simplistic and definitive solutions to the myriad of puzzling and difficult problems in our complex world, regardless of the requirements of constitutional democracy. (Chapter 7 examines this theme in the public opinion literature.)

It is not only the working class who may suffer distortions due to adverse job conditions. The 18 percent of Americans in the managerial and executive ranks might also do so, although in a different way. In 1956 William H. Whyte Jr., in *The Organization Man* emphasized the theme that such upwardly mobile people who "get along by going along," by conforming, are susceptible to engaging in pathological corporate actions.[54] In a June 1979 interview, he assessed this possibility as having grown even stronger. Whyte and others cite examples of the implications of this: (1) General Electric knowingly dumped chemical PCBs, which were highly poisonous, into the Hudson River for years and then put up a legal battle (ultimately unsuccessful) until 1976, disclaiming culpability; (2) at about the same time, the Ford Motor Company allowed the hatchback model of its Pinto to be driven for many months after it was virtually certain that the gas tank was so situated as to make the car a firebomb in the event of rear-end collisions; (3) McDonnel-Douglas actively defended the DC-10 and promoted sales worldwide even

---

[52]Studs Terkel, *Working* (New York: Random House, 1972), pp. xii–xxiv. See also his "Work without Meaning," *Business and Society Review* 9 (Spring 1974), pp. 15–22.

[53]The term comes from Seymour M. Lipset, *Political Man* (Garden City, New York: Anchor Books, 1963), pp. 87–126. For an empirical test of this phenomenon, specifically Lipset's analysis, see Edward G. Grabb, "Working-Class Authoritarianism and Tolerance of Outgroups: A Reassessment," *Public Opinion Quarterly* 33 (Spring 1979), pp. 37–47. A useful analysis of this genre of American social science literature is Peter Bachrach, *Theory of Democratic Elitism: A Critique* (Boston, Mass.: Little, Brown, 1967), pp. 26–46.

[54]William H. Whyte, Jr., *The Organization Man* (New York: Simon and Schuster, 1956); see also an interview with Whyte entitled "Organization Man—Alive But Not Well," *New York Times*, June 11, 1979.

after the worst air crash in history to that time (France, 1974) and the worst in the United States (Chicago, 1979) plus other "incidents" raised serious questions about the airplane's design.

The possibility that nondemocratic job situations might be a major factor in promoting authoritarian inclinations in the working class and amoral conformity in managerial ranks is disturbing. Such severe thwarting of human possibilities is compared by Reich, a major proponent of "work democracy," to the situation of a seed which takes root in a weeded area.

Those [fir] seedlings that are not surrounded by many weeds grow fully on all sides; hardly above the ground, the stem shoots forth far-reaching branches. The needles are full and sappy. The plant strives upward toward the sun free of any hindrances; it is "healthy"; its development is "free." But if the fir seed has chanced to fall on a spot where there are a lot of weeds, then it develops, hemmed in by weeds, a needless, crooked stem. It does not develop full branches; the needles are shriveled, others don't develop at all. Many such seedlings are not capable of pushing their way up through the weeds. The influences of the weeds is directly manifested in the deformity of the plant. It has to fight a hard battle to get to the sun, and it is distorted in the process.[55]

Conclusion

In contemporary America large-scale, centralized secondary social agencies assume growing importance for political consciousness. One of these is television, which was examined in the preceding chapter. Another is government itself, which attempts to structure the interpretation of information and images—emphasizing the favorable and deemphasizing the unfavorable material—about itself to the citizenry. Two others are schooling and the economic workplace.

For several reasons schooling in America has become an enormous enterprise. The last several decades have seen a diploma become a requirement for an ever-increasing number of jobs. Also, as society has become more complex, education is imperative to functional literacy. Because of these things, plus the push of the educational lobby and international stimuli such as the successful launch of Sputnik by the Russians in 1957, a lengthier and more

[55]Wilhelm Reich, *The Mass Psychology of Fascism*, trans. Vincent R. Carfagno (New York: Farrar, Straus and Giroux, 1970), pp. 348–49.

intensive educational experience is of much greater significance to the political consciousness of current generations than of previous ones. This experience inducts people into the patterns of dominant myths and—to a great degree—prepares them for particular adult economic roles.

There is little doubt that the developmental function of education—which is closely aligned with the Jeffersonian model of democracy and a prerequisite for the Socratic consciousness—plays a distinctly secondary role to conditioning and instrumental ones in the United States. Structurally, judicial and administrative elites promise to exercise more control each year, with parents and students playing lesser ones. Regimentation and often biased competition most accurately characterize the process of American education. As for politically significant content, there is extensive manipulation of regime symbols, courses that promote free enterprise, and extensive vocational tracking and accelerating pre-professionalism. The structure, process, content, and instrumental orientation of American schooling do not go unchallenged. Classroom insurgencies, dropping out, and vandalism can all be viewed as sociopolitical counterrituals.

Perhaps of even more importance to political consciousness is the work experience. Whether or not we equate it with love as one of the two most basic human experiences, adult Americans spend more of their time engaged in working, approximately 10,000 days, than in the pursuit of any other activity. Proponents of both socialism and capitalism, the two most prominent theories of economics, agree that economic organization and functioning greatly affect human consciousness. Of course, they disagree bitterly over the respective merits of the private versus the public economy.

Melville's classic about work and human nature, "Bartleby, the Scrivener," appeared just as America embarked on its midnineteenth-century industrial revolution. As I noted above, the populace was transformed from a largely self-employed work force to one in which most people received a wage or salary. Melville portrayed in Bartleby the ultimate destruction of the human spirit by a work experience within an authoritarian structure, and with an alienating process and deadening content. Fortunately, the structure, process, and content of the contemporary American workplace is not so oppressive as was Bartleby's. Still, it is far from a democratic and essentially developmental experience. Ownership, perhaps the most important feature in the structure of any workplace, is not widespread. Moreover, American labor unions, more than in many other countries, have abdicated to management and owners decision-making prerogatives over the work experience. They have done so in return for higher salaries and greater job security, with the key unions representing some 11 percent of the work force attaining these to a great degree. The particular content of the goods and services produced in our $3.0 trillion economy is much less clear. While it does not approximate a deadletter office, still, far too many workers are engaged in the production of life-threatening substances, from weapons to carcinogenic chemicals.

The negative implications of these two socialization experiences may dovetail. In Pirsig's fictional critique of American schooling, as well as in the assessments of real-life critics such as John Holt, conformity is the major lesson that is learned in our schools. If this lesson is combined with those conveyed by an undemocratic work experience, it can produce, according to the findings of many social scientists, authoritarian inclinations in the working class. At the managerial level of the workplace, the conformity demanded by corporate structures makes for an "organization" mentality which lends itself to the most pathological institutional endeavors. This bodes ill for either Socratic consciousness or Jeffersonian democracy.

Part Three

Political Consciousness
and American Democracy

VII

Conceptions of Citizenship, Mass Behavior, Culture, and Consciousness

We are what we learn.
It often takes a long and painful time.
Doris Lessing, *The Summer Before The Dark*

As you believe, so shall you do.   New Testament

What effectively distinguishes the citizen from all others is
his participation in Judgment and Authority, that is,
holding office, legal, political, administrative. . . . Our
definition is best applied in a democracy.
Aristotle, *The Politics*

In a democracy citizens relate consciously to politics in two basic ways. One is through their perceptions of and feelings about political authority and leadership in their society. The other is through their views, feelings, and orientations toward all those campaigns and elections, parties, and pressure groups and other processes that allow for self-rule. The nature of these two major dimensions of political consciousness in America—conceptions of citizenship and conceptions of leadership and authority—can significantly affect the behavioral orientations of the population to their political processes and officials. As one recent public opinion text puts it, the major importance of the study of attitudes and conceptions, "after all, is that it helps us to understand and predict what people *do.*"[1]

As the twin conceptions of citizenship and leadership evolve and take on a more precise shape in a human community, they increasingly channel political thinking and influence the way citizens behave. Indeed, Kenneth Dolbeare writes that "our most basic personal identities are shaped by particular consciousness-dictated understanding of who and what we are. What we do, how we live, and what are right and wrong things in our world are all bound together and integrated with our consciousness."[2] Thus an under-

[1]Bruce A. Campbell *The American Electorate: Attitudes and Action* (New York: Holt, Rinehart and Winston, 1979), p. 9.
[2]Kenneth Dolbeare, *Political Change in the United States* (New York: McGraw-Hill, 1974), p. 10.

standing of the characteristic political consciousness of one's society is important for self-knowledge and/or understanding of the possibilities of politics.

The desirable shape of a democratic political consciousness is clearly stated in the basic liberal Jeffersonian democratic theory discussed earlier. In a responsive, well-functioning democracy, the citizens' socialization experience and their involvement with all those campaigns and elections, parties, pressure groups, and other processes that theoretically allow for self-government would engender a sense of efficacy, community, tolerance, and independence. Public attitudes on the issues and the persons involved in these political processes would be based on sufficient attentiveness and information to allow for measured judgment. This consciousness and these attitudes would stimulate the maximum possible political involvement of the population. Consequently there would be the widest possible airing of political matters and the widest possible contribution to the common good. In terms of the citizens' feelings and orientations toward their political leaders, democratic theory expects: (1) the public to accord basic legitimacy, trust, and support to duly selected officials, so as to allow for effective leadership and (2) the people to avoid being so unrealistic as to bring about public cynicism when incumbents fail to measure up to false or unrealistic standards or so uncritical as to induce arrogance in leaders.

Classical democratic theory clearly demands much of its citizens. This is because political citizenship in a democracy involves a complex social network of human relations with a high moral purpose, the development and enjoyment of human capacities. Jefferson's use, in the Declaration of Independence, of that enigmatic phrase "the pursuit of happiness" was an expression of that moral purpose and capacity. Happiness was a concept borrowed, in part, from an eighteenth-century Scottish philosopher, Francis Hutcheson. The pursuit of happiness involves public activity; "the surest way to promote . . . private happiness . . . [is] to do publicly useful actions."[3] Thus happiness is to be achieved in the social or public realm, and its emotive purpose is to "be pleased and happy when we reflect upon our having done virtuous actions . . . [and consider] how much superior we esteem the happiness of virtue to any other

[3]Quoted in Garry Wills, *Inventing America: Jefferson's Declaration of Independence* (New York: Vintage Books, 1978), p. 252.

enjoyment."[4] Further, the egalitarian thrust of classic democratic thought demands that this happiness, this virtue which is so essential to human development, be available to all. Such democratic thought insists that the dignity, growth, and development of the citizen "as a functioning and responsive individual in a free society is dependent upon an opportunity to participate actively in decisions that significantly affect him."[5]

Political participation itself is, for the classic democratic theorist, a fundamental educational and developmental experience. A private life of pursuing individual or group self-interest is not sufficient. The private realm of family and friends, of work and play, is a necessary component of one's life, but it is not enough. As Lane Davis so aptly characterizes the matter:

The road to intellectual and moral growth must lead to participation in the practical problems of public affairs. Full moral development for most men is only to be attained by taking part in, and accepting some responsibility for, the realization of the common good.[6]

It is precisely this democratic consciousness and citizenship, no matter how demanding, that is needed in order to rationally address the major problems faced by a technological society like the United States.

With this belief in the need for a democratic political consciousness in mind, I shall now attempt to describe, analyze, and assess the conceptions of citizenship—and consequent behavioral inclinations —and of leadership and authority that characterize contemporary American society. What about those powerful social laws of the American political culture—in particular, the equation of liberty with property rights, a limited view of equality excluding economics, emphasis on radical individualism, a manipulative and materialistic approach to the natural world, the harsh and distrustful view of man, and the competitive view of human society in Federalist No. 10? As they are transmitted within the American social structure by family and subgroups, language and television, schooling and the work experience, plus other agencies, do such

[4]Ibid.

[5]Peter Bachrach, *A Theory of Democratic Elitism: A Critique* (Boston: Little, Brown 1967), p. 98.

[6]Lane Davis, "The Cost of the New Realism," in *Frontiers of Democratic Theory,* ed. Henry S. Kariel (New York: Random House, 1970), p. 218.

social laws assist in developing a political consciousness more compatible with the majoritarian model of democracy upheld by Jefferson or the other, more elite models advanced by the Federalists and pluralists?

Chapter 7 asks this question about culturally induced beliefs concerning the role of citizens and explores how these beliefs lead to certain levels and types of participation or to nonparticipation. I make no pretense of offering an exhaustive study of this very large topic of citizenship, mass behavior, culture, and consciousness, but I hope to clarify some general trends. For a case study of the interplay of leadership, culture, and consciousness, we shall look in chapter 8 at the situation of the American president, the most visible political leader in the society. I shall examine the presidential role in American political consciousness, its sources within the political culture and the socialization process, and its consequences for American democracy.

In closing the exploration of the sociocultural base of American political life, I shall abandon the descriptive and analytical approach in an effort to evaluate the implications of American political culture, socialization, and consciousness for American democracy. I shall also suggest a first step that might be taken toward enhancing the political understanding of individuals. But first we must ask to what degree and to what particular extent are American conceptions of citizenship and leadership, as shaped by the political culture and the socialization experience, more compatible with the classical liberal Jeffersonian model of democracy, the conservative Federalist model, or the contemporary pluralist model. We begin by looking at American conceptions of citizenship.

Contemporary Conceptions of the Rights, Responsibilities, and Roles of Citizens

In his seminal work on the Western political tradition, *Politics and Vision*, Sheldon Wolin explores—in turn—Greek, Roman, Christian, and other views of citizenship.[7] The key elements of each of these were closely related to the cultural values of the particular society and prescribed certain rights, responsibilities, and roles for the citizens. Our knowledge of these conceptions is derived from writings on political matters that remain from the respective

---

[7]Sheldon Wolin, *Politics and Vision* (Boston: Little, Brown, 1960).

periods and from our reading of history. When one seeks to gain some understanding of the contemporary sense of citizenship held by the American population, then he or she looks to the enormous data on public opinion that have been compiled over the past three to four decades. The major sources of this data are: (1) commercial polling organizations, such as the well-known firms of Gallup (American Institute of Public Opinion) and Louis Harris; (2) university research institutes, the most prominent of which is the University of Michigan's Center for Political Studies; (3) a large number of scholarly studies, reaching back into the 1940s; and (4) numerous government studies. There has also been some comparison of American attitudes with those of other peoples, such as in Almond and Verba, *The Civic Culture: Political Attitudes and Democracy in Five Nations*.[8]

This public opinion research is patterned after physical science with its empirical bias. The citizens are probed and poked to "quantify" their perceptual patterns, belief systems, attitudes, sense of politics, and behavioral inclinations. The instruments of this social research are attitude scales of direct and indirect projective measurements, statistical analysis of opinion poll data, and electoral research.

There is a great deal of controversy over the validity of the data which result from this empirical-behavioral research. Critics say that for a host of reasons, such data may be the scientific equivalent of those flickering and deceptive images cast on the cave walls by fire in Plato's famous allegory. Nevertheless, the depiction of American citizens offered by these social science findings holds great authority in a society constantly exposed to an equation of science with specialized, quantitative research. This enters the belief system of policymakers, is purveyed by the mass media, and is entertained by different segments of the general citizenry. The beliefs of people in these various walks of life regarding the nature of public opinion and attitudes obviously affect what they are inclined to do.[9]

If one looks at the details of the social science portrait of how the American people view political life and their role in it then—as suggested in chapter 3—on the whole it is not a very pleasing or

[8]Gabriel A. Almond and Sidney Verba, *The Civic Culture: Political Attitudes and Democracy in Five Nations* (Boston: Little, Brown, 1963).

[9]M. Brewster Smith, "A Psychologists' Perspective on Public Opinion Theory," *Public Opinion Quarterly* 36 (1972), p. 37.

optimistic picture. Four general features, in particular, seriously call into question the extent to which a Jeffersonian democratic political consciousness is being fostered in America. They depict a populace which: (1) lacks a public spirit and is confused about political matters; (2) is intolerant, with no real understanding of or appreciation for democratic principles; (3) tends to be subservient, alienated, and apathetic, with no real sense of their political potential or responsibility; and (4) possesses authoritarian inclinations that are endemic in mass culture.

It should be emphasized that to highlight these four features of the public opinion literature and data is, in some ways, to depict the worst case. Some scholars in the area find reason for a more optimistic interpretation. For example, the late V. O. Key, Jr., insisted that his reading of the public's attitudes and political behavior indicated that "the voters are not fools."[10] And Elmer Schattschneider believed it "an outrage to attribute the failures of American democracy to the ignorance and stupidity of the masses."[11] Similarly, Christian Bay and other "radical" democratic theorists who came to prominence during the tumultuous 1960s asserted that rather than the people suffering the kinds of democratic deficiencies cited above, the fault lay with pseudointellectuals who misread public opinion and political officials who mislead it.[12] Still, in the final analysis those who peruse the literature of the last three to four decades will find, .in the words of Dennis Thompson, a "seemingly pessimistic picture of democratic citizens evoked by contemporary social science."[13]

The most fundamental charge pervading the public opinion data is that from one-third to one-half of the American population knows little about political life and cares less. As Christopher Achen notes, the many studies based upon the public opinion surveys of the Center of Political Studies draw upon data which suggest "that the average citizen has little understanding of political matters" and that in the terms of political affairs, for many people "preferences

[10]V. O. Key, Jr., *The Responsible Electorate* (New York: Random House, 1966), p. 7.

[11]E. E. Schattschneider, *The Semi-Sovereign People* (1960; reprinted., Hinsdale, Ill.: Dryden Press, 1975), p. 132.

[12]Christian Bay, "Politics and Pseudopolitics: a Critical Evaluation of Some Behavioral Literature," *American Political Science Review* 59 (December 1965), pp. 39–51.

[13]Dennis F. Thompson, *The Democratic Citizen: Social Science and Democratic Theory in the Twentieth Century* (Cambridge, England: Cambridge University Press, 1970), p. 6.

are absent from the beginning."[14] An early and especially influential example of such studies was *The Voter Decides* by Angus Campbell and others in 1954.[15] Philip Converse, in a highly significant article published in 1965, asserted that a large segment of the population thinks little about its political life and displays only minimal logical consistency among their (temporarily adopted) attitudes when they do confront public matters.[16]

Turning to book-length studies, Lane and Sears in their analysis of public opinion reasearch held that most citizens are not notably rational in their political thinking. "Their main interest lies in defending emotionally derived and poorly considered opinions— opinions based on early imitation of parental beliefs, partisan adherences, and selfish economic or personal interests."[17]

Harry Holloway and John George believe, on the basis of the extensive research which went into their 1979 text, *Public Opinion*, that an individualistic privatism prevails among the masses. A "plausible case can be made," they contend, "that the bulk of the population sees politics as a peripheral matter and divorces the personal sector from the public sector"—and this is "in large measure normal."[18] On the scale of a broader social criticism, Christopher Lasch sees individualistic privatism as tending to narcissism[19] while Daniel Bell sees an increasingly "hedonistic way of life."[20] None finds much promise of a renascent public spirit or what some call a public "regardingness," although some do believe that increased educational levels among the population might add to public concern and understanding.

A second democratic liability said to characterize the average American's conception of the rights, responsibilities, and roles of

[14]Christopher Achen, "Mass Political Attitudes and the Survey Response," *American Political Science Review*, vol. 69, no. 4 (December 1975), p. 1218.

[15]Angus Campbell et al., *The American Voter* (Detroit, Mich.: John Wiley and Son, 1960).

[16]Philip Converse, "The Nature of Belief Systems in Mass Publics," in *Ideology and Discontent*, ed. David E. Apter. (Glencoe, Ill.: Free Press, 1964), pp. 206–61.

[17]Robert Lane and David Sears, *Public Opinion* (Englewood Cliffs, N.J.: Prentice-Hall, 1964), p. 81.

[18]Harry Holloway and John George, *Public Opinion* (New York: St. Martin's Press, 1979), pp. 271, 66–67.

[19]Christopher Lasch, *The Culture of Narcissism* (New York: W. W. Norton, 1979). Unlike most political science analysts, Lasch finds the historical roots of this phenomenon in capitalistic culture and the pervasive bureaucratic setting of America.

[20]Daniel Bell, *The Coming of Postindustrial Society* (New York: Basic Books, 1973), p. 477.

political citizenship is the lack of appreciation for democratic principles and intolerance toward those with whom one differs. Several studies have researched this. A major one was conducted by Samuel Stouffer in 1954. Over 500 interviewers questioned more than 6,000 Americans from all walks of life about their interrelated attitudes toward communism and civil liberties. It was found that a majority of Americans were quite willing to suspend civil liberties for nonconformists such as communists, socialists, and atheists.[21]

Two parallel articles on this theme of mass misunderstanding and intolerance were published in 1960 and 1964. The former, by James Prothro and Charles Grigg, was based on surveys in Tallahassee and Ann Arbor.[22] The latter, by Herbert McClosky, was based on a Gallup survey and a survey of the delegates to the national party conventions in 1956.[23] Both sought to measure the understanding of and commitment to democratic ideals in America. And both studies concluded that except for the better educated and more politically active segments of the population, there was a minimal understanding of such ideals and little support for their concrete application. McClosky wrote that for many people it seems, "the presuppositions and complex obligations of democracy, the rights it grants and the self-restraints it imposes, cannot be quickly comprehended. Even in a highly developed democratic nation like the United States, millions of people continue to possess only the most rudimentary understanding of democratic ideology." Joseph Femia notes, in a useful critique of these two studies which assesses the bias inhering in such value judgments as McClosky's statement about the highly democratic nature of the United States, that they cast a spell over many subsequent researchers on American public attitudes.[24]

As for the democratic expectation that the citizens will not adopt a subject and subservient social and political orientation and will comprehend their political potential and act upon it, there are—in the public opinion literature—some findings indicating that Americans deviate significantly from this ideal. Perhaps the definitive

[21]Samuel A. Stouffer, *Communism, Conformity, and Civil Liberties* (New York: Doubleday, 1955).

[22]James W. Prothro and Charles M. Grigg, "Fundamental Principles of Democracy: Bases of Agreement and Disagreement," *Journal of Politics* 22 (1960), pp. 276–94.

[23]Herbert McClosky, "Consensus and Ideology in American Politics," *American Political Science Review* 58 (1964), pp. 361–82.

[24]Joseph V. Femia, "Elites, Participation, and the Democratic Creed," *Political Studies*, vol. 27, no. 1 (March 1979), pp. 1–20.

study identifying a willingness of average Americans to accept subordinate roles was done by Robert Lane in his 1962 work *Political Ideology*. Lane conducted in-depth interviews with twenty-eight white, working-class Americans, paying particular attention to their feelings and beliefs about social stratification. He assessed their responses as indicating a general belief in the appropriateness of inequality and an unwillingness to assume the responsibility for governing. In other words, the sample seemed to feel that educated and more successful people should make more money and exercise more sociopolitical authority. And they seemed to feel that the society was better off with such people and not themselves making decisions. Lane concludes: "The fact of the matter is that these men, by and large, prefer an inequalitarian society, and even prefer a society graced by some men of great wealth. As they look out upon the social scene, they feel that an equalitarian society would present them with too many problems of moral adjustment, which they fear and dislike."[25] Perhaps the deference to expertise which emerged so strongly in America in the early 1960s is a manifestation of this trait.

The major device by which public opinion researchers have sought to measure the degree to which Americans comprehend their potential power as democratic citizens is the efficacy scale. The pollsters determine the percentage of Americans who disagree with the proposition "People like me don't have any say about what the government does." One study in 1960 found the United States to have the highest efficacy scores of eleven countries which were compared. (And as we shall see, it was in 1960 that we had the highest voter turnout in the post-World War II era). Still, that appeared to have declined slightly in 1964, and by the time of the 1968 measurement, the score had most certainly dropped, and dropped substantially.[26] Political observer Bill Moyers wrote at the time of the Bicentennial: "As I travel the country today, the mood is resignation and perplexity. . . . In America today, individual citizens live immersed in a political environment but have lost their personal political value."[27]

[25]Robert Lane, *Political Ideology* (New York: Free Press, 1962), p. 70.

[26]Douglas Madsen, "A Structural Approach to the Explanation of Political Efficacy Levels under Democratic Regimes," *American Journal of Political Science*, vol. 22 no. 4 (November 1978), pp. 881–82.

[27]Bill Moyers, "Bill Moyers Discovers A New Mood in America," *National Observer*, January 30, 1976, p. 13.

Tied to this declining estimate of political efficacy is a growing sense that life is uncontrollable and that the future may be worse than the past. In his 1978 study of voting behavior, Authur Hadley noted that "more and more Americans find their lives spinning out of control.[28] As the decade ended, for the first time ever, the public opinion polls began registering an American belief that the nation's future would be worse than the present. President Carter said in his controversial "malaise" speech: "We've always believed in something called progress. We've always had a faith that the days of our children would be better than our own. Our people are losing that faith."[29] (Interestingly enough, people continued to be optimistic about their own personal lives but not about that of the nation as a whole.)

Finally, American public opinion research is finding that increasingly the populace moves in a chaotic, unstable mass culture within which many are receptive to authoritarian appeals of demagogues. Four influential studies on this phenomenon have been particularly important. The first, appropriately entitled *The Authoritarian Personality*, was written by T.W. Adorno and several associates and appeared in 1950. It has since become a classic. Adorno and his colleagues defined the authoritarian individual as characterized by hostility, insecurity, and frustration, a person who detests weakness, is intolerant of ambiguity, and desperately seeks quick, simplistic solutions to complex social, economic, and political problems. They designed instruments to measure varying degrees of authoritarian characteristics which people displayed. One of their major findings was that the lower classes possessed significantly more authoritarian traits than did people higher on the socioeconomic scale.[30]

Another important study relating authoritarian tendencies to the evolving mass culture in post-World War II America, *The Politics of Mass Society*, was published in 1959 by William Kornhauser. Kornhauser saw American society as having changed from the communal form of its early years to the pluralist one of its years of industrialization and immigration and finally to a mass type. Mass

[28]See Arthur Hadley, "The Rich, Happy, Educated Nonvoter," *Washington Post*, November 12, 1978.

[29]See text of June 15, 1979, television address, *Congressional Quarterly Weekly Report*, vol. 37, no. 29 (July 21, 1979), p. 1470.

[30]T. W. Adorno et al., *The Authoritarian Personality* (New York: Harper and Row, 1950).

society, in his analysis, has characteristics that include the break-down of social groupings, the emergence of mass communications, impersonality and mobility, complex issues, and large-scale in-stitutions. These make for a somewhat perplexed and anxious, uprooted and atomized populace who lack traditional group or class identities, structures, and leaders to mediate between them-selves and the political world. In normal times mass society is characterized by widespread apathy. But because elites become directly accessible to the masses and the masses become directly accessible to elites, there is the omnipresent possibility of dema-gogic, extremist, and violent mass movements. All that is needed to crystallize this is the right combination of issues, circumstances, and leaders. The most extreme forms of mass, authoritarian move-ments result in totalitarianism.[31]

A year later Seymour Martin Lipset reconfirmed the existence of widespread "working-class authoritariansim" in America and, like the authors of the other studies, sought to clarify its nature and the factors producing it. He was persuaded that social isolation, a punishing childhood, economic and occupational insecurities, and a lack of sophistication about the world were the main contributors to this personality type.[32] He and Earl Rabb published, in 1970, another relevant study, *The Politics of Unreason*. This exploration of right-wing extremism included extensive analyses of Wallace's supporters. They concluded that many were authoritarians who had experienced the deprivations that Lipset identified in his 1960 work and who responded to such demagogic appeals in the 1968 campaign as Wallace's pledge to solve the crime problem in the na-tion's capital by putting an army battalion on every street corner and to discourage protest (the first protestor who lay down in front of his car, Wallace remarked, would not lay down in front of any more cars).[33]

The studies cited above are only a small sample of the enormous literature on public opinion in America. They are, however, some of those which have exercised the greatest influence on the people—politicians, media commentators, and social analysts—who must,

[31]William Kornhauser, *The Politics of Mass Society* (New York: Free Press, 1959). For an excellent critical analysis of Kornhauser see Sandor Halebsky, *Mass Society and Political Conflict* (New York: Cambridge University Press, 1976).

[32]Seymour Martin Lipset, *Political Man* (Doubleday 1960), p. 47.

[33]Seymour Martin Lipset and Earl Raab, *The Politics of Unreason* (New York: Harper and Row, 1970).

of necessity, strive to understand public attitudes and conceptions. This is not to say that the methodology used goes unchallenged, or that they represent the last word on the subject, or that one cannot find contrary evidence in the research. Just to take one example of the latter point, the poll cited in chapter 3 on lower-class attitudes supporting ameliorative programs to alleviate the high cost of utilities and housing for the poor and to provide government-sponsored jobs and health insurance suggests the presence of a stronger egalitarian strain than Lane perceived, at least on economic issues. Also, many critics see the entire methodological thrust of public opinion studies as scientistic rather than scientific, as a very narrow technical and ideological restriction of scientific reasoning, knowledge, illumination, and understanding.

Still, the most persistent view of mass opinion about political life is that sketched above. Our next task is to relate these conceptions of the rights, responsibilities, and roles of political citizenship to their sociocultural sources and to assess the implications of this political consciousness for participation.

Sociocultural Bases for Conceptions of Citizenship and Their Implications for Political Participation

To the degree that individualistic privatism, intolerance, confusion, apathy, and authoritarianism characterize American conceptions of citizenship, they merely echo the underlying political culture and the socialization process which transmits it. The egoistic, materialistic values of Federalist No. 10, the Constitution, and the latest television commercial all vitiate a public spiritedness. *The absence of ideological choices and lack of debate over the first premises of America (or their prohibition, as in the example of the House Un-American Activities Committee), reduce the citizen's ability to understand and tolerate fundamentally different points of view. Americans simply have no significant cultural experience doing this. The hierarchy inherent in the unequal economic structure and in that of a technological society, along with the impersonal, bureaucratized nature of modern life, weigh heavily on citizens.* They may indeed become apathetic and may conclude that they have little potential for effecting change through politics or other channels. A combination of all these things within a society which places on individuals a heavy burden for their own fate may make them long for simplistic, even authoritarian, solutions to persistent problems.

Turning to the socialization process, it is likely that—given the way various agencies operate—feelings of powerlessness and desires for authoritarian solutions would be generated. The family experience is all too often dominated by feelings of anxiety. The family is torn between a set of traditional values and a traditional role as the primary agency, on the one hand, and a situation where the nuclear unit is in disarray, on the other. It is being overrun by institutions in the private and public sectors. Key subgroups, such as women and blacks, find their socioeconomic conditions so adverse that they may internalize negative perceptions about themselves. Language, so important to the way Americans view themselves, their community, and the world, is imbued with antiegalitarian codes and is increasingly technical and quantitative. Television, the most important new socializing force to emerge in postwar America, is controlled not by the many but by the few and offers a normal fare of materialistic, centrist, and escapist values along with a heavy dose of negativism about politics and politicians. Schooling is more and more within larger and larger impersonal, bureaucratic structures, with the content all too often verging on outright propaganda. And in the workplace citizens own less and less of the means of production as concentration accelerates. There is less worker input than in any other Western society, and the end products are all too often of questionable utility to the quality of human life. Fortunately, these negative dimensions are somewhat alleviated by the many positive ones discussed in part 2 as well as by the imperfect coordination of the agencies. Still, the negativistic tone of American political socialization is powerful.

The cultural values and attitudes transmitted by the socialization process significantly affect the many citizens residing within a hierarchical and increasingly inflexible social structure of roles with a radically unequal wealth and income distribution. First, the socioeconomic structure—the material conditions of political existence—interacts with the cultural values and socialization process or the mental conditions of political existence, to inhibit, more than with any other segment of the population, the development of an activist or democratic outlook on the part of those at the base of the society. This dampening effect contributes directly to the low levels of participation in ranks of lower status, as is noted below. Second, the socioeconomic structure places certain unique contextual constraints on the possibilities for effective citizenship of the same group, further diminishing participation.

So we find certain antipolitical and nondemocratic values of the political culture, the negative dimensions of the socialization process itself, and the inhibitions of the socioeconomic structure all reflected in the diminished conceptions of democratic citizenship found in American public opinion literature. In turn, these reduce the level of participation engaged in by Americans, particularly for certain population cohorts, and also affect the types of participation engaged in by Americans. This question of participation is our next concern.

"It has been observed," begins a journal article on American political participation, "that political apathy is a very widespread phenomenon in American culture."[34] A major government study says, "the primary reason people do not register and vote is because they are not interested."[35] The former piece appeared in 1954, the latter in 1980. A disinclination to participate appears more persistent and widespread in the United States than in virtually any other Western democracy. This is certainly proven by a comparison of voter turnout. One study found that turnout rates in major elections average 71 percent in Great Britain, 74 percent in Canada, 82 percent in France, and 91 percent in West Germany.[36] Yet only 52½ percent voted in the 1980 American presidential elections, continuing a decade long decline that approaches the post-World War II low of 51 percent. Many Americans would no doubt be surprised to learn that: (1) 1928 was the first year that a majority of the population voted; (2) turnout was higher in the depression and war years of 1936-1944 than in the 1970s; and (3) nonvoters have outnumbered the winning total in every presidential election. And in off-year elections the turnout plummets to about one-third of the electorate.

There are, of course, many other and more important ways of participating. While data on participation in spheres other than voting are inadequate to provide a clear picture, one oft-cited study concluded that the voting-age population participates in politics at the following rates (expressed as a percentage of voting-age population).[37]

[34]Morris Rosenberg, "Some Determinants of Political Apathy," *Public Opinion Quarterly*, vol. 18, no. 4 (1954), p. 349.

[35]Charles E. Johnson, Jr., "Nonvoting Americans," *Current Population Reports*, Special Studies, Series P-23, No. 102 (Washington, D.C.: U.S. Department of Commerce, Bureau of the Census, 1980), p. 18.

[36]William F. Stone, *The Psychology of Politics* (New York: Free Press, 1974), p. 187.

[37]Charles E. Lindblom, *The Policy-Making Process* (New York: Prentice-Hall, 1968), p. 45.

Holding public and party office	
Being a candidate for office	Less than 1%
Soliciting political funds	
Attending a caucus or a strategy meeting	4-5%
Becoming active member of a political party	
Contributing time in a political campaign	
Attending a political meeting or rally	
Making monetary contribution to party or candidate	10%
Contacting a public official or a political leader	13%
Wearing a button or putting a sticker on the car	15%
Attempting to talk another into voting a certain way	25-30%
Initiating a political discussion	
Voting	40-70%
Exposing oneself to political stimuli	

These findings are paralleled by other major studies.[38] Virtually all observers have concluded that some one-third of the population is not at all involved in politics. At the other end of the spectrum, it is estimated that only 4-5 percent engage in what Milbrath terms gladiatorial acitivies such as running for office, fundraising, or being active in a party.

Many factors contribute to the disinterest in voting and the extreme scarcity of Americans engaged in significant political activity. The nature of campaigns, parties, and candidates, the issues that are raised, and the institutional matters of how citizens are registered and where and when an election is held are all important. Still, the fact that procedural changes like the easing of residency requirements, a succession of highly varied candidates for national office, and powerful issues ranging from a controversial war to urban violence to runaway inflation, have all failed to alter the steady twenty-year decline in presidential balloting or to increase the percentage displaying higher levels of involvement suggests a much more deep-seated problem. Indications are that many people, and particularly those segments of the population that participate least, are being socialized to nonparticipation.

As would be predicted by our analysis of political socialization, those Americans who show the greatest disinclination to vote and who are the least active in the higher type of participation are those

[38]For example see, Lester Milbrath, *Political Participation* (Chicago: Rand McNally 1965); and Norman Nie and Sidney Verba, *Participation in America* (New York: Harper and Row, 1972).

of lower-class standing. In a useful study which appeared in the mid-1970s, Robert Gilmour and Robert Lamb wrote:

Those who have withdrawn from American politics, who have become so alienated from and disinterested in governmental affairs that they have ceased to participate, are most typically not the disaffected student demonstrators and dropouts who gained so much notoriety a few years ago. Numerically they are likely to be the men and women, more often the women, of any age who are lowest on the social and economic ladders. More than a third of the apathetic Americans are found in the lowest income category, coming from families that earned less than $4,000 in 1972. Almost two-thirds of these apathetic people are from families that earned less than $6,000 in 1972. A low level of formal education intensifies this effect. Of those found in the lowest two income categories and who dropped out before completing high school, 40 percent expressed apathy toward American politics. These were also the people who were least likely to vote in elections or otherwise to participate politically.[39]

The 1980 government study mentioned above found these class-conditioned proclivities reflected in participation rates.

1. High school graduates who did not vote totalled 34 percent in 1976 compared with 54 percent for nongraduates. Only 20 percent of college graduates did not vote, whereas 71 percent of those with fewer than 4 years of schooling did not vote.
2. The number of white-collar workers was slightly larger than the total of workers in other occupations; however, only 28 percent of the former failed to vote compared with 49 percent of the latter. White collar workers comprised 60 percent of the voters but only 38 percent of the non-voters.
3. Median family income was $9,807 for nonvoters and $13,485 for voters. Only 23 percent of families with incomes of $25,000 or more did not vote compared with 45 percent of those with incomes under $5,000.[40]

Since blacks, like women, suffer disproportionately high membership in lower socioeconomic ranks, they are less inclined by their sociocultural experiences to participate. Blacks are consistently found to show much higher levels of alienation, and whites have a

[39]Robert S. Gilmour and Robert B. Lamb, *Political Alienation in Contemporary America* (New York: St. Martin's Press, 1975), p. 106.
[40]Johnson, *Current Population Reports*, pp. 9–14.

voter turnout rate approximately 20 percent higher than that of blacks. A black candidate, a strong community organization, or a civil-rights-oriented campaign can alter the pattern. As to sex, one analyst noted that "As of 1972 . . . , a clear pattern of less interest in participation (except for voting in primaries) and in politics characterized American women."[41]

This class conditioning and the skewed participation rates are not found in all democracies. For example, one study comparing voter turnout in American with that of Sweden discovered that "the number of voting Americans drops off noticeably at the lower end of the socio-economic scale in the United States, but there is much less variation among Swedish voters."[42]

Such skewed participation rates obviously have consequences for public policy, which in turn affects the socioeconomic opportunities for population groups. As Key noted in his classic study, *Southern Politics*, "The blunt truth is that politicians and officials are under no compulsion to pay much heed to classes and groups of citizens that do not vote."[43] This is even more true for those inactive in more significant areas of political behavior. As we noted in chapter 3, the United States, which has—with France—the most unequal distribution of wealth and income of the industrial democracies, spends less of its GNP on social welfare programs than any other such country. Partly for this reason and partly because the United States has slid since the early 1960s from first to approximately tenth among the industrial nations in per capita income while also experiencing double-digit inflation for almost a decade, the actual standard of living of at least that bottom one-third of the population who participate very little is deteriorating. Yet there is surprising calm in the nation's poor neighborhoods, with the isolated exceptions of the looting during the New York blackout of July 1977 and the Miami riots of May 1980—which were stimulated by anger over police brutality against blacks—and other, lesser disturbances. (It is true, however, that the "normal" level of participation in criminal activity is exceedingly high).

Almost fifty years ago Whilhelm Reich suggested that the real question to be asked about a society is not why men sometimes rebel

[41]Susan B. Hansen et al., "Women's Political Participation and Policy Preferences," *Social Science Quarterly* vol. 56, no. 4 (March 1976), p. 581.

[42]Richard H. Kraemer et al., *American Democracy: The Third Century* (St. Paul, Minn.: West Publishing, 1978), pp. 176–77.

[43]V. O. Key, Jr., *Southern Politics* (New York: Vintage Books, 1949), p. 527.

Figure 1.
Voting Participation Rates by Class:
Two National Surveys: (A) United States, 1968; (B) Sweden, 1960

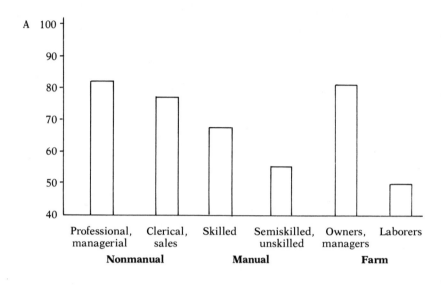

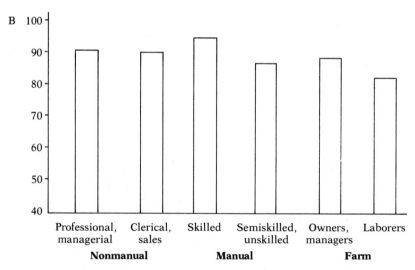

against it but why those in the lower ranks do not rebel.[44] In America, the reason seems to lie in the inordinate power of the legitimating values and symbols of the political culture, as perpetuated by the political socialization process, and the inhibitions instilled by that process, along with those inherent in the socio-economic structure. It is a great and controlling irony that alongside the disenchantment with politics and the withdrawal from public affairs noted above, is maintained—in the consciousness of the citizens—a strong affection for systemic values and symbols.

By the manipulation of symbols, appeal to dominant values and identities, and rigorous adherence to the prescribed rules of the political game which limit political conflict, the unequal system is legitimized. Edelman asserts that "the American poor have required less coercion and less in social security guarantees to maintain their quiescence than has been true in other developed countries."[45] And Devine finds that in a world of change, "The United States seems to be one of the few countries which have been characterized by relative regime stability." This is so even though "traditional means of regime maintenance such as coercion and resource allocation to relevant groups have seemed inadequate" in this stressful age. It is, he concludes, "American support attitudes"[46] that provide the most significant basis for this extraordinary stability. Is it possible that Marcuse is more correct than we would like to think possible? "In this society, for which the ideologists have proclaimed the 'end of ideology,' the false consciousness has become the general consciousness—from the government down to its last object."[47]

DEMOCRATIC ELITISM: DENYING THE NECESSITY OF MASS PARTICIPATION

As the social science data on American political behavior accumulated in the 1950s and 1960s, it became abundantly clear that Americans were a long way from the classical ideal of the par-

[44]Wilhelm Reich, *The Mass Psychology of Fascism*, trans. Vincent R. Carfagno (1933; reprint ed., New York: Farrar, Straus and Giroux, 1970), p. 19.

[45]J. Murray Edelman, *Politics as Symbolic Action* (Chicago: Markham Publishing, 1971), p. 56.

[46]Donald J. Devine, *The Political Culture of the United States* (New York: Little, Brown, 1972), pp. 1–2.

[47]Herbert Marcuse, "Repressive Tolerance," in Herbert Marcuse, Barrington Moore, and Robert Paul Wolff, *A Critique of Pure Tolerance* (Boston: Beacon Press, 1965), p. 110.

ticipatory citizen striving for moral fulfillment. Political reality, concluded many political leaders, commentators, and academic observers, was not only unlike the ideal but in many ways contrary to it. Finding irrational, uninformed, and disinterested citizens who, when and if they do participate in politics, are likely to be motivated by authoritarian rather than democratic motives presented a difficult choice to leaders in and observers of American democracy. They could either attempt the feat of trying to change the sociocultural environment restricting American conceptions of citizenship and constricting democratic behaviors, or they could change the operative view of democracy and in particular of the kind of citizen participation it requires. For a host of reasons, most political elites and political analysts—both academics and commentators—chose to redefine democracy in such a way that it would better describe the reality of citizens' beliefs and behavior.

There was enormous academic debate on this subject in the 1960s and the 1970s. The key questions were: what are the theoretical alternatives? How can a "democratic" system be built upon citizen irrationality and noninvolvement? Economic theorist Joseph Schumpeter provided the key answers to these questions for many pluralists and other contemporary thinkers more conservative than latter-day Jeffersonians.

Schumpeter began his revision of classical democratic thought by asserting democracy is to be understood as a method and not as an end in itself. This sufficiently narrowed the scope of democracy to those institutional arrangements necessary for "arriving at political—legislative and administrative—decisions." Schumpeter's insistence on democracy as means rather than purpose was also in keeping with the desire on the part of many post–World War II social scientists to be value free and thereby allegedly resemble natural scientists. Institutional arrangements can be described and analyzed, whereas discussions of purpose leave one in the murky realms of nonverifiable values. Schumpeter's definition took all of this into account.

We now take the view that the role of the people is to produce a government. . . . And we define the democratic method as that institutional arrangement for arriving at political decisions in which individuals acquire power to decide by means of a competitive struggle for the people's vote.[48]

[48]Joseph Schumpeter, *Capitalism, Socialism, and Democracy* (New York: Harper and Row, 1942), pp. 242, 269.

From the standpoint of participation, the critical dimension of classical theory, and the means to self-improvement, Schumpeter's descriptive theory of democrary is dependent only upon high levels of involvement from a small number of political activists, elites. Nonparticipation on the part of the mass of citizenry not only is an empirical reality but a logical necessity if the system is to maintain stability, given the proclivities of the people.

American political scientists were quick to adopt Schumpeter's lead, and Robert Dahl, mentioned earlier in our discussion of pluralism, was most prominent among them.[49] Dahl argues that democracy is a *political method*, a series of institutional arrangements that focus on the electoral process and, since the larger part of the citizenry is politically inactive and most likely to be authoritarian in political mood, the political system is better off, more stable, if they do not participate. It is not difficult to see that what C. B. Macpherson calls the Schumpeter-Dahl axis is a theory which "treats democracy as a *mechanism*, the essential function of which is to maintain equilibrium."[50] Nor is it difficult to perceive that in spite of the desire to be value-free, the existing Anglo-American democratic system is, for these modern democratic elitists, "the ideal democratic policy."[51]

Nonetheless, from these meager theoretical beginnings, the Schumpeter-Dahl axis developed into the dominant theory of democratic theory and behavior. It was the logical conclusion of pluralist and Federalist thought. Just how dominant the theory has become can be seen from the fully rationalized form in a popular text on political participation by Lester W. Milbrath and M. L. Goel.[52]

Milbrath and Goel tell us that modern society has evolved into a highly specialized and differentiated system in politics as well as economics. Thus political roles are highly differentiated and specialized, permitting some citizens, primarily elected officials

[49]Dahl, *Preface to Democratic Theory*. See also H. Ekstein, "A Theory of Stable Democracy," in *Division and Cohesion in Democracy* (Princeton, N.J.: Princeton University Press, 1968); B. R. Berelson, "Democratic Theory and Public Opinion," *Public Opinion Quarterly* 16 (1952), pp. 313–30; and G. Sartori, *Democratic Theory* (Detroit, Mich.: Wayne State University Press, 1962).

[50]C. B. Macpherson, *Democratic Theory: Essays in Retrieval* (New York: Oxford University Press, 1973), p. 78.

[51]Carole Pateman, *Participation and Democratic Theory* (New York: Cambridge University Press, 1970), p. 15.

[52]Lester W. Milbrath and M. L. Goel, *Political Participation*, 2nd ed. (Chicago: Rand McNally, 1977).

(elites), to devote their full attention to matters of public policy, while others, the bulk of the citizenry, need expend very little time and energy in public affairs. At periodic intervals these elites come before the people to see who will have the privilege of governing. Political parties are useful economizing devices in this process because they simplify our perceptions of the elites' records in office. Parties, coupled with a free and open communications media and vigilant interest groups, keep elites responsive to the people. Milbrath and Goel admit that it is essential that these elites be committed to democratic values and that elite recruitment must come from a broad base, from many different sectors of society. But they are rather sanguine about the success of such a system of democratic elites.[53] Others are not so uncritical.

The supposed scientific neutrality of the new democratic elitism is, in fact, a defense of a particular set of values. As Jack Walker aptly points out, the elite theorists "have substituted stability and efficiency as the prime goals of democracy."[54] Low levels of citizen participation are acceptable because stability will be the result. This attachment to the status quo of equilibrium has a definite policy and class bias as well. Significant issues of poverty, discrimination, waste, and violence remain untouched by elites and elite theorists alike. C. B. Macpherson puts the matter most succinctly: "Democracy is reduced from a humanist aspiration to a market equilibrium system. And although the new orthodox theory claims scientific neutrality, its value judgment is clear enough: whatever works is right—that is, whatever enables the existing class-stratified society to operate without intolerable friction is best."[55]

Both Theodore Lowi and Jack Walker have been in the forefront of contemporary critics of democratic elite theory. They point to its essentially apologetic character. Lowi's *End of Liberalism* argues persuasively that the emphasis on elite groups, one of the more rigid aspects of our political system, is apology, the emphasis on equilibrium is apology, and the attempt to separate fact from value is

[53]Ibid., pp. 145–48. One of the most popular American government textbooks of the 1970s interprets this theory of democratic elitism very well. See Thomas R. Dye and L. Harmon Ziegler, *The Irony of Democracy: An Uncommon Introduction to American Politics*, 4th ed. (Belmont, Calif.: Duxbury Press, 1978).

[54]Jack L. Walker, "Normative Consequences of 'Democratic' Theory," in *Frontiers of Democratic Theory*, ed. Henry Kariel (New York: Random House, 1970), p. 234.

[55]Macpherson, *Democratic Theory*, pp. 78–79.

apology.[56] Many political scientists, Walker concludes, have "become sophisticated apologists for the existing political order."[57]

In addition to the class and issue biases, wittingly or unwittingly supported by democratic elitism, there are two additional, serious consequences of the theory. First, the emphasis on a "realistic" process theory of democracy—with elite rule and citizen apathy leading to homeostasis—results in a theory which is "bound in time and space by its realistic description of a political reality." It has no utopian quality to it, no sense of the possible. In a world of rapid change, it provides little if any guidance for the future. Such a theory of democracy, in Lane Davis's words, "lacks the radical bite of classical theory" and becomes "a system to be preserved, not an end to be sought."[58]

Second, the assessment democratic elitism makes of human nature is excessively negative. The elite theorists see human beings motivated by interest, ambition, and power. In this they share their view with earlier Federalist theorists such as James Madison and John Adams. They neglect, however, characteristics of human beings which emphasize friendship, brotherhood, and piety. In so doing, they have created a theory which justifies a static and self-fulfilling view of human beings—which is to say, we are motivated by our inclinations to self-interest and *we shall always be so.* They have thus destroyed the last and most crucial vestige of classical democratic thought, the possibility that humans, through participation in the public realm, might rise above self-interest and realize greater potential. In the final chapter I shall have more to say about the possibilities of achieving that potential, in other words, of reviving classical democratic theory.

Conclusion

The classical view of democracy anticipated the presence of at least a certain degree of public attentiveness, tolerance, and understanding, plus some willingness to participate, among its citizenry. The resulting political involvement would, to the Jeffersonian democrat, further educate and interest the population in public affairs and develop their skills as citizens. Still, the findings of modern

[56]Theodore J. Lowi, *The End of Liberalism* (New York: W. W. Norton, 1969), p. 313.
[57]Walker, "Normative Consequences of 'Democratic' Theory," p. 234.
[58]Davis, "The Cost of the New Realism," p. 226.

social science raised serious questions about this ideal. It came to appear to many who did this research, or perused the results, that contemporary conceptions of political life held by Americans were characterized to a large degree by intolerance, confusion, and authoritarianism, along with a disinclination to participate in public affairs. Many polls, surveys, questionnaires, and other devices proclaimed this social inquiry scientific, and research progressed in the 1950s and 1960s.

If American political consciousness is as restricted and diminished as the bulk of social science findings indicate, then this may be a—possibly the—major explanation for the low rates of participation in American politics. Interestingly enough, even if the findings are untrue, some analysts feel that their very popularization diminishes participation and structures the quality of the relationship between citizens and officials. On the former point, Richard Hamilton—who challenges much of the research on mass authoritarianism and ignorance versus elite tolerance and intelligence—believes that because these findings are so widely trumpeted they become authoritative components of the social knowledge. If the masses themselves internalize a belief in this picture of their consciousness, then such findings can become "restraining myths" depressing levels of self-confidence which are important to participation.[59] And Key explains how elites can be influenced in their approach to the population by their acceptance of the negative tenets about public attitudes. In his view the perceptions that leadership elements of democracies hold of the electorate

condition, if they do not fix, the types of appeals politicians employ as they seek popular support. . . . If politicians perceive the electorate as responsive to father images, they will give it father images. If they see voters as most certainly responsive to nonsense, they will give them nonsense. If they see voters as susceptible to delusion, they will delude them.[60]

In contemporary America it seems clear that to some degree, the real nature of political consciousness, and to a great degree the widespread perceptions as to the negative nature of that consciousness, vie against mass participation. Thus we find low participation rates. We also have the least participation on the part of the lower

[59]Richard Hamilton, *Restraining Myths* (New York: Sage, 1975).
[60]Key, *The Responsible Electorate*, pp. 6–7.

ranks of the population, who have the least control over the agencies of political socialization. They may be most influenced by the antipolitical dimensions of the American political culture and the negative dimensions of the socialization experience. And they certainly are the most constrained by the unequal distribution of socioeconomic resources in America.

Many academicians and other observers of American democracy have, under the stimuli of the negative conclusions about mass consciousness and low participation levels, engaged in rethinking the nature of democracy. They have focused particularly on what role mass participation should play. One of the more prominent theorists to lead in this was Joseph Schumpeter. He and others like Robert Dahl redefined democracy in such a way as to accommodate the particular nature of American politics as they found it. The major goal was to justify the status quo theoretically by denying the need in a democracy for large-scale involvement by the citizenry in public affairs. The masses were relegated, in theory, to the role of simply choosing at periodic elections among elites who were empowered to make decisions. Intimate involvement by such a confused populace was seen as the greatest threat to the system. This view recalls the conservative one of Madison, Hamilton, and Adams, articulated in chapter 2 as the Federalist theory of democracy. And it merged with the pluralists, a major representative of whom was Dahl. They had never adhered to the Jeffersonian view of citizenship and had always been much closer to the elite view of the Federalists. Indeed, the theoretical origins of pluralist democracy reside in Madison's Federalist No. 10.

VIII

Conceptions of Leadership, Culture, and Consciousness: The Case of the Presidency

"The President is a 'lightning rod' or object of displacement."   Fred I. Greenstein, "The Psychological Function of the Presidency for Citizens"

"The more we study the Presidency, the more we learn about ourselves."   Bill Moyers, "Bill Moyers Journal"

"None of us wants to restore an imperial presidency, but neither can we afford an imperiled presidency."
Gerald Ford, 1978 speech, Washington, D.C.

The relationship of political leaders in governing institutions with the citizenry is shaped by many things. History, circumstance, issues, and individual figures can all be very influential. These can incline official conduct and institutional behavior to a particular direction at a given moment. And they can affect the attitudes toward political officials and interaction with the institutions of government on the part of the citizenry. Still, the center of gravity governing the general pattern of such relationships of government, leaders, and people lies always in the cultural foundations of a polity. As Erwin Hargrove wrote "Our institutions are manifestations of our culture with all its defects and virtues."[1] Or, as is indicated in chapter 1, the "interaction between culture and consciousness is crucial in determining what kind of political system emerges into reality."

This is so for the four branches of our Madisonian system and for any social institution intimately involved with political life. Indeed, one could study the presidency, Congress, the judiciary, or the bureaucracy in terms of their grounding in political culture and the socialization process. Still, clarification of the status and function of the most visible institution of leadership in the political society should be most revealing of the interrelationship of political institutions, political culture, and political consciousness. In the

[1] Erwin Hargrove, *The Power of the Modern Presidency* (New York: Alfred A. Knopf, 1974), p. ix.

United States, this prominent institution is the presidency. To quote Hargrove, "As we study the presidency, we find that we come face-to-face with ourselves as Americans, our beliefs, prejudices and values."[2]

The first aim of this chapter is to analyze the reciprocal relationship of president and political consciousness. What are the implications of American political culture and socialization for the standing and function of this office in the hearts and minds of the nation? In addressing this question one must explore the major sociocultural elements of the process by which, between the presidencies of Franklin D. Roosevelt and Richard Nixon, the presidency was enshrined as a political icon. The resulting creation came to be called the imperial presidency. This imperial cast of the office was most clearly demonstrated in the abortive Johnson and Nixon presidencies, from November 22, 1963, to August 9, 1974. The deep disillusionment occasioned by these two administrations led to such skepticism that Gerald Ford and others began to express concern over a possibly imperiled president. How is it possible for attitudes toward the foremost political leader in America to vary so dramatically over such a short span of time? To what degree are salient features of political culture and socialization culpable, as distinguished from incumbents' actions, in this political schizophrenia? What are the implications of such attitudinal instability for effective citizen control and the democratic leadership required of a president? These and related questions will be the concern of the initial sections of this chapter.

The second goal is a prescriptive one. If we understand the curious and unparalleled role played by the president in American political consciousness and have some idea of its consequences for political life, then perhaps we can make the stature of the office in our political culture and socialization more realistic. Clearly, former president Ford is correct. Neither an imperial presidency nor an imperiled presidency advances the effort at a rational and moral ordering of the affairs of the community that is grounded in a democratic political consciousness. How can that lightning rod function attributed to the office by Greenstein, which gives rise to these two undesirable extremes, be moderated? Before embarking on an effort at prescriptive theory, however, it is necessary to examine the place of the presidency in our political consciousness.

[2]Ibid.

Enshrining the Presidential Icon: Sociocultural Factors

St. Augustine in the fifth century described idolatry as "mankind tyrannized over by the work of his own hands." If modern America has had an idol, it has been that of power.

Why has power been idolized? Lowi gives one account in his analysis of the political and economic intricacies of the depression years as a crisis that culminated in a spectacular but unrevolutionary turn to government.[3] Coupled with the development of economics of gigantic scale, this turn to government meant that political and economic institutions and the individuals manning them experienced an exponentially explosive increase in their activities in all areas of American life. These activities inevitably involve questions about and conflicts over power. Presidents, Pentagon generals and bureaucrats, industrialists, union leaders, and all those at the apex of the pyramidal institutions of postindustrial America strive feverishly to maintain a power base once they have attained it. Their daily, never-ending struggle to gain and retain a seat of power reminds one of Bellamy's brilliant stagecoach analogy of capitalism. "It was naturally regarded as a terrible misfortune to lose one's seat, and the apprehension that this might happen to them or their friends was a constant cloud upon the happiness of those who rode."[4] Bellamy, like Marx, was only partially correct in emphasizing the economic motivation. While power often grows from wealth, it is still something distinct and the chief prize.

We suffered during the decade leading up to the American Bicentennial from a perverse form of political idolatry of the American presidency. Samuel Dubois Cook addressed this problem in his presidential speech to the Southern Political Science Association convention in 1973. "Our political and governmental institutions and processes have been corrupted by the blind and tragic worship of power as a self-validating and self-fulfilling reality."[5] Cook's comment has pertinence beyond the Watergate-related crimes of the early seventies which prompted it.

If one applies this analysis to recent presidents, it is easier to understand why a socially and intellectually insecure incumbent

---

[3]Theodore J. Lowi, *The End of Liberalism* (New York: W. W. Norton & Company, Inc., 1969).

[4]Edward Bellamy, *Looking Backward, 2000–1887* (New York: Random House, The Modern Library, 1942), p. 4.

[5]Samuel Dubois Cook, "Presidential Address" (Paper delivered at the annual meeting of the Southern Political Science Association, Atlanta, November 2-5, 1973).

like Lyndon Johnson, surrounded by people whom David Halberstam termed the best and brightest,[6] would go to such enormous lengths to protect his power. One is reminded of the tale Johnson related to Doris Kearns about a recurring nightmare that he had as president. In his recounting, Johnson explained how he would dream that he was paralyzed (as Wilson had been) and could overhear his aides parceling out his authority among themselves in the next room. Unable to stop this emasculation, he would experience the ultimate terror of a power-driven politician. Upon awakening, Johnson would be in a cold sweat. He would rise and walk down the hall of the White House till he reached Wilson's picture. Touching it would somehow relieve the fear.[7]

Watergate also becomes somewhat more intelligible from this perspective. Nixon and his entourage of advisers would do virtually anything to protect themselves. Personalities, acquaintances, and beliefs are inevitably drawn into such struggles. All become crucial to the contest to maintain power which characterized the later years of both the Johnson and Nixon administrations. This official power madness in the presidency (and also in other private and public institutions) became a central element of contemporary reality. Such a development is tragic in itself, and it clearly contributed to the catastrophic policy failure of the Indochina War and to Watergate. There are however, deeper, broader, and more elemental levels where other than purely official personages were embroiled in the idolatrous process.

Major participants in the ever-increasing idolatry of power over roughly the middle third of the twentieth century were many intellectuals. There were necessarily deep intellectual implications involved in the turn to executive government in the 1930s. Dewey explained in 1935 that the way to distributive justice and effective liberty was through organized social intelligence. "It is useless to talk about the failure of democracy until the source of its failure has been grasped and steps are taken to bring about that type of social organization that will encourage the socialized extension of intelligence."[8] To a large degree the United States adopted Dewey's path, emphasizing organization equally with intelligence in the process.

[6]David Halberstam, *The Best and the Brightest* (New York: Random House, 1969).
[7]Doris Kearns, *Lyndon Johnson and the American Dream* (New York: Harper and Row, 1976), p. 342.
[8]John Dewey, *Liberalism and Social Action* (New York: G. P. Putnam's Sons, 1935), p. 53.

Stress was placed on the application of specialized knowledge to policy concerns. As the process evolved, intellectuals, who are normally responsible for dissident inquiry concerning questions of power and policy, were subtly incorporated into the existing socioeconomic and political structure. Establishment intellectuals came to be subsidized through tax-free grants from the U.S. Department of Education, Guggenheim funds, Pentagon research funds, quasi-public think tanks, foundation awards, and prestigious academic and governmental positions. They were assimilated into the expanding establishment in the same manner as defense contractors, the maritime industry, corporate farmers, and other leading members of the status quo.

Potentially influential intellectuals thus lost their independent base for criticism, perhaps permanently. Some few resisted, but most willingly accepted their comfortable prostitution. This militated against diversity and dissent and contributed to a narrowed sterile conformity. The resulting primacy of a one-dimensional set of establishment intellectuals had grave implications for the presidency.

Such primacy resulted in the blind, headlong hubris of American intellectuals in government (particularly the executive branch) which was particularly visible in the Kennedy administration. They shared a "sense of power and glory, omnipotence and omniscience of America in this century. They *were* America, and they had been ready for what the world offered, the challenges posed."[9] Certainly the world offered numerous challenges. Many domestic and foreign issues could only be dealt with through some centralization of power in the presidency, the center of action in the system. Thus events created a need for swift, decisive, presidential action, reinforcing and rationalizing the sense of "power and glory" of those in power. Not only did intellectuals in government directly participate in the accumulation of presidential power; perhaps more importantly, their colleagues in the universities were at the same time enshrining the presidential icon.

The Johnson and Nixon excesses stimulated a large body of analysis on the relationship of contemporary academics to the imperial presidency. It revolved around the question of the degree to which the executive office and surrounding sociopolitical environment which allowed for widespread abuses in the pre-Bi-

[9]Halberstam, *The Best and the Brightest*, p. 655.

centennial decade was, to paraphrase Augustine, "the work of academic hands." A study by Malcom Parsons found a homogeneous intellectual predeliction—until the later Johnson years and the Nixon presidency—thoughout academia to strong, dominating chief executives. "So far as rank and ordering goes, the shared values and status of economists as opposed to political scientists or historians, make virtually no measurable difference in perceptions of presidential performance."[10] William Andrews identified eleven major books appearing within three or four years of 1960, that is, just before the fruition of those trends to an imperial presidency, praising the office as a noble, virtuous, and glorious burden. The authors of those books generally perceived the president as possessing too little power to carry out domestic responsibilities and having his foreign affairs authority continually threatened by the Congress."[11] Such writers offered many proposals to strengthen the presidency, with one, Louis Koenig, calling for "more power to the president (not less)."[12]

In looking for an explanation of why a shared political bias to the strong presidency was elevated into constitutional theory in the 1960s, Andrews discovered that most of the presidency's glorifiers had common personal commitments to Roosevelt, Truman, or Stevenson, plus service in Democratic administrations, and no congressional experience. This impelled them to what many call the "stewardship" theory of the strong presidency that was initially promoted by Alexander Hamilton and was given its classic formulation just over a century later by Theodore Roosevelt. To Roosevelt, the chief executive

was limited only by specific restrictions and prohibitions appearing in the Constitution or imposed by the Congress under its Constitutional powers. My view was that every executive officer . . . was a steward of the people bound actively and affirmatively to do all he could for the people, and not to content himself with the negative merit of keeping his talents undamaged

[10]Malcolm Parsons, "The Presidential Rating Game," in *The Future of the American Presidency*, ed. Charles W. Dunn (Morristown, N.J.: General Learning Press, 1975), p. 86.

[11]William A. Andrews, "The Presidency, Congress, and Constitutional Theory," in *The Presidency in Contemporary Context*, ed. Norman C. Thomas (New York: Dodd, Mead, 1975), pp. 13–33.

[12]Louis W. Koenig, "More Power to the President (Not Less)," in *Congress and the President*, ed. Ronald C. Moe (Pacific Palisades, Calif.: Goodyear Publishing, 1971), pp. 69–73.

in a napkin. I declined to adopt the view that what was imperatively necessary for the Nation could not be done by the President unless he could find some specific authorization to do it. . . . I believe that the efficiency of this Government depends upon its possessing a strong central executive.[13]

As the Indochina war and other events of the 1960s unfolded, and again in the 1970s during Watergate, doubts sprang up about this view. By 1971, when Andrews surveyed the relevant literature, most students "preached an almost contradictory doctrine. The Glorified Presidency, erected and exalted by the 1960 group, was being destroyed—at least abstractly—by the 1970 group."[14] He went on to caution against permitting a weak president to become established in constitutional theory. Yet when the 1980s began, the "stewardship" theory appeared to be regaining prominence, at least temporarily.

One might find this phenomenon rather interesting and still ask, as indeed Malcolm Parsons does, what (if any) difference does it make? For an answer we move to the third and most important aspect of the idolatry of power that was chiefly responsible for the ever-increasing authority of the president in the Johnson and Nixon terms, namely the attitude of the citizenry. The "textbook" presidency created by academics was partially to blame for the citizens' misplaced belief in the institution, as Thomas Cronin makes clear.[15] And the intense effort of incumbent presidents and their advisers to aggrandize the office, in Edwin Crowin's phrase, also had an impact. These factors were supplemented, reinforced, and enormously magnified by the secular thrust of contemporary American culture.

Theodore Roszak, a perceptive social critic, recognizes the significance of this trend in raising questions about the "religious dimensions of political life" in an era where secular figures, institutions, and issues tend to overshadow spiritual ones. "How else," he asks, "to talk politics in a apocalyptic era?" He traces the manner in which the Western Protestant and scientific tradition, which we have inherited, has moved steadily and irrevocably against the transcendent authority of myth, magic, and miracle. It has denied the authority of experiential values. This tradition is derived from

[13]Quoted in James MacGregor Burns, *Presidential Government: The Crucible of Leadership* (Boston: Houghton Mifflin, 1965), pp. 58–59.

[14]Andrews, "The Presidency, Congress and Constitutional Theory," p. 26.

[15]Thomas E. Cronin, "The Textbook Presidency and Political Science," *Congressional Record*, October 5, 1970, p. 34920.

the Reformation purism and the mind-body dichotomy of Descartes. Western man has substituted political and scientific phenomena for religious transcendence and existential vitalism. With the denial of otherworldly reality and the domination of the natural world, man has come to pay homage to the technological imperatives of urban-industrial necessity, as we saw in chapter 3. The most prominent of these imperatives are executive power politics and the bureaucratization of life. In the meantime there has been "the terrible possibility that a society wielding such inordinate power may release negative forces within the human psyche, as well as within the repressed natural environment, that will never allow it to survive the fifty or one hundred years it needs to exploit its capabilities."[16]

There is yet another sense in which the presidency rose to the psychological apex of the technocratic political system. In a political society that came to worship power, the president alone possessed the ultimate power that for the first time in history involves a veto over mankind. This is the ultimate irony. We have not destroyed myth, magic, and miracle but have merely made them immanent. We have transferred a sense of religion and magic to a secular religion. As Roszak says, "The truth of the matter is: no society, not even our highly secularized technocracy, can ever dispense with mystery and magic ritual."[17] One manifestation of this complex, deep strain of political religion in the United States was apparent in the centralization of moral, as well as political, authority in the presidency immediately before Watergate. Fawn Brodie aptly wrote near the end of the 1960s that the "political hero is more than ever essential to the emotional health of the nation. The decline of religion has resulted in what psychoanalyst Erik Erikson describes as increasing 'charisma hunger.' "[18]

Reinforcing such a craving is the role that presidents assumed in setting America's course to the hallowed secular ideal of progress. All presidents promise to get the country moving once more (although the destination they have in mind is not always clear). As

---

[16]Theodore Roszak, *Where the Wasteland Ends* (New York: Anchor Books, Doubleday, 1973), pp. xiv, 200. An excellent study of the religious origins and ideological functions of the effort at domination of nature is William Leiss, *The Domination of Nature* (Boston: Beacon Press, 1974).

[17]Roszak, *Where the Wasteland Ends*, p. 148.

[18]Fawn Brodie, "Political Hero in America: His Fate and His Future," *Virginia Quarterly Review* 46 (Winter 1970), p. 48. The most absurd manifestation of this is the preoccupation of president and public with the "athletic image" of incumbents.

Cronin noted, by the end of the 1960s Americans looked "toward their presidents to articulate national goals, unite the nation, explain the state of the nation—or the 'state of the world'—forecast the future and protect us from alien ideologies." We came to "regard our 'sense of purpose' and pious presidential pronouncements as nearly one and the same."[19] Is this why we speak of eras in terms of presidents?

Theodore White was the most widely read commentator on the presidency in the decade of the 1960s. He has, therefore, special significance for popular perceptions. White drew together many of these themes in his analysis of Nixon. He wrote of the necessity of secular faith, myth, and symbolism as means to unite our diverse people. Consensus would be impossible in America "unless its people were bound by a common faith." And "politics in America is the binding social religion." Turning to the significance of the president, he explained: "Of all the political myths out of which the Republic was born, however, none was more hopeful than the crowning myth of the Presidency." To White the myth is composed of a belief that the supreme office would ennoble occupants. "The office would burn the dross from his character; his duties would, by their very weight, make him a superior man, fit to sustain the burden of the law, wise and enduring enough to resist the clash of all selfish interests." That myth "held for almost two centuries."[20] Even discounting White's tendency for a dramatic overstatement, such conceptions were widely held by the populace in the period under discussion. They resulted inevitably in the royal aura of the American chief executive of the late 1960s, which was unparalleled in any but the few theocracies still extant. Such a development involved the gravest implications.

In sum, as the United States completed its second century, the beneficent potential of the presidency came to be a dominant psychosymbolic paradigm of the political culture, rivaled in symbolic power only by the U.S. Constitution. Donald Devine says flatly, "Presidents, in fact, provide the major symbol system emphasis."[21]

[19]Cronin, "The Textbook Presidency," p. 34919.

[20]Theodore H. White, Breach of Faith (New York: Reader's Digest Press, 1975), pp. 323–24. One is reminded of the theory of "giveness" explicated by Daniel J. Boorstin in The Genius of American Politics (Chicago: University of Chicago Press, 1953). For an interesting discussion of Boorstin's theory as it applies to the presidency, see Vukan Kuic, "Theory and Practice of the American Presidency," Review of Politics, 23 (July 1961), p. 323.

[21]Donald J. Devine, The Political Culture of the United States (Boston: Little, Brown,

Furthermore, the executive office, unlike the much misunderstood Constitution, is personified by an incumbent who can confer symbolic and material favors. Thus the presidency loomed larger than life in the American mind in the era from the depression until the abuses of Watergate. This is illustrated by Fred Greenstein's well-known classification of five psychological functions of the president which magnified his status. He (1) simplifies perception of government and politics; (2) provides an outlet for emotional expression; (3) is a symbol of unity; (4) provides people with a vicarious means of taking political action; and (5) is a symbol of social stability.[22] That a disgraced president might symbolize the reverse only attests further to his radically unequal status. This psychosymbolic primacy is enormously significant, for as Justice Frankfurter wrote four decades ago, "we live by symbols." The unwarranted and unfulfillable expectations attached to the symbolic presidency have rendered our political society vulnerable to schizophrenic swings from excessive veneration to extreme disenchantment with incumbents.

POLITICAL SCHIZOPHRENIA: THE IMPERIAL
AND IMPERILED PRESIDENCY

Almost two centuries ago James Madison in Federalist No. 51 stated the classic case of the problems of governance: "In framing a government which is to be administered by men over men, the great difficulty lies in this: you must first enable the government to control the governed; and in the next place *oblige it to control*

1972), p. 126. Murray Edelman, *The Symbolic Uses of Politics* (Urbana: University of Illinois Press, 1964), p. 193, believes that anxious, insecure citizens give "their allegiance most wholeheartedly to the chief executive whose gestures proclaim that he can deal with the enemy, quite apart from the concrete results."

[22]Fred I. Greenstein, "The Psychological Functions of the Presidency for Citizens," in *The American Presidency: Vital Center*, ed. Elmer E. Cornell (Chicago: Scott, Foresman, 1966), pp. 29–36. David Easton and Jack Dennis, *Children in the Political System: Origins of Political Legitimacy* (New York: McGraw-Hill, 1969), pp. 206–07, explain: "In the United States the President as a personalized figure is a towering, glittering mountain peak for the younger child, easy to single out from the whole range of authority. . . . The positive feelings for political authority generated there can be expected to have lasting consequences." Other significant literature on this point includes David Easton and Jack Dennis, "The Child's Image of Government," *Annals of the American Academy of Political and Social Science* 361 (1965), pp. 41–57; Fred I. Greenstein, *Children and Politics* (New Haven, Conn.: Yale University Press, 1965); Fred I. Greenstein, "Popular Images of the President," *American Journal of*

itself."[23] Madison knew that a democratic government, no matter the form, was not immune from these difficulties of control. If the people are the government, they must limit themselves. Indeed, it may be argued that one of the fundamental requisites of democratic citizenship is self-restraint. Ironically, with the rise of democratic governments in the nineteenth century, the belief in the need for such limits was severely weakened. Another spokesman and observer of democratic behavior, John Stuart Mill, echoed Madison's warning. The people, Mill asserted, are a danger to themselves when they act as an intolerant mass and when they place excessive faith in their leaders. "The limitation, therefore, of the power of government over individuals loses none of its importance when the holders of power are regularly accountable to the community, that is, the strongest power therein."[24] In being persuaded by incumbents and establishment intellectuals to worship the major office of American democracy, and in placing unrealistic demands upon that office, the populace ignored Mill's caution. As we have seen, the result was presidential abuse of power.

A good deal of debate and discussion appeared in the 1970s as both scholarly and popular forums explored the relationship of popular perceptions of the presidency to its monarchical cast by occupants in the office.[25] Two major issues were raised by that debate. One is whether or not the political society in which we live tends to look for the wrong qualities in presidential candidates. Do we seek an imaginary ideal president that no human being could possibly attain? Similarly, once the successful candidate takes office, do we have expectations of performance that far exceed human

---

Psychiatry 122 (November 1965), pp. 523–29; Robert D. Hess and Judith Torney, *The Development of Political Attitudes in Children* (Chicago: Aldine Publishing, 1967); and Roberta Sigel, "Image of a President: Some Insights into the Political View of School Children," *American Political Science Review* 62 (March 1968), pp. 216–26. This authoritative figure, like government itself, does not have the same significance for all children, although political socialization studies have not always made this clear. For an excellent collection of articles organized around the consensus and dissent theme, with an informative introduction, see Edward S. Greenberg, ed., *Political Socialization* (New York: Lieber-Atherton, 1970).

[23] James Madison, Federalist, No. 51, in *The Federalist*, p. 337.
[24] John S. Mill, *On Liberty*, 6th ed. (New York: Bobbs-Merrill, 1966), p. 6.
[25] See, for example: "In Defense of Politicians: Do We Ask Too Much?" *Time*, January 27, 1975, p. 32; Stephen Hess, *The Presidential Campaign: The Leadership Selection Process after Watergate* (Washington, D.C.: Brookings Institution, 1974), pp. 4–22; and Michael Novak, *Choosing Our King: Powerful Symbols in Presidential Politics* (New York: Macmillan, 1974).

capacity? It may well be that we have a symbolically oriented, apolitical presidency bent upon aggrandizement because we demand not political but "presidential" behavior from our most important political leader. Thomas Cronin goes so far as to say that "today the principal ground of reproach against president and citizens alike should be that he or she is not a politician."[26] The implications of both the selection process and the cues given incumbents are of critical importance to the interaction of people and president.

Questions of whether we look for the wrong qualities in a candidate, or of how candidates attempt to offer themselves to the public, are increasingly complex. They are made so by modern campaign technology, particularly the use of the electronic media. The superhuman or—with Carter—saintly ideal, or the movie star quality with Reagan, is the image that we seek via the airwaves. All are unattainable ideals. Thus candidates that are too frank in their inevitable inconsistencies, too spontaneous, and all too human violate the image. They convey the wrong message and have fared poorly over the past decade. Packaged, managed candidates do much better. Even a small, confused, and thoroughly political candidate can be made to appear statesmanlike, heroic. McGinnis quotes one memo circulated in the Nixon campaign of 1967: "Potential candidates are measured against an ideal that's a combination of leading man, God, father, hero, pope-king, with maybe just a touch of the avenging Furies thrown in." Knowing that Nixon did not fulfill this model (and who does?), the memo suggested "improvements that would have to be made—not upon Nixon himself, but upon the image of him which is received by the voter."[27]

Elections of the past decade offer overwhelming evidence that such improvements work all too well. It was, after all, the paternalistic peace candidate who won in 1964 and the moralistic law-and-order candidate in 1968 and 1972. The first and last of these elections produced record majorities. In 1976, the successful candidate was the one whose most oft-repeated pledge was not to act on a policy issue but that "he would never tell a lie." Historical

---

[26]Thomas E. Cronin, "The Presidency and Politics," in *The Future of the American Presidency*, ed. Charles W. Dunn, p. 285.

[27]Joe McGinnis, *The Selling of the President, 1968* (New York: Trident Press, 1969), p. 26. The new industry that tailors candidates to culture has been explored by David L. Rosenbloom, *The Election Men* (New York: Quadrangle Books, 1973), and other analysts.

myth can be played very well in the media age. And in 1980 America elected its first president to have had a career in movies and television. In such a tragicomic politics there are no winners, certainly not the people and not even the victors. When celebrity, not leadership, becomes the key,

Like the praying mantis, it consumes the consummator. It stands mischievously by the gates to the citadel of power and destroys those select few it permits to enter. . . . The winners, at least in the short run, are those who have clowned away their souls and thus can no longer use the power they have.[28]

Once in office the successful candidates do their best to maintain the "myth of the president."[29] Building upon the symbolic primacy of the office, incumbents endeavor to manipulate public sentiment by offering an idealized portrait of themselves. They try to control and structure the flow of words, images, symbols, and information to the populace. Obvious examples are Johnson wrapping himself in the flag, Nixon doing likewise with the office, Carter's efforts to use the "bully pulpit," and Reagan's use of television plus his tight control over the conduct of press conferences. This tendency has always existed in the presidency. Still, it has experienced such a quantitative evolution in the past few decades as to make for a qualitative change in our democratic politics. The process has been greatly accelerated by the periodic political crisis since 1933 and by presidential access to the media, particularly television. The telegenic Kennedy administration benefited enormously from such access.[30]

One of the most astute commentators on the presidency sums up what may well be the major result of all this: "The real problem of the Presidency is the pressure on the Chief Executive, especially in

[28]Benjamin Barber, "Command Performance," Harper's, April 1975, p. 54.

[29]See the article of that title by Alfred de Grazia, in Congress and the President, ed. Ronald C. Moe, p. 88.

[30]David Halberstam, "Press and Prejudice," Esquire, April 1970, p. 113: "Kennedy's Presidency helped change the entire balance of American politics. By the time he left office, the Presidency, in large part because of television, in part because of his own life style, had come to play a dominant role in American life; he and the men around him began to take on the roles previously relegated to Hollywood stars—proxy lives. We led our lives through him and his successors, for better or for worse. Even his death and his funeral were almost more affairs of theatre than affairs of politics." An authoritative study of the presidency and the media is Newton W. Minow et al., Presidential Television (New York: Basic Books, 1973).

times of crisis, to forsake his function as majority leader and to assume the more exhilarating role of acting for the whole people as Chief of State." Incumbents are of a "disposition to give in to that pressure. Here we reach the nub of the issue of presidential power."[31] Another highly respected analyst has concisely described the duality of symbolic-psychological and political roles as conferring a schizophrenic aspect to the executive office.[32] Incumbents increasingly veer to the former, avoiding the latter. In doing so they take their cues from the traditional ambivalence to politics within the American political culture. Cronin contends, for example, that Nixon's seeking out of nonpartisan issues, particularly foreign policy, so as to avoid the appearance of playing politics, "had its roots in his perception of the mood of the people."[33] This is certainly one possible explanation of Carter's moralistic emphasis on human rights and Reagan's oft-stated claim that no appointments or policy decisions would be made in response to political considerations.

The dangers of such a distancing of president from politics, as well as abuse of the easy access to media, are many. Monologues, fireside chats, and royal statements often involving distortion and abuse of language to alleviate conflict were characteristic of the Johnson and Nixon administrations. Similar use of the media for other than democratic conversation is an ever-present possibility for subsequent ones. Other dangers are secrecy, isolation, paternalistic decision making, arrogance, self-deceit, moral and political rigidity, a sense of limitlessness, and the tyranny of benevolence and distrust. Such things are deadly for a political society. As one failed presidential aspirant says, "The idea of a president who is above politics, in my judgment, is hostile to the genius of democracy."[34]

The attempt of both public and president to fit men for Superman's costume, the holy cloth of sainthood, or stardom was always doomed. The most important component, human nature, cannot in the end be manipulated. Aristotle knew this: "Strong feelings lead astray rulers and the very best of men." And a leader, even one who

[31]James McGregor Burns, "The Politics of the Presidency," in *Congress and the President,* ed. Ronald C. Moe, p. 295.

[32]Joseph Kallenbach, "The Presidency and the Constitution: A Look Ahead," in *The Presidency in Contemporary Context,* ed. Norman C. Thomas, p. 36.

[33]Cronin, "The Presidency and Politics," p. 277.

[34]Morris K. Udall, "A Democrat Looks at the Presidency," in *Congress and the President,* ed. Ronald C. Moe, p. 248.

is lawful and trustworthy "has only one pair of eyes and ears, one pair of feet and hands, and cannot possibly be expected to judge and to act better than many men with many pairs."[35] Machiavelli, the much misunderstood Florentine, knew this also. No ruler is

so wise as to be able to adapt himself to such changes, [i.e., of fortune], both because we cannot be other than as nature inclines us and because one who has prospered by following one kind of policy will not be persuaded to abandon it. Hence the cautious man, when the time comes for bold action, is incapable of it and so falls, for if nature could be changed with the variation of time and circumstances fortune would not change.[36]

The inevitable disillusionment with incumbents' inadequacies is accelerated by the fact that at least in domestic policy areas, few presidents find their actual power sufficient even to begin fulfilling the expectations flowing from their symbolic primacy. In late 1978 Jimmy Carter broached this subject in an interesting interview with Bill Moyers. It is, in Carter's words, "a fond hope, I guess, of every politician to be universally admired . . . , to have one's character be recognized clearly and to have universal approbation of the people that you try to represent." In a tone of real regret he added: "All those things are hopeless dreams." They are so partially because the expectations are unrealistic and the incumbents are all too human, no matter how much they may try to hide this fact. This desire for "universal approbation" is frustrated because in the immediate post-Watergate era the institutional power of the office was weakened, hence ex-President Ford's concern about the imperiled presidency. Carter bemoaned this: "I have limited powers, limited authority, and I try to overcome these inherent defects in the office itself the best I can."[37] (Ironically, Carter—who explicitly and repeatedly rejected the imperial model—may have accepted its presuppositions if he concluded that democratic and institutional limits on the presidency constitute defects.) The combined effects of limits in both office and incumbents within a context of the inordinate symbolic significance of the presidency may produce (perhaps

[35]Aristotle, *The Politics*, trans. Benjamin Jowett (New York: Random House, The Modern Library, 1943), pp. 163–64.

[36]Niccolo Machiavelli, *The Prince*, ed. T.G. Bergin (New York: Appleton-Century-Crofts, 1947), p. 74.

[37]"Bill Moyers' Journal: An Interview with President Carter," transcript (New York: WNET, Educational Broadcasting Corp., November 13, 1978).

make inevitable) political alienation on the part of occupants of the office as well as citizens being governed by it.

Ralph Nader once described the body politic as having moved from the delegation of its responsibilities to itself to abdication of them to the "final stage of vegetation."[38] To him this is a man watching Johnny Carson over the rim of his belly. This loss of personal will, energy, direction, force, and purpose in politics is inextricably related to the deep cultural currents of our technological age that I explored in chapter 3. This vacuity of will occurs precisely at the time when Americans must take ever-increasing responsibility for crucial choices in leisure activities, sexual relations, and politics. Yet in these late decades of the twentieth century, the normative criteria for responsible personal choice are chaotic, and the reliability of authoritative symbols, leaders, and institutions, like the presidency, are in question. The ensuing uncertainty and confusion comprise what one author calls "a failure of followership."[39] This involves not only the apathy Nader referred to but also at times violence. Both phenomena—apathy and violence —are present in Americans' relation to their preeminent political leader. They each reduce the possibility of effective democratic interaction of president and public.

Whenever presidents, the ultimate political celebrities, are revealed as finite and flawed mortals by the crises of war, scandal, and economic problems, and the political means of controlling and directing them become ineffective, there are only two alternatives. One is to turn away, as many do in their disenchantment. The other is to lash out.

Assassination in America has fed on quite homicidal rages born of paranoia and polarization. The selectivity with which targets were chosen and the efficiency with which the killings were carried out support the terrible suspicion that a large public, against its better instincts, in some way wished these deaths.[40]

The assassination of John Kennedy in 1963 began a frightening series of attempts on the lives of presidents and presidential candidates. Accountability by the gun supplanted accountability by

[38]Quoted by Nicholas V. Hoffman, "A System of Checks and Silencers," *Washington Post*, July 18, 1975.
[39]Barber, "Command Performance," p. 52.
[40]Ibid., p. 56.

political channels, and the presidency became the most dangerous job in America.

The facts that no other comparable industrial nation assassinates as many executives and that we assassinate no state, local, judicial, or congressional political figures support this analysis. As Greenstein says, the president truly is "a 'lightning rod' or object of displacement."[41] Squeaky Fromme's and Sara Jane Moore's courtroom comments linking their respective attempts on Ford's life in the mid-1970s with his alleged responsibility for the cutting of the redwoods, environmental pollution, and various other ills of our society are manifestations of this irrationalism. Cory C. Moore, one of the many terrorists so prevalent in the early months of 1977, was granted his demand to speak with Carter before releasing his hostages in Cleveland, providing yet another example, as does the shooting of Reagan on March 30, 1981, by John Hinckley. It is with good reason that incumbents (and prominent candidates) move about only within a cordon of highly trained and well-armed security forces. They *know* the true dialectic by which the imperial presidency became the imperiled one.

American Democracy and the Symbolic Presidency

The conclusion is inescapable. The pendulum of cultural attitudes must avoid the extreme ranges of excessive veneration and deep disillusionment. There must be a more balanced and realistic appraisal of the presidency if the environment is to be conducive to responsive and responsible democratic leadership in the office. And tinkering with devices to refashion formal checks and balances and pursuing new laws to meet this need clearly will not suffice. Hargrove makes the point well. "There are no structural or institutional gurantees of private or public virtue. Therefore, there is no faith that reforms in the mechanism of institutions can do much to resolve fundamental ills in the functioning." Specific reforms might meet limited, specific problems. But "old habits and folkways are likely to shape such changes into old paths. It is much more difficult to change the folkways and the underlying ways of thinking and feeling that nourish them."[42] But this must be attempted if we are to

[41]Fred I. Greenstein, "What the President Means to Americans: Presidential 'Choice' between Elections," in *Choosing the President*, ed. James David Barber (Englewood Cliffs, N.J.: Prentice-Hall, 1974), p. 146.
[42]Hargrove, *The Power of the Modern Presidency*, p. ix.

permanently reduce, not destroy, the president's psychosymbolic authority in our culture and our political consciousness.

Unfortunately, fallout from the Indochina war and Watergate failed to stimulate as much prescriptive theory on methods for concretely restructuring the symbolic power of the presidency as it did proposals for institutional reform. There are, however, a few obvious measures which some commentators have touched on and which have been adopted to varying degrees. While space precludes an exhaustive analysis, we may nevertheless consider four of the more important: resocialization; demythologizing the presidency; reforming the selection process; and restricting the president's access to the media. The significance of the first of these, resocialization, is pointed out by Greenstein. "The most probable source of change in the tendency for the President *either* to be unrealistically idealized or to assume the status of handy scapegoat would appear to be in the formal and informal political socialization process." This includes "learning from peers and from one's own thought and experience as well as from 'authorities.' " It involves "the learning of nonconformity and autonomy as well as conformity."[43]

The Indochina war, Watergate, domestic spying at executive command, and other incidents of abuse in the Johnson and Nixon years constituted a decade of learning experience that affected attitudes toward the president. Most significantly for the long run, it is arguable that the young generation of that era was affected the most. One study concluded, "It may well be that the enduring distinction of the Nixon administration will not be the 'opening to the East' or a 'generation of peace' or even the sordid episodes of corruption and misuse of power." Instead it may be "a vital breakdown in the political system's socialization of its youngest members."[44] It is impossible as yet to determine the accuracy of this statement. The 1970s found many of the youth seeking good magic

[43]Greenstein, "What the President Means to Americans," p. 147.

[44]Robert S. Gilmore and Robert B. Lamb, *Political Alienation in Contemporary America* (New York: St. Martin's Press, 1975), p. 147. The literature on the impact of Watergate on youthful attitudes is extensive. See F. Christopher Atherton's "The Impact of Watergate on Children's Attitudes toward Political Authority," *Political Science Quarterly* 89 (June 1974), pp. 269–324; and "Watergate and Children's Attitudes toward Political Authority Revisited," *Political Science Quarterly* 80 (Fall 1975), pp. 477–96; Marjorie Hershey and David B. Hill, "Watergate and Preadults' Attitudes toward the President," *American Journal of Political Science* 19 (November 1975), pp. 703–26; Fred I. Greenstein, "The Benevolent Leader Revisited: Children's

to replace the bad, with religions of various sorts attracting many. Others became cynical and apathetic, which is, of course, the other side of the coin from excessive veneration and equally undesirable. Still others may have become more effective at practical politics with their new realism toward the system and its head. No one can say which of these trends will strengthen in the 1980s.

A second strategy proposed in the immediate post-Watergate period was to demythologize the presidency, which Eugene McCarthy whimsically proclaimed that we could accomplish by turning the White House into a museum, plowing over the Rose Garden, and planting a cabbage patch.[45] Wisconsin Congressman Henry Reuss offered an amendment to create a separate office of "Chief of State" to help dispel the undemocratic attitude that the king can do no wrong. And, of course, recent incumbents other than Johnson and Nixon have made their undeniable although inadvertent contributions to destroying our illusions. The widespread perception of both the Ford and Carter administrations as inept further weakened Americans' illusions. Even academics contributed; one text appearing in 1976 concluded with a chapter on "The Theory and Practice" of the presidency by asking whether we were experiencing an "end to Superman."[46]

These are positive signs, until and unless the process destroys the requisite symbolic power of the office needed in our fragmented Madisonian system to permit democratic leadership. The cultural forces on each side of the Watergate political divide bring into sharp focus this danger within the traditional ambivalence of Americans to political leadership. From the depression years to Watergate, America witnessed the domination, as discussed above, of cultural attitudes reinforcing the tendency to a monarchical cast in the office, which in turn was conducive, given the right personalities and events, to the arrogance of power of the Johnson and Nixon

---

Images of Political Leaders in Three Democracies," *American Political Science Review*, 69 (December 1975), pp. 1371–99; Robert R. Hawkins, Suzanne P. Hawkins, and Donald F. Roberts, "Political Socialization of Children: Two Studies of Responses to Watergate," in *Watergate and Mass Communications*, ed. Sidney Kraus (Bloomington, Ind.: University of Indiana Press, 1976). See also the special issue devoted solely to Watergate of the *American Politics Quarterly* 3 (October 1975) and *Communications Research* 1 (October, 1974).

[45]See *The Hard Years* (New York: Viking Press, 1976).

[46]William W. Lammers, *Presidential Politics: Patterns and Prospects* (New York: Harper and Row, 1976).

administrations. The disillusionment of Indochina and Watergate stimulated great anxiety for a restoration of both morality and human dimensions in the office. In the ultimate irony, the understandable intensity of this public anxiety may have found the citizenry in the mid-1970s as ill prepared as before, although in a reverse fashion, for effective democratic interaction with presidential leadership. Carter clearly felt this to be the situation during his term of office. Citizens must accord incumbents basic legitimacy, trust, and tolerance.

Third, the presidential selection process must allow for a clearer spotlight on candidates' characters. It must not merely showcase their public image, nor exaggerate their human foibles. Nixon's and Johnson's Watergate and war experiences were, as is now obvious, intimately related to flaws in their personalities, just as Carter's problems were related to his personality. If personality bears so closely on policy and if people often, as in 1976, must judge more on character than issues, then it is critical that the judgmental process be bettered. This requires certain reforms, such as improving the debate format used in 1976 and 1980. Inadequate as the debates were, some observers suggested that they greatly revealed the essential nature of the candidates, which often contrasted dramatically with the advertised images. Not only must the selection process be bettered, but citizens must be stimulated and enabled by media, party, and campaign process to face up to their responsibility. As one scholar remarked, "The citizenry must be willing to do what is necessary to identify, develop and support those who are qualified to lead."[47] A more involved citizenry attuned to character, not image; better debates; coverage of other than major-party candidates to enhance comparisons; and more penetrating reporting of personal and political backgrounds, perhaps along the lines indicated by James D. Barber,[48] would be just a few ways to increase the likelihood of a better selection.

Finally, there has been recognition that if we are to have democratic presidential leadership, incumbents' access to public opinion channels must be offset, which is not to say denied. This can be done in a number of ways. First, the networks need to give the loyal

[47]Address by Henry J. Abraham, "The Presidency at the Threshold of the Last Quarter of the Century" (paper delivered in the Honors Lecture Series, University of Southern Mississippi, Hattiesburg, Miss., October 21, 1977).

[48]James D. Barber, *Presidential Character* (Englewood Cliffs, N.J.: Prentice-Hall, 1972).

opposition air time to answer a presidential announcement or respond to a radio talkathon. Second, they should be more bold in questioning presidential requests for air time. In the immediate post-Watergate period the networks were more willing than before or since to do both of these.[49] Legislation is badly needed in these and related areas. A third necessity is greater Congressional and public caution in acquiescing to large staffs of presidential image makers on the public dole. Of possible significance in this regard was the Federal Election Commission's well-publicized inquiry into Ford's appointment in the 1976 election year of Rogers B. Morton to a $44,000 staff position for essentially political advice for the campaign. This precedent, no matter how weak, might be useful in the future to those concerned about public subsidies of political image makers for presidents. On the other hand, Carter maintained his image maker, Gerald Rafshoon, and pollster Patrick Caddell on the White House staff, and no questions were asked. In addition, Congress must overcome its fear of the American people and should televise its proceedings, at least in part, preferably live, with the networks providing the coverage (not doing as the House does at present, that is, televising selected procedures over its fixed cameras, reserving the authority to edit all tape). If the judiciary committee impeachment hearings of 1974 are any kind of guide, airing important legislative matters would help to equalize the disparity of power with the president. While the latter has had almost unlimited access to television, the Congress has had considerably less. Similarly, more attention to bureaucratic, corporate, foundation, and other arenas of decision making is needed. This brings up a central point. The media could show, through their coverage, that much decision making occurs outside the presidency.[50] To ignore this and focus inordinately on the presidency is to perpetuate a misperception.

These are but a few of the obvious ways that the perceptions and values of our political culture relating to the presidency might be

[49]Richard Salant of CBS has expressed regret ("Talking Back to CBS—Discussion," February 15, 1976) that his network has allowed presidents such free and unlimited use of their communications facilities. He explained that in 1973 CBS adopted a policy of allowing the opposition equivalent air time to respond within seven days of a presidential address. The network has also ceased automatically granting presidential requests for air time, particularly during election periods.

[50]For a study with a great deal to say about the problem, see Todd Gitlin, *The Whole World Is Watching* (Berkeley: University of California Press, 1980).

made more realistic. They may or may not be of sufficient significance. As noted above, prescriptive theory on the methods for restructuring the symbolic power of the presidency is woefully lacking. Certainly if this analysis has any merit, it will assist in stimulating exploration of ways of effecting change in the American political culture. Such changes should permit the presidency to retain enough symbolic status for democratic leadership without going to extremes.

Conclusion

To maximize the leadership potential of the presidency an incumbent requires favorable economic and international conditions, carefully crafted policies, political skill, and allies in Congress and throughout the political system. Still, one other ingredient in the equation of presidential leadership may be of even more importance: the particular nature of those feelings, perceptions, and expectations about the presidency which attach to the person in office and pervade the political culture. This political consciousness is affected by a host of socialization agencies, incumbents, and events, as I have sought to explain. The components of American awareness of the most visible leadership role in the political society should, ideally, accord basic legitimacy, trust, and support while avoiding being so uncritical as to induce presidential arrogance or so unrealistic as to bring about public cynicism when incumbents do not measure up.

To what degree will inclinations to the reforms outlined above lead to fundamental change in the role and status of the presidency? Will changing folkways prove so difficult, as Hargrove notes, that they and habits "are likely to shape such changes into old paths?" In a book published the year Nixon resigned, Barber presented a less than optimistic assessment. "Absent some revolution in deep public attitudes, Presidents will continue to be chosen in part to satisfy our hunger for a Superman, a hunger made all the more intense by a decade of deprivation."[51] (Some would interpret the Reagan victory as verification of Barber's prophecy.) If so, this hunger will never be satisfied because, as we noted, the domestic policy process appears ever less susceptible to presidential control. Whatever the solution

---

[51]Barber, "Introduction," *Choosing the President*, p. 5.

to this dilemma may be (and there may be none), it must be thought through with sensitivity to the realization that schizophrenic swings to an imperialistic towering office or an imperiled presidency gutted of authority and functioning as a lightning rod for disillusionment are intimately tied to cultural folkways. Such extremes poorly serve the need for legitimate democratic leadership exercised under effective popular control. Ultimately "the triumph or tragedy of each Presidency, is in some measure at least, also our own."[52]

[52]Milton C. Cummings, Jr., and David Wise, *Democracy Under Pressure*, 2nd ed. (New York: Harcourt Brace Jovanovich, 1974), p. 370.

IX

Political Consciousness and the Future of American Democracy

Man is not what he thinks he knows, but what he thinks he can know, can become.   Archibald MacLeish, quoted in
The Consent of the Governed

Rationality and politics distinguish teleological man from beasts and plants.
Mulford Q. Sibley, *Nature and Civilization*

To change the world in a conscious way one must first have a conscious understanding of what the world is like. Lack of such understanding is a dismal portent.
Marvin Harris, *Cannibals and Kings*

In this book I have sought to clarify to what degree and in what particular respects the foundations of American political life—political culture, socialization, and consciousness—support a majoritarian democracy in the Jeffersonian mold as opposed to an elite type like that envisioned by the more conservative Federalists and pluralists. While the former does exist to a degree it is probably true that, on the whole, the greatest restraint on the realization of majority rule democracy in America is the nature and functioning of these very foundations of the political society. This is not to deny that often inadequate party competition, sometimes ineffective and sometimes corrupt political leadership, and the increased complexity of public issues also inhibit participation. Still, Americans' ambivalence to political leadership and their diminished conceptions of citizens' rights, roles, and responsibilities are too persistent and deep-seated to be eliminated by spasmodic and fluctuating trends. The underdeveloped political consciousness appears firmly tied to political culture values and the socialization process, plus the attendant socioeconomic structure of roles and the distribution of wealth. The inhibitions on political awareness and involvement inhering in these are doubly important for those at the lower ranks of the socioeconomic structure who have the least input into the agencies of socialization. Hence they participate least.

At several points in the foregoing exploration of American political life it has been suggested that such a diminished political consciousness and the ambivalent view of leadership it encour-

197

ages—along with the disinclination to participate—ill serve the political society, and have become particularly acute as America has moved into the technological age. One goal of this last chapter is to specify why this is the case by discussing key items on the political agenda. The second goal is to suggest a necessary first step toward a solution. This can only come about by recognizing the political nature of man, and moving to encourage the realization of the political self. The ability of America to deal with its increasingly perplexing problems turns on this, as does—to some degree—the future of American democracy. Holding to such a position need not lead one to despair. For, as Jean-Paul Sartre wrote: "Men are free, and life begins on the far side of despair."[1]

THE TRANSITIONAL POLITICAL AGENDA AND AMERICAN CONSCIOUSNESS

At about the time the United States was celebrating its Bicentennial, there emerged a growing sense that the country was entering a major political transition. While the Bicentennial itself stimulated thinking about the country's past and future, other factors provoked concern. Of particular importance were interrelated setbacks during the 1970s in the areas of foreign and military policy, the economy, and energy. In their cumulative impact these strongly suggested a new and possibly ominous turn for America.

Two particularly dramatic and widely publicized failures of American military and foreign policy greatly shocked Americans in the 1970s. The first was the total failure of the nation's Indochina policy. This was brought home vividly in the television age by the spectacle in late April 1975 of the hurried, chaotic evacuation of embassy and other key personnel from Saigon, as the North Vietnamese and Viet Cong forces overran the city. Americans were treated to, among other things, pictures of marines beating off the embassy walls South Vietnamese allies who desperately sought to board the American planes and helicopters and escape the country. These images were followed by accounts of the triumphant enemy forces. Such news staggered a people accustomed to considering their nation an invincible superpower, especially since the nation had lost more than fifty-five thousand soldiers in Indochina, with

[1]Jean-Paul Sartre, *No Exit* and *The Flies*, trans. Stuart Gilbert (New York: Alfred A. Knopf, 1947), p. 121.

hundreds of thousands more wounded. The second searing failure was the taking of fifty-three American hostages by student revolutionaries in Teheran on November 4, 1979. They were held for fourteen and one-half months, and the American government proved able to do little about the situation. The one effort at a rescue on May 1, 1980, ended in catastrophic failure, with eight American soldiers losing their lives in airplane collisions as they were trying to abort and return to their home bases.

On the economic front, the news was little better for Americans. Just as the population had become accustomed to think of this nation as militarily invincible, so had they become accustomed to think of the modern economy as an inexhaustible cornucopia. In 1957 John Kenneth Galbraith termed America an affluent society, and the boom years of the 1960s seemed to bear this out. Yet by 1973 Paul Ehrlich had published a book prophesying a "scarcity society." In 1974–1975 and again in 1979–1980 the nation experienced its two worst recessions since the 1930s. The decade closed with unemployment at 8.5 percent and inflation running at between 12 percent and 15 percent per year. In 1980 the Gross National Product, after adjustments for inflation, actually dropped. Political and economic leaders were lecturing the population about a new era of limits. These international and economic failures provoked increased concern about what the future might hold in store for Americans, as did the meteoric rise on the newly emerging political agenda of the energy issue.

Americans entered the 1970s with little concern about energy supplies. This was partially due to a misplaced faith in the potential of nuclear power. President Eisenhower had expressed a belief promoted by an important segment of our economic and technical elites (our "wizards," Harry Caudill called them), when he supposedly remarked in the late 1950s that once nuclear plants were brought on line, electricty would be so plentiful and cheap that there would be no need to meter it as it entered people's homes. This complacency was also the result of the abundance of domestic oil and natural gas supplies. In the mid to late 1960s America imported only about 10 percent of its petroleum supplies. And American companies, acting in concert with the government, could command those foreign supplies at a very low cost.

Consequently, the United States developed the most energy-intensive socioeconomic system in the world. By the 1970s its citizens consumed approximately twice the energy per person that

West Germans did. C. J. Haug, among others, noted that the spectacular advances made this century in living conditions were due precisely to this extensive "replacement of human and animal energy with energy drawn from inanimate sources—wood, coal, natural gas, uranium, and particularly petroleum."[2]

Americans became increasingly dependent on the so-called "Seven Sisters," those multinational energy conglomerates who control 60–70 percent of all inanimate sources in the country (plus virtually all imports), and upon external energy suppliers. As the 1970s ended some 50 percent of the nation's crude oil was being imported from foreign nations at an annual cost of $60 billion. The dislocations of this supply caused by the 1973 oil embargo or the Iranian Revolution of 1978–1979, and the exponential price increases by the "Seven Sisters" and the Organization of Petroleum Exporting Countries shook the very foundations of our political society.

The immediate response to the energy crisis highlighted the dilemma facing a nation whose cultural values, socialization experiences, and sociocultural structure were geared to consumption, privatism, competition, unequal distribution, and a disregard for politics. The world environment has unalterably changed in such a way that the old values, experiences, and sociopolitical structures actually hamper attempts to confront the new items on the transitional agenda. Truckers and farmers struggled against one another for dwindling supplies, the latter occasionally using violence in the summer of 1979 to protect their economic well-being. Spokesmen for eastern, southern, and western regions castigated one another for failing to conserve and/or produce to the maximum. Northerners worried that if a severe winter found supplies short, home heating bills would skyrocket and there would be widespread suffering and death. During one summer of long gas lines someone grimly joked: "If you happen to be contemplating suicide but lack the nerve, just break into a gasoline line." Some Americans died, in fact, for this transgression. Then, too, a near melt-down at a nuclear plant at Three Mile Island, Pennsylvania, in April 1979, caused the

---

[2]C.J. Haug, "Energy and the Mythology of Historical Optimism," *The Humanities and Public Policy*, ed. Dennis J. Mitchell and Peyton W. Williams, Jr. (Jackson, Miss.: Mississippi Committee for the Humanities, 1979), p. 17. For a historical perspective on the "energy crises," see Richard Barnett, *The Lean Years* (New York: Simon and Schuster, 1980).

evacuation of thousands of people and threatened an unthinkable catastrophe. These and similar occurrences confounded an anxious population.

In a famous and distrubing anthropological study, *The Mountain People,* Colin Turnbull describes the destruction of one society caused by decades of intensifying scarcity, like that sensed by some as beginning in the United States. "The Ik," writes Turnbull, gradually "relinquished all luxury [of human feeling] in the name of individual survival, and the result is they live on as a people without life, without passion, beyond humanity." The Ik even lost the will to make the choices required to retain human values.[3] Some extreme pessimists wondered if America might someday in a distant future follow the Ik.

Not only did the initial response to the energy issue arouse concern about the future direction of the nation. The worst fear of some political observers—which may have been overblown—was that the economic situation might deteriorate sufficiently to crystallize fascistic tendencies within the political society. Carter's second treasury secretary, G. William Miller, warned on several occasions, as the seventies ended and the eighties began, that inflation presented "a clear and present danger" that could erode social stability and the nation's freedoms. Chairman Paul A. Volcker of the Federal Reserve Board was asked, when testifying before a congressional committee in late April 1980, whether he thought rampant inflation could undermine the political system. He responded, without elaborating, "I agree."[4] But it was Arthur Burns, Volcker's predecessor, who headed the board for over a quarter of a century, who expressed the gravest fears.

It was no accident, Burns is quoted as saying, that Hitler came into power in Germany in 1933 on the heels of a disastrous inflation rate in that country. The situation reached the point where the "middle class was wiped out and there was a destabilizing sense of frustration in the country, something Hitler was able to capitalize on." The economy of the United States is nowhere near as badly off as Germany's between the wars, but Burns noted that inflation "tends to raise questions in people's minds about the workings of

[3]Colin Turnbull, *The Mountain People* (New York: Simon and Schuster, 1972), p. 295.
[4]Quoted in R. Gregory Nokes, "Leaders Worry Inflation Will Hurt U.S. Democracy," *Hattiesburg American,* March 2, 1980.

democracy." He worries that "if no one in our two parties takes hold of the inflation problem and provides leadership, some demagogue may arise and capture the public imagination."[5] While these comments focus on inflation, the fact is that unemployment and underemployment, declining rates of productivity increases, an aging industrial base, and increased competition from abroad present a wide range of economic liabilities as the 1980s begin.

What Burns, Miller, and Volcker were all saying has been suggested above—there may be a danagerous tilt in the value structure, socialization experience, and sociocultural structures of American society that points in the direction of anxiety, violence, and repression in case of a catastrophic crisis.

But if peril inheres in the conflicts of American political culture and consciousness and the transitional political agenda, there is also possibility and even promise. Possibly America will learn to accept and perhaps even welcome the end of a quarter-century of Pax Americana signaled by the international setbacks of the 1970s. The burden, in money and lives, associated with being the dominant world power and the likelihood of unwise military involvement that attaches to such status became clear in Vietnam. The energy crisis may bring renewed efficiency and leaner, less frenetic, healthier life-styles, plus the sharing of resources. Maybe the new shape of the poltiical economy will accelerate a movement away from surplus material consumption—the quantitative standard of life—to a concern for other values, like a love of nature, family, place, and community, spiritual appreciation, and a regard for the ethical dimensions of existence—or qualitative standards. Also, Americans might learn thrift with compassion, to quote a popular slogan, and share economic opportunities and production with those heretofore dispossessed.

It is very unlikely that the promise residing in the new agenda will be actualized through decisions of elites. To expect decision makers in the public and private sectors who have flourished during America's emergence as a superpower, the expansion of the political economy, and increase in energy consumption and needs to lead the nation in such a new and very different direction would be illogical. It is not only contrary to the interests of those at the apex of these spheres of American life to do this, it may be—given their institutional roles and socialization experiences—beyond their imagination. Anyway, as Key says, ruling groups have "so inveterate a habit

[5]Ibid.

of being wrong" that the "health of a democratic order" cannot be restored until they feel the hot breath of the populace on the back of their necks.[6] It may be more than mere coincidence that the decline in voter participation rates after 1960 was accompanied by many policy failures—such as the ones mentioned above—and abuses of power like Watergate, Koreagate, and Abscam, to name only three.

It is in the interests of the vast majority of Americans and in their untapped potential for self-rule that the greatest hope for the promise of the United States in the third century resides. All Americans have a direct stake in avoiding future Vietnams, and most have a stake in a greater sharing of resources and in restructuring the political economy, as well as in such things as decentralization and throughgoing political-governmental reforms. All these are needed to democratize life. And if Jefferson is right, the people have the capability—undeveloped though it may be—to participate in a political community in such a way as to advance rationally such common interests. What is needed is a way to revive Jeffersonian democracy in America. And the prerequisite for this lies in cultural conceptions of the possibilities of man, politics, and society altered from the negativistic neo-Madisonian view which dominates America and flavors so strongly the socialization experience of education, economics, the media, and other agencies.

Put very simply, American political culture and socialization are fundamentally unable to develop a sense of the political self and an understanding of the community on the part of the citizenry. Hence the ability to envision the manifold possibilities of individual and collective political life is thwarted. This vision, understanding, and imagination are essential to revitalize American democracy in such a way that the nation will be able to deal with the transitional agenda as it moves toward the twenty-first century. The last task of this study is to suggest a way of thinking about man and his political life that suits the need of a renascent American democracy. This is the "teleological persepective."

Envisioning the Possibilities of Political Life: The Teleological Perspective

"Telos," meaning "end, goal, or purpose," began to be used extensively as a philosophical concept when the Greek world asked about the meaning and design of the cosmos and the nature—that

---

[6]V.O. Key, Jr., *Southern Politics* (New York: Vintage Books, 1949), p. 310.

is, the end—of things within it. The teleological view found its greatest application to politics in the classical period in the thought of Aristotle. The most prominent proponent of this perspective among contemporary American political thinkers is Mulford Q. Sibley. This conception of man, politics, and society is diametrically opposed to the neo-Madisonian view and reveals the unrealized possibilities of political life.

Aristotle

Aristotle begins *The Politics* by setting forth the teleological perspective that guided his study. The nature of any object is the "end-product of the perfecting process; . . . that which man, house, household, or anything else aims at being." Focusing on man he arrives at the famous assertion that man is by nature a political animal. And there is a natural impulse among all men toward political partnership. Combining the concept that the purpose or goal of all things is perfection of its nature with the analysis of man as by nature political, Aristotle concludes that the good, just, active, and happy social life is the perfection of man's telos. Indeed, "man is the best of all animals when he has reached his full development." But where justice is absent,where the good society does not exist, then man's political telos rather than being perfected may be so distorted as to become the opposite. Man "is worst of all animals when divorced from law and morals. . . . Man without goodness is the most savage, the most unrighteous, and the worst in regard to sexual license and gluttony."[7] So for the perfection of man's nature justice must exist in state and society.

Inhering in teleology is the presupposition that the processes and structure of a thing are designed to facilitate the perfection of its nature or telos. Applying this to man, Aristotle found two abilities —possessed by no other animal—essential to the construction of a just political existence. They are speech and ethical reasoning. These make man a "political animal in a sense in which a bee is not, or any gregarious animal." While other animals have a verbal ability to express pleasure or pain and to communicate, human speech "serves to indicate what is useful and what is harmful, and so also what is right and what is wrong." The ability to distinguish right from wrong, good from evil, and justice from injustice, as well

[7]Aristotle,*The Politics*, trans. T.A. Sinclair (Baltimore, Md.: Penguin Books, 1962), pp. 25–29.

as to communicate this, is "the real difference between man and other animals." A city is based on "the sharing of a common view in these matters." Hence, "*right* is the basis of the political association and right is the criterion for deciding what is just."[8]

Modern thinkers who, like Aristotle, hold that man's telos is to be a conscious, rational, active political being—as symolized by Socrates—do not deny the influences of biological or sociocultural factors on political abilities, attitudes, and behavioral inclinations. But they assert that the human being is free to react to these determinants, to absorb them, change them, overcome them. Freedom and the estrangement that goes with it are essential parts of the human condition. This freedom includes the capability for a final moral decision, not simply action that responds to genes, customary morality, class, "operant conditioning," or other biological or sociocultural factors.

As previously noted, utopian political thinker Mulford Sibley is the most important contemporary exponent of this teleological perspective. Since he offers the clearest exposition of this powerful conception, Sibley's thought merits detailed consideration.

Sibley

In *Nature and Civilization: Some Implications for Politics*, which grew out of his presentation of the 1973 Lecture in Political Analysis at Loyola University of Chicago, Sibley sets forth in detailed fashion his understanding of the teleological model and its implications for contemporary America. To him, man cannot be comprehended merely as a biological or social construct, although what Sibley terms man's "existential self"—man as he is in the world—is shaped by both dimensions to some extent. But more important, man must also "be seen through the goals implicit in his nature, teleologically understood." While he is a creature comprised of molecules and animal lusts, there is a telos, or end, working within him. This represents him, man, as the "kind of whole that is more than the sum of all its possible parts." This end, which Sibley defines,like Aristotle, as that of being rational and political, shapes man as the "idea" of victory shapes the athlete, even though the victory may never be made "actual."[9]

---

[8]Ibid.

[9]Mulford Q. Sibley, *Nature and Civilization: Some Implications for Politics* (Itasca, Ill.: F.E. Peacock, 1977). Page numbers in the text refer to this edition.

Man can only be fully understood by transcending his primitive elements and by asking "what he is implicitly striving to become." While civilization is necessary for man's rational, political nature to develop, if it is not directed "through deliberate rational collective planning," civilization can frustrate man's teleological nature. By taking into account sociocultural influences, primitive human nature, and teleological human nature, man can develop "an integrated human nature." This will not, however, "arise automatically or unconsciously, any more than an adult human being's personal life can be adequately integrated without deliberation and thought" (p. 60).

Like Aristotle, Sibley sees humans—and no other creatures—as possessing the many talents and abilities which are necessary for the perfection of the telos of rational, political existence. Potentially at least, we are "rational, creative, free . . . , just, and appreciators of the world of beauty." The idea of humanity is seeking its way within us through these talents, "not to command us but rather to goad us and to ask questions to which we must respond" (p. 81). To say that man is capable of freedom is not to imply that man always decides freely. In many situations "we probably do not. But it does imply that we have the potentiality for doing so" (p. 215). Humans can free themselves both from biologically "natural" reactions to things and from the power of sociocultural values. Sibley gives as an example of the former the instances where men respond to violence with nonviolence, rather than the supposedly more natural violent reaction. As for the latter, he emphasizes that man can, even within the most materialistic of societies, like our own, transcend the fetish of acquisition and consumption in the quest for intellectual, ethical, and spiritual goods.

To Sibley, we are workers par excellence. Creative work and the tool making which is a central part of labor activity not only produces objects but also perfects human nature and improves men's lives together. Unlike those who see man as wishing to *avoid* the expenditure of his energies, to Sibley man not only desires to employ them but "hopes to use them in ways which help the community and challenge his own powers" (p. 215). The technology that emerges from this creative work allows men collectively to move away from the constraints and inhibitions of primitive nature (although they may move to the constraints and inhibitions of a technological society).

A most important teleological ability is the potential for awareness of self and of others, and of deriving moral, or ethical, principles from this awareness with which to govern the proper relation of man to men. Sibley contends that we are ultimately capable of almost a complete view of "personhood." This recognizes that while the group is essential for human fulfillment, yet at the same time an individual soul transcends the group and has "legitimate ends and purposes of its own upon which the group has no legitimate claim." To him, "the indestructible human soul develops its personhood in the community of souls." But the group is only a necessary and not a sufficient condition for personhood (p. 77).

Lastly, man is also the only creature which has the capacity to struggle toward his own apprehension of the good, the true, and the beautiful. Unlike the beasts and the gods, man's essence is "to grow to the desirable by always running the risk of thinking or doing and having a certain amount of power to do or think the undesirable" (p. 97). In fact, this difficult struggle itself to do that which is desirable is an "element of the desirable"(p. 98).

Due to these abilities and the fact that man's telos is rational and moral political ordering, Sibley believes—like Socrates in Hegel's interpretation—that human thought and attention are inevitably drawn to the questions of politics. That freedom which is man's renders him uncertain as to how all these dimensions of his teleological nature—his technological ability, his struggle for the good, his sense of self among other selves, and so forth—can and should best be expressed. He seeks to reduce that uncertainty "by using his powers of reason, analysis, and imagination" (p. 259) in formulating the best societies or utopias. This utopia building "may be thought of as central to man's teleological nature" (p. 254). There is within even primitive man, to Sibley, "an implicit, albeit ragged, vision of how and why human nature should transform the nonhuman world." (p. 254). The human role as "utopist" is his most basic one, in Sibley's view.

THE FAILURE AND FUTURE OF AMERICAN DEMOCRACY: TO REALIZE THE POLITICAL SELF

Three questions that quickly present themselves in light of Aristotle's and Sibley's assertions about the political nature of man and his inherent political attentiveness are: (1) why isn't the political world in a better state? (2) why isn't political involvement and participation of higher quality? and (3) how can we realize the teleological self? Sibley responds to the first query by emphasizing that there is nothing inevitable about the actualization of man's teleological nature. While existential man foreshadows teleological man, still everyone is "existentially only a partial human being when measured by what he might or ought to become" (p. 81). Indeed, "most are probably not what they ought to be or can be" (p. 78). The aspects of human nature which are developed and emphasized depend on "the degree to which deliberation and developing consciousness can organize and control the structures of civilization" (p. 33). This only became a possibility with the emergence of civilization which weakened the traditional ordering forces of custom and instinct. Civilization freed personality from gods, custom, and instinct, thereby creating a puzzle as to how it, personality, "ought to order itself." This issue "is posed by civilization; the answer must be found by political reflection" (p. 82). The ultimate goal of such political reflection is to devise conscious ways—rather than relying on invisible hands, pluralistic chaos, or dialectical history—of organizing and controlling the structures of civilization to facilitate realization of the "self-governing, fully aware personality" (p. 87).

Sibley's own political reflection leads him to conclude, in the final chapter of *Nature and Civilization*, that such a personality can only flourish in a small-scale, self-reliant political community, surrounded by wilderness and linked in a world confederation, with minimum socioeconomic specialization and maximum participation. The community would operate by consensus, not majority rule, and on the premise that whatever touches or affects "all is to be decided upon by all." Individuals would be liberated from excessive concerns about the material realm by application of the social principle of contribution by ability, distribution by need, with income disparities no greater than one and one-half to one. The principle of selective technology would guide the introduction—but not the development—of new innovations. And there would be maximum tolerance of individual eccentricities combined with a heavy social responsibility placed on each individual to make the contribution to which he or she is best suited. Sibley emphasizes two things in particular about his ideal community which would also be applicable to the utopian vision of other thinkers. One is that it cannot be imposed on men, but must evolve from trends, ideas, and suggestions present in any given preutopian society (p. 292). The other is that the existence of some rebellion of existential man against "his own rationally derived conclusions" would still be present. It always is, Sibley notes, in no matter how small a degree, due to the freedom that will always be man's (p. 232).

With the question of why, if man is by nature political, there is often such a low level and such an unreflective type of political involvement—for example, in many American elections—we come to a central concern of contemporary political inquiry. Sibley argues that existential man can become so greatly separated from his teleological nature that the development of his politically relevant skills is arrested and they are, to some degree, forgotten. It is not only that most men are probably "divorced from what they should be" but all too often that they "are not even aware that this is so" (p. 78). If man is not actively utilizing his teleological abilities, they become less visible to other men (maybe leading them to view man as by nature nonpolitical), and they will also become less omnipresent to the invidual. So the memory of one's teleological end and teleologically significant abilities is contingent upon existential man participating in political life in such a way as to be progressing toward his teleologically natural self. As Sibley puts it, to become fully human, man must "participate actively in a small community" (p. 267). Like Jefferson and other democratic theorists, Sibley stresses both the self-creative and communitarian implications of participation.

Indeed, it is precisely the democratic ideal of a participatory citizen striving for moral fulfillment that Sibley insists is the telos of man. Where participation is not invited and encouraged, the gap of existential man and teleological man widens, skills fall into disuse, and there may occur a forgetting of the human telos.

It is with this recognition of the possibility of forgetting that we begin to understand how the teleological self might be realized. Mark Warren has approached the politics of forgetting in a way similar to Sibley that sheds light on the discussion. Warren sees forgetting as "a necessary covering of the nonidentity of human desire and human existence" and interprets it as central to the thought of such apparently diverse figures as Freud, Nietzsche, and Marx. The relevant terms are "repression," "nihilism," and "false consciousness." Memory, to Warren, turns upon the satisfaction of internal desire in external nature. Where the painful gap between the two is too great, forgetting occurs. Even so, "forgetting always contains a suppressed remembrance of truth" which can lead to the recovery of truth. To the Freudian, therapy would be the best way to

such recovery. To the Marxist, class politics leads to true consciousness. And to the Nietzschean, rejecting slave morality is the appropriate path. The task and the responsibility, in Warren's view, of the
most attentive students of politics—such as political activists and
political scientists, media commentators, community leaders—and
all citizens, is clear. They must facilitate a thinking back, a remembrance by the individual and society of basic needs and full potentiality, as against perceived needs and present development. Only
through such "articulation of forgetting" into memory can a better
political order occur. In his closing sentence, Warren links up with
classical Greek throught: "Self-knowledge, as Socrates knew,
cannot be politically neutral."[10]

Sibley's thoughts on the role of students of society and politics
who are at the same time—and foremost—citizens parallel Warren's. To Sibley the key to the realization of man's teleological nature is a concerted effort aimed at the "development of a much
more sensitive political consciousness on the part of individuals"
(p. 153). Everyone must work toward this end, and particularly
those citizens who are best suited to such work. This will lead both
to individual freedom and to community. On the individual level,
Sibley contends that we can largely understand the "psychological
and social roots of slavishness and, with that understanding, seek to
destroy them" (p. 121). At the level of community, he writes that
heightened self-awareness brings to an individual soul greater
"consciousness of its intimate ties to other souls and the would-be
community of souls." There comes a recognition that any "personal
utopia" is "related to, if not wholly dependent on, the utopias which
are proposed for the community" (p. 254). A political society
achieves such ennobling self-knowledge through a combination of
scientific and subjective approaches.

The scientific approach, such as predominates in contemporary
political research in the United States, allows us to measure—with
some accuracy—existential man. (We explored some of this measurement in America in chapter 7.) And since existential men have
failed to establish fraternity, equality, and justice in their human
communities, "they are confronted with such phenomena as alienation, violence, war, and in general, what Plato termed political

[10]Mark Warren, "Remembrance and Forgetting: An Essay on Memory, Desire, and
Social Criticism" (Paper delivered at the annual meeting of the American Political
Science Association, New York, August 31–September 3, 1978).

'illness' " (p. 82). These things frustrate existential man's teleological nature. Measurements of this frustrated existential condition are imperative if humans are to become aware of the gap between this and their teleological selves. As a result, a scientific account of human beings is "perfectly legitimate and necessary" (p. 83). Still, in such an account we must remember that what is being measured is the existential self—what men are rather than what they might be and ought to be.

To know teleological man and facilitate his knowing himself Sibley insists that one—like a political scientist—must adopt a subjective, intuitive approach. "Consciousness itself is best apprehended by the so-called subjective approach which psychological science tends to spurn" (p. 11). The Socratic devices of self-examination and dialogue characterize Sibley's methodological recommendations. He suggests several specific things, one of which is introspection. Certain dimensions of the soul to Sibley, "can only be comprehended" by introspection (p. 10). Also, we should compare the feelings and direct perceptions of oneself with that which is perceived through introspection with others. By introspection and sharing, man achieves at least some understanding of those "motions of the soul which the behavioralist can at best get at only indirectly through experiments" (p. 11). There must be, if we are to know ourselves and one another, direct experiences of one another, for the soul "can be fully known only by direct experiences" (p. 83). We must compare our experiences and values because that is how we can "refine our statements, hopefully making them clearer (for much turns on precision of langauge)" (p. 66). Through our own intuition and introspection and discussions with our fellows we come to discover "starting points for discussion of justice" (p. 66); we find the stirrings "of a broad new political awareness quite different from that of traditional Marxist, liberal, or conservative outlooks" (p. 230); and we witness a growing movement of people toward the realization of their teleological natures. We begin discovering utopia.

Conclusion

If American political society is to avoid a perilous response to such issues as its loss of international stature, the end of energy abundance, and the emergence of a steady-state economy, then it must reconstitute itself as a democratic political community on a level as yet never realized in the American experience. This is a vital necessity because, as Wolin points out, "human existence is not going to be decided at the lesser level of small associations: it is the political order that is making fateful decisions about man's survival. . . ."[11]

The failure of American democracy has been in the inadequate utilization of the potential inhering in the individual political self of Americans and in the political community. Consequently, there is a deficient ability to envision democratic political resolutions to the perplexing new agenda which confronts the nation as it moves toward the twenty-first century. Such resolutions must speak to the interests of the vast majority of the population and must utilize the long atrophied political skills and talents of the population.

In order to realize the promise and possibility of American democracy it is first necessary to alter the heretofore largely unchallenged neo-Madisonian perspective on man, politics, and society which stresses human selfishness, materialistic urges, competitiveness, natural inequality, and man's apolitical and privatized nature. This pervades the political system and the socialization experience and rationalizes the stratified sociopolitical and economic structure. This is not an easy task, yet there is no reason to think that it is an impossible one either. It is clear that the political and sociocultural process which generally promotes this perspective is far from being either solely one-dimensional or so closed and well coordinated that a change in social outlook and social values is impossible.

The initial step in this process of revisioning the possibilities of politics in America is to consider an alternate conception of man and political society. A powerful and persuasive perspective that well suits the needs of a revitalized democratic community is the teleological one. In this view, which is traceable to Aristotle, man is revealed to be inherently political rather than apolitical. This is indicated by his unique abilities for abstract thought and speech, freedom, technology, morality, self-awareness, and sense of community. All of these propel man to questions of politics and make possible a political society different from that of all other species.

Existential man as he presently is in American society has found his teleological self stunted, and his political skills go largely unrealized. Because public opinion measurements of the self reveal

[11]Sheldon Wolin, *Politics and Vision* (Boston: Little, Brown, 1960), p. 434.

frustration, confusion, ambivalence to community and leadership, anxiety, and privatism, there is an unwarranted tendency to classify this as human nature. But human nature is not necessarily indicated by man as he currently is; rather, we need a clearer understanding of what man might become. As Archibald MacLeish remarked, "Man is not what he thinks he knows, but what he thinks he can know, can become."[12] Democracy is based on the proposition that man can know and fully understand his political world and can become a self-motivated, effective political citizen.

The challenge confronting America is to go beyond a set of cultural values, a political socialization process, and a socioeconomic structure which largely reinforce the negative and undeveloped dimensions of man as he is, to a society which encourages and facilitates the realization of what he might become. The unsettling conditions of this transititional moment present a rare, open-ended opportunity for beginning the process of transformation. As William Irwin Thompson says, we are truly at "the edge of history."

The future is beyond knowing, but the present is beyond belief. We make so much noise with our technology that we cannot discover that the stargate is in our foreheads. But the time has come; the revelation has already occurred, and the guardian seers have seen the lightning strike the darkness we call reality. And now we sleep in the brief interval between the lightning and the thunder.[13]

---

[12]Quoted in John C. Livingston and Robert G. Thompson, *The Consent of the Governed*, 3rd ed. (New York: Macmillan, 1971), p. 63.

[13]William Irwin Thompson, *At the Edge of History: Speculations on the Transformation of Culture* (New York: Harper and Row, 1972), p. 230.

Index

Adams, John: and Federalists, 23; on human nature, 23-24; conservatism, 24-25; on checks and balances, 24-25; letter from Jefferson, 34.

Aeschylus: *Oresteia*, 4-6.

Anderson, Walt: on awareness and repression, 36; on politics and psychology, 41.

Apathy: Rollo May's analysis, 53; Herbert Marcuse's analysis, 53-54; and nonparticipation, 154-55. *See also* Political participation.

Apollo: and scientific mind, 51.

Aristotle: *The Politics* on man's defects and abilities, 9; on speech and politics, 90-91; on education and politics, 119; on economics, 136; on leaders, 187-88; teleological perspective, 204-05; mentioned, 59.

Articles of Confederation: goal of friendship, 35.

Assassinations: presidential, 189-90.

Behavioralism: distinguished from behaviorism, 13; and positive science, 13.

Behaviorism: denial of consciousness, 13; operant conditioning, 13-14; B. F. Skinner, 13-14; mentioned, 15.

Bell, Daniel: end of ideology thesis, 37; postindustrial thesis, 60.

Bicentennial: and American transition, 198; mentioned, 38, 40.

Black Americans: education, income, occupation, 83-84; attitudes, 84-86; and genetic endowment theory, 126. *See also* Discrimination.

Boorstin, Daniel: on paucity of American political philosophy, 19; theory of giveness, 37.

Burger, Warren: "melting pot" metaphor, 40; ruling on obscenity, 95.

Burns, Arthur: on perils of economic crisis, 201-02.

Calhoun, John C.: political theory, 26-28.

Campaigns: financing, 44-45; presidential, 184-87.

Career Incentive Education Act, 1978: and vocational tracking, 129.

Carnegie Council on Children: study, 73; policy recommendations, 77.

Carter, Jimmy: "life isn't fair", 63; State of the Union Address, 1979, 93-94; 1972 campaign-planning memo, 102-03; "malaise" speech, 1979, 158; saint image, 185, 195; public relations style, 186-87; on limits of presidency, 188; mentioned, 108, 192, 193.

Children: class-conditioned attitudes, 80-81.

Communications Act of 1978: and television, 116.

Communism: *See* Marx, Karl.

Conscience: and political consciousness, 5-6.

Consensus theory: exponents, 36-37; and political socialization studies, 80, 87.

Declaration of Independence: goals of security and happiness, 34-35.

Desegregation: affirmative action, 46-47; busing, 55; centralized control of schools, 124.

Determinism: rejected, 17-18.

Dionysus: and romantic sensibility, 51.

Discrimination: and language, 98-102; and self-image, 101-02. *See also* Black Americans; Women.

Disintegration: social factors, 68-69.

Dissent: in 1960s, 37-38, 114.

Dostoevsky, Fyodor: on freedom, 17.

Economic distribution: in U.S., by families, 76; and ownership, 136-38.

Education: in Jefferson's thought, 22; discussed, 117-132; alternative mean-

215